SOUNDING FOR COOL

Sounding for Cool

Donald Morrill

Michigan State University Press

East Lansing

∞ The paper used in this publication meets the minimum requirements of ANSI/NISO Z39.48-1992 (R 1997) (Permanence of Paper).

Michigan State University Press
East Lansing, Michigan 48823-5202

Printed and bound in the United States of America.

08 07 06 05 04 03 02   1 2 3 4 5 6 7 8 9 10

LIBRARY OF CONGRESS CATALOGING-IN-PUBLICATION DATA
Morrill, Donald, 1955–
Sounding for cool / Donald Morrill.
p. cm.
ISBN 0-87013-611-9 (cloth : alk. paper)
1. Group homes for youth—United States—Case studies. 2. Problem youth—Rehabilitation—United States—Case studies. I. Title.
HV863 .M67 2002
305.3'1'0973—dc21
2001007862

Cover photography by King Thackston
Cover design by Heather L. Truelove
Book design by Sharp Des!gns, Inc., Lansing, MI

Visit Michigan State University Press on the World Wide Web at *www.msupress.msu.edu*

ACKNOWLEDGMENTS

My deepest thanks to the following organizations and people:

To the University of Tampa for the sabbatical leave that allowed me extended time at the TLP, and to the Dana Foundation for a summer grant that allowed me to write portions of this book;

To Lisa Birnbaum, my first reader and toughest editor;

To the staff of the TLP and its parent organization for allowing me to observe their difficult undertaking;

And, most important, to the residents of the TLP for allowing me, yet another strange adult, into their company.

NOTE: The names of private individuals, as well as a few details, have been changed to maintain confidentiality.

SOUNDING FOR COOL

ONE

I SIT IN THE OFFICE of the Transitional Living Program and ice my busted lip. During basketball—the residents' group activity of the week—I reached too far in on Andre, just when he drove for the hoop. His elbow in my mug. I deserved it, more than twice Andre's seventeen years, secretly proud of a purported instinct for the game, pitiable feet slower now than ever.

Andre said nothing about the wound. A pro forma "sorry" doesn't lodge in his repertoire. I didn't expect one. Still, his shyness from such niceties, his awkwardness about such a simple exchange, astonishes me and enlarges his foreignness.

The iron tang in my blood. And I think, again, about Andre holding the gun to the woman's head while his father rifled her purse. He told me that he was ready to pull the trigger, there in that dim parking lot behind a grocery store in his Tampa neighborhood. Andre and his father had watched the woman go to the ATM, had waited, patiently, for her to return to her car. Andre told me that his father always preached to him that a man must help himself, must watch his own back. He recruited his son for this robbery—this man, now in prison on other charges, who fights his war against the world that spits into his black hand rather than shaking it, who spits into his own palm as well, into the lifeline there, the undressable and malignant wounds.

I try to envision Andre with the gun to *my* head. But I can't quite escape from thinking of him on the basketball court—tall, his muscular abdomen rippling like a leather shoe tongue no longer banded by laces. All of him so lean: the wing of an ultralight plane. This boy-man with lint pills in his hair after a nap. Hardly ominous.

That woman who felt the hard tube of the barrel jammed against her skull, however, would disagree, no doubt.

What did she think when she heard Andre's father tell Andre to keep the pistol on her, and then heard this man say "I love you" to his young partner?

"That's the only time my old man ever said anything like that to me," Andre told me one afternoon. "He never had no time for me, 'less he had a job for us . . ."

Frank, the staff resident of the TLP, says Andre's record contains some B&Es, some car thefts, some drug arrests, but no violence of this sort. Andre could not have been admitted to the program otherwise. But, then, Andre's records are incomplete, as are the records of all the TLP residents—as are all our records.

And maybe the robbery is Andre's invention, his true tale: *The Pistol of My Father's Love*. Tales of every sort echo in this place, mostly the stories that the self tells the self. Some of them are worthy lies.

Everybody has a story, people say, meaning (when they're talking about teenage males with damned autobiographies) *get over your tale, and don't bother (us) with it*. And it's true that more horrific narratives than those of the TLP residents emanate from the daily media. Too many. But who can escape his story?

I daub my lip and think again that soon, our tribe—adults—will not excuse Andre any longer for his fortunes. A few years, or months, from now and that will be the end of our indulgence, our patience and public compassion. He will have passed the age of forgiveness for his follies, if he hasn't already. The clock is ticking for him and the rest of the TLP residents, and who among them knows that, really? With them, we adults are nearly always in the position of the audience of some Greek tragedy brimming with dramatic irony. *Don't go in there,* we cry to each of them, our doomed protagonists. *Do this. Want this. Think this.*

Andre glances toward me on his way out of the office. Checking on me, maybe. Frank might not be telling me the whole truth about Andre's record. He's taken a shine to Andre. He sometimes slap-boxes a little with him on the steps. Or he swoops across the green in the center of the TLP and wrestles Andre to the ground like a lion bringing down an impala. Andre grins sickly and happily as he tries to deflect these playful assaults. Though he doesn't say it, Frank believes that Andre has a good chance to succeed in the program, even though—like Galvin, Salim, Quovonne, and Matt—he's still in Phase One, has been here only a month.

I've been here longer than a month—hanging around since the inception of the program nearly two years ago. Yet I'm somehow also in Phase One, of my own devising. Andre and the others are, as the TLP material says, young men "unable to live with their families as a result of family conflict, or for whom there are no safe alternatives." They have come here for nine to twenty-four months to "achieve self-sufficiency and avoid long-term dependency on social services by gaining employment skills through educational assistance and life skills training."

In other words: to grow up . . . at least enough.

They used to call me "the book guy" because I was introduced as the man who wanted to write about them. I had proposed this self-involved idea. But the months yielded no coherent pages. Like many men, I don't understand what I'm talking about when I talk about men of any age or sort, though I believe I know them, beneath articulation. That's probably why I'm lingering over this adventitious blow from Andre like some rite of passage, and why I'm unduly affected when Matt, say, or Galvin or Quovonne draws close or allows me near. It's also inescapable that while I'm childless by choice, encounters of this latter sort have, more than once, caused a tear to rim my eye, that stinging. And I blink this effusion to the periphery of things, where, I suspect, most of our crucial matters remain within our vision, if we will notice.

One day, riding in the back of Frank's pickup, another of the residents, Tim, joked about me, "He's not writing any book. He just wants to hang with us."

Not entirely false.

I'd like to know them. I'd like to help. I'd like to understand, also, the nature of that tear, its source, how it connects—as intuition insists—to the ocean of human longing and necessity, to others.

About his purpose at the TLP, Andre once told me, "I know this is my last chance."

"Which last chance is that?" I asked, sensing that he believes he should console adults with such platitudes from time to time.

He squinted off like a homesteader facing his agonized crops. Courtesy of his fastidious iron, a sharp crease ran down the front and back of each leg of his starched blue jeans.

"To get myself right," he said, turning suddenly toward me. "At least here I don't have to worry about no crooked cops and good cops and gettin' shot."

In their faces, I sometimes sense I am looking into our age as into a broken mirror. Accurate shards, distorted angles, flawed lights, with the cracks like a web, a mesh holding the whole together. From where did the impact come that shattered and rearranged the reflection?

And what reflection do they see in me, in all adults, here at the last chance?

I go out with the final sliver of my ice and sit under the oak tree edging the little green between the two facing banks of white-washed rooms that comprise the TLP: once a parking lot and its motel, built just after World War II. Andre tends coals on a grill donated by the local neighborhood association—decent, anxious citizens with children and property values to protect, most of whom still want to do what's right and helpful for the Delinquent Youth of America.

Chops and burgers and chicken sizzle as some of the residents gather around the grill. Ghostly smoke. Frank banters with Andre about his jump shot, and I remember another of Andre's unofficial tales.

One night he rendezvoused to sell crack to another teenager, a dealer, in his neighborhood in Tampa.

"The dude looked all crazy," Andre told me, "his face buggy, whirlin' dark. He didn't have no money, I guessed, so I was fixin' to split. No reason to be hangin' on no dark corner with a weirdo.

"Then he comes at me. I think he's got a knife. I don't know.

"I grab this brick and hit him in the head. And his eyes go white, like he's blind, or somethin,' and he falls on the curb.

"I'm runnin' and not lookin' back, man . . .

"My friends told me the dude died. I done looked in the paper, but there wasn't nothin' I could find 'bout it. I wasn't askin' around at the police or the hospital. No way.

"I had some nightmares 'bout that dude's eyes all white . . . He was crazy, that guy. I know it was him or me. I know . . ."

All the residents but Quovonne reach for cigarettes. (Smoking is banned everywhere on the property except under the oak.) Showing off, Matt and Tim flip out lighters. Matt opens his by snapping his fingers. In one motion, Tim shakes his as though tossing something away and rakes it down his thigh until it fires. Perfected, by practice, for this moment.

"So, you've taken up smoking," I say to Tim, teasing. He's in Phase Two and, at seventeen, might still be mistaken in the evening light for a cream-cheeked girl.

"Yeah, black and sweets," he replies, pinching a cigarillo, sounding for cool.

"He be thinkin' he a G funk pimp daddy," Salim declares, putting on his parodic basso thug-voice, and he laughs mockingly.

two

PHASE ONE: Monday–Friday (*first two weeks*)

8:30	Wake-up, shower, breakfast
9:00	Life Skills
12:00	Lunch
1:00	Chores
1:30	Life Skills: Employment Training
3:00	Group
4:00	Free time
5:00	Dinner
6:00	Free time
8:00	Curfew

Life Skills is a joke. Everyone knows it. That's the way things have been . . . well . . . since the beginning of the world. Ask Matt or Bill or Salim. Ask any of the residents. They'll tell you.

Life Skills is shut your mouth, sit up straight, early to bed. Life Skills is yum-yumming the rules every day, yes sir and no ma'am. It's wait, wait—forget it. Stupid boss. The big hand of budget, detention, be good and die.

Mostly, it's the mess adults make of things. Who would want to live like adults? Look at them.

What are you gonna do?

"Have you ever thought about killing yourself?" Jen, one of the staff, asks Matt in his assessment interview, at the start of Phase One.

"I have," Matt replies matter-of-factly. "But there's no way I could do it. I'm afraid of the pain." He pauses, summoning. "But life doesn't have that great of an appeal. It doesn't really matter if I die or not."

"When did you think of it?" Jen asks.

"When my stepfather and I had trouble. Counselors said I was passive-aggressive. They said that I was angry that he married my mom, but I didn't care about that. It's her life . . . It's just that he lied. He said he wouldn't yell and things like that."

"Did you ever think of killing him?"

Matt leans back on his chair. "Oh yeah. But I never was a match for him. He was a lot bigger."

"Any plans to hurt anybody lately? Homicidal thoughts?"

"Not really an impulse. I just get an image in my mind of killing someone. That only happened for about a month. My parents took me to counseling when I didn't want it. When I did, they wouldn't take me. 'It's too much money,' they said. But that was a while ago. I've changed a lot in six or eight months."

"Do you carry any weapons?"

"Just a couple of small knives, for protection. But I don't have them now."

"We've heard about the conflict with your stepdad. Any others?"

"My stepmom."

"What about her?"

"She lies."

"You know, you said the same thing about your stepdad."

A long pause wells up in the room. Jen waits skillfully, but Matt is accustomed to this stratagem. Jen, at last, continues.

"Your parents divorced when you were seven and got married to others when you were eight. Right?"

"Yeah."

"Significant deaths?"

"Three deaths. One I just found out about. Sort of my uncle. He died one and a half to two years ago. Then my aunt's old boyfriend died a year ago. We did a lot of fishing. I'm like my aunt's favorite . . . And then there was my mom's dad. He just died. He had Alzheimer's."

"History of mental health problems?"

"Well, my dad. He spent all he had on private investigators. I guess he had them following my mom around."

"You said your dad has a drinking problem. Has he had treatment?"

"Nope. He drinks about a case of beer a day. Me and my stepsister tried to get him in, but it hasn't worked . . . I don't drink but to relax."

"Does it worry you?"

"Yeah, I saw what it did to my grandfather . . ."

On another morning, Jen stands before a flip chart in the office. On it, she writes:

Life Skills: Goals of the Day

- *Public Agencies*
- *Electoral Process*
- *Juries*

Bill, aged sixteen, aims his enduring, Popeye the Sailor squint at Jen.

"Can you get outta this if you already know it?" he snaps. "I've had most of this since I was eleven."

"Well, we can work on your patience skills," Jen replies.

"I've got plenty of patience!" He turns in his chair and puffs.

"Do you know how to register to vote?" Jen asks.

"I don't want to vote. I don't care about President Clinton or whoever he's running against. I know all I need to know to do my work."

"We're not just thinking of tomorrow but three years from now."

"I'm going to work in construction!" Bill pleads with exasperated assurance. "That's all I'm going to work. That's what I know, and that's all I've wanted to do."

Jen glances at me. Beyond a brief stint policing rubbish on building sites for his uncle's renovation business in Cleveland, Bill has no experience in the construction line. Jen turns back to him. "You don't want to be a foreman someday?"

"Why would I want to be that? Before I came here I was gettin' a job that pays $11 an hour." He turns to Clark, a social worker from the local runaway shelter, who first brought him to the TLP and who has stopped by to check his progress. "That's more than *you* make!"

Clark laughs, eyeing Jen sidelong as he speaks to his former charge. "How would you know?"

"I know!" Bill sneers.

Clark looks at Jen coolly, but a tremor of restrained humiliation teases his corner of the room.

Jen resumes. Bill shakes his head.

"This stinks," he puffs.

"We encourage residents to purchase an alarm clock and umbrella with their first check," Jen says with managerial briskness, "so that they can get up in the morning and have no excuse to stay home from work on a rainy day."

"I don't care about the rain," Bill mumbles. "I'll sleep in the rain."

Flip the chart.

The goal of Phase One is to swathe the new resident in structure not organized by the sovereignty of familial despair, violence, or the rituals and necessities of the street. Bill's bravado aside, residents generally embrace this order at first. It beats skimming bits of Daddy's heroin stash to trade for food or sliding between that freaky, friendly couple shaking a fifty at you from the back seat of their Buick. It beats a night crashed on the roof of the Wal-Mart. The newcomer hunkers down in the plain luxury of his own room with bath and kitchenette and forty dollars' worth of groceries each week until he can find a job and/or return to school or acquire his GED. The Phase One schedule is his introduction—or re-introduction—to what Salim calls "red-tape life." You know, security and incremental prosperity born of steady labor and coupon-cutting; the suburban mire that the baby boom generation rejected temporarily three decades ago, and that the Kerouac-offs of current youth culture ritually denounce now in poetry slams, desperate for the vital fluids coursing through the soul "on the road"; stable life and life in the stable, unglamorous, amortized, functionally sober—with the trash taken out regularly.

I confess that I wonder, as Jen instructs Andre in résumé writing, as she works out model monthly budgets with Bill and Quovonne, as she proctors Tim and Salim's GED pretest, how much the program is an attempt to exchange a life of tumultuous, dangerous desperation for an existence differently desperate—clearly safer, yes, legal and more wholesome, but socially hushable and with the limitations of the merely tamed. But then I am still a sentimentalist of potential. "The mass of men lead lives of quiet desperation," Thoreau once famously observed, casting off from the crowd of grubbing red-tapers. That mass now includes those among us quietly desperate to undo or cast off the life of quiet desperation.

So, Phase One. Give the boy—aged sixteen to twenty—a place to stay. Show him how to get a job, encourage him to take responsibility for his future, offer him therapy. Sign him up for Selective Service, get his inoculations, take him and his peers to the grocery store once a week. Provide a model for behavior during the intricate fittings of each day. Push him and pull him and let him fall and, sometimes, pick him up.

Hope that he'll learn to care for himself in ways that will allow him promotion to Phase Two—semi-independence—and then to the more or less landlord-tenant relationship of the final portion of the program, Phase Three. Hope, then, that he can move beyond this.

According to Frank, there are, at present, between 75 and 100 such programs in the country, most of them having emerged in the past five years. The first appeared in California in the 1970s, no doubt in response to yet another grim manifestation in that leader among cruel American Edens. The wave of need, however, or the recognition of need, has rolled from there back east and south—including here: St. Petersburg, another frontier, another dubious paradise. Frank says this is the only program in the country lodged in what was a motor inn—with separate living quarters for each resident—and, as such, it is something of an experiment. (Most programs are single-house or barracks-style arrangements.) It's also an architecture of necessity, since suitable, affordable real estate here was difficult to locate.

Thus, frugality—imposed by the modest government grant, which underwrites the place—deems that the ten current residents sprawl in motel chairs from the 1950s and '60s. They curl up on beds into which ten thousand tourist dreams have sunk, agitated by sunburned beach trips, and they pin their middle-of-the-night stares on ceilings blankly doting since before their parents were born. Not guests, they are, it sometimes seems, the foundlings of our moment. Romuluses and Remuses suckled by the she-wolf of ignorance and blind force, poverty or the indigent heart. Latch-key kids grown a little older, who came home and found the lock changed. Who swallowed the key and now feel that small weight settled as an ulcerous hunger—an appetite then easily imputed to the surroundings.

CAREER ESSAY *(Andre)*

I wouldn't mind being a welder because you meet alot of people, make alot of money and it doesn't take alot of working I could go to school like a tech college and take up welding. And get my license for welding they make at least a couple thousand a month probably more. And the good thing is that I don't have to stick with that because I can learn alot on a trade. I could have another job and do welding on the side.

Life Skills. Andre leans over a job application. He flipped burgers at a fast food restaurant in North Tampa four days a week, even after he began peddling crack. He gave the burger money to his two younger brothers as their allowance, standing in as their father. This, until his mother procured a court order to separate him from them.

"She didn't want me messing them up with my thing," he tells me.

He claims that he pulled down $500 a day from his crack business. He says he stopped it all because a creeping terror finally tapped him. He began to freeze at the head of dim streets. One of the parked cars there he just knew hid a rival gangbanger with a gun.

"They was wantin' to spray me," he says.

He detoured down alleys. He dipped out of sight.

Now he tells me that more than anything, he wants to be a rapper. He saunters through the day, often taciturn to the larger world, almost fey at times, muttering his verses to himself like a praying pilgrim. At other times, he sings out loud, proud, improvising like a jazz player.

I'm in Queens so I'm night.
Got my 44 on my waist and half a stick of dynamite.
Got some beef with some niggas cross town.
They beat my man to the ground. I gotta shut 'em down.

As he heads off to the bus stop on the morning's search, as the potential employers do not call him, Frank and I wonder aloud how enticing his former entrepreneurship might begin to appear to him.

CAREER ESSAY *(Quovonne)*

I will like to do cosmotology work, working in the salon. I like doing this job because I love working with people and making them look good I would like my salary to be about $100 per hour cosmotology education is necessary and a high school diploma or a GED this job is necessary because that's my goal in life. I became interested in this job because I was born into it and looking at my family doing this same job. I was about 6 years old when I decided to be came a cosmetology. I can receive cosmetology education at a school called P-TEC in St. Petersburg or in a school called PIC in West Palm Beach.

Quovonne, Matt, and Salim listen to Jen outline dress codes during a Work Ethics session. Matt, from a military family in the Florida Panhandle, with his long, polished fingernails which he will daub black in honor of Halloween. A mohawk of locks which would usually cascade down the sides of his shaved head is tucked under a white surfer beanie. Despite the blond goatee, he resembles a hefty infant. At twelve, he began ripping off the cash register at his stepfather's video store.

And Salim, from Orlando, "just shouting distance from Disney World, dude." Silver chains drape his wrists. The blade of a pocketknife dangles around his neck. A silver skull ring stares over the words he writes in the opposing columns of his personal inventory: *Strengths: Sports, Math . . . Weaknesses: Don't finish things, Don't Want to Fail . . .* His older brother, he tells me, ruled their turf and was his idol. He once shot a classmate at his high school with a stun gun and hung him, unconscious, from a gym locker with a sign *Don't mess with the Burgus* pinned to his chest. Salim sighs and repeats that injunction. Clan glory. The Burgus were the shit in their part of Orlando.

His light clay complexion, his oval face and shaved head, his eyes pinching into feline angles as he smiles (made more suggestive of a cat by the right brow razored into tiger stripes). He resembles the novice monk who greeted me with "Welcome! Welcome!" (his only word of English) deep in the core of the Potala Palace in Lhasa, Tibet—a boy scooping, with his hands, mounds of yak butter from a cabinet and pressing this fuel into metal lamps. A boy who also, it seems, knew his place in the scheme of things.

Inspired by his older brother—now in prison—Salim says he rose quickly in his gang, "mostly with brains, but sometimes with muscle." His biggest promotion came when he discredited a senior member of the gang.

That was the word Salim used. *Discredited.*

He engineered a situation in which the senior gangbanger appeared untrustworthy to his peers.

"You could probably do quite well in a corporation with that savvy," I say. "Why not turn in your gang rack for a blue suit? It's got a better life expectancy, probably."

He searches me, the wish to believe like a lamp flickering in a back window.

And that light spurs my memory toward another boy in Lhasa, much less healthy looking. In the middle of the bazaar, he gathered a crowd around him by pushing a six-inch knife between the ulna and radius of his left forearm. Then he held out his beggar's cup.

CAREER ESSAY *(Matt)*

I want, and plan to, own my own video store. My parents owned it before and it seemed to get good business, so it sounds like a good idea. All the education I should need is a G.E.D. Whatever money is left over from business expenses will be my salary.

Hesitantly, Galvin approaches me with a job application for the post office. I'm surprised, given his showy remoteness. In his few weeks here, he and Andre—strangers to each other when they arrived—have fastened themselves to a common slouch of toughness and indifference at least partly styled on music videos. Andre has declared "this white boy is a good nigger," and their right fists gently hammer and submit to the other's in greeting.

Galvin's current problem: the blanks marked *employment history.* He's just turned twenty (at twenty-one, a resident must leave the program), and he drags a chain of botched chances.

"He loves programs," Jen says, "the kind of kid who never has followed through on anything. He sits in a program for a while, gets bounced, and then drifts to the next thing."

At Job Corps, for instance, Galvin dropped out of an introductory psychology class three days before it ended. Most recently, he sabotaged a chance to join the military. Sam, another staff member and currently in his twelfth year in the Air Force, had arranged for an enlistment interview, even though few new applicants are accepted these days, and Galvin is not an ideal candidate. On the day of the interview, Galvin hopped the bus to "run a few errands" and returned after curfew, feigning confusion as to the appointment time.

Now he wants to fill the white spaces with dependability, continuity, responsibility. He knows about these requisite virtues, even if he hasn't made their acquaintance.

"What should I put down?" he asks, timidly.

He can't tell about the oil change job. He lasted a week at it.

He can't include carpet laying. Fired. Electrician's apprentice. Quit. And there are those vacant zones of elongated sleeps, TV, and general fucking around.

I think of his fathers—blood and step—the former, by Galvin's own description, "a biker who let me do anything" and the latter, in Frank's assessment, "an authoritarian pounding the shit out of him twenty-four/seven."

I wonder how much they spur Galvin's rash confusion, his usual smartass, sidelong attitude, his cheek to me always as though he expects a blow. That same expectation, I now realize, may have caused Andre to shy from me after our collision on the basketball court. Maybe he sensed a violence lurking within me, the anger that has defined so many of my early relationships, that puzzlement which I fear most in myself.

As I sit with Galvin, my terror at that old prospect resurfaces and broadens. Shame pours over me.

What to put in those blanks that are not blank?

A Letter That Frank Made Me Write About My Career *(Tim)*

I want to be a Marine Biologist.

signed,

Tim

—JUST KIDDING—

It's not easy to just come up with a whole load of reasons why I want to be a Marine Biologist. Okay well here's a few. I like the ocean and I like the environment. I have my whole life, grown up by the intercoastal waterway and the gulf. I have watched from my back sea wall the water go from disgusting to putrid to worse. The water and (when it was low tide, since ours was a corner sea wall) the sand would get darker and smellier over the years. I always wanted to find a way to cleanout the tires and oil and crap and even I sometimes did. Of course it barely made a dent but it made me feel better. The main reason for the oil were the power boats and the wave runners and the jet ski's. I always liked them but I always hated the pollution they left.

On a seperate note, I have always liked the sea life itself. Sea turtles and dolphins have always fascinated me. As I think you already know I have done the sea turtle watch for two years in a row. It by the way is a corrupt organisation which has as much backstabbing as Little League. I have learned though that the frequency of sea turtles nesting on the gulf beaches has deminished severely in the past years.

I guess I do care a little after all. Well Frank you really got me thinking for the first time in a while. How mean of you, and I don't think you really meant to either. It must be a gift.

signed environmentally,

Tim

THREE

"WHY DON'T YOU TALK to me?" Quovonne asks, sounding almost hurt, "You talk to everybody but me."

And he is nearly correct. In the two months since his arrival, I have chatted with him amiably in the company of others under the oak tree. I have helped him a little with a school essay. I have been present while he has discussed some of his problems in a session with Jen. But I have otherwise shied from him. The morning we first met, passing on the balcony, I thought he was a *she,* perhaps Andre's visiting sister. He wore blue pedal pushers and white sandals, his hairless legs smooth and shapely, his coiffure waxed tight like some flapper with curlicuing sideburns. Faint traces of white lotion swirled on his brow, and white powder dusted his shaved underarms. He seemed possessed of breasts, girlish nubbins. Yet an instant later, an enveloping ambiguity redefined them as muscular male pectorals. The perceptual longing for clear distinctions, for assured order, jittered among the paradigms.

"We debated a long time about letting Quovonne into the program," Frank told me. "He was insistent during intake interviews that he was going to become a female one day, and we told him that we had no problem with him being gay but that as long as he was here, we would treat him as a male. It's a male program, after all."

Quovonne's presence has altered the daily pattern of agitation and compromise at the TLP. Each newcomer confronts strangers all around. But since he is assigned his own room, he can, for the most part, harbor himself in solitude if he chooses. Frank, Jen, and the program manager Paul designed this option into the TLP—the goal is to help the guys become independent, not merely part of a managed group policing itself. Most of the residents, however, also suffer too much isolation. Public life bewilders and challenges them, so a regular round of group meetings, house meetings, and group activities forces each resident into the arena of company and competing wills.

"We want to build a community, as much as possible," Paul told me, in the first months of the program. "We try to navigate between making the resident responsible for his own status in the program and encouraging him to deal with others.

"There've been problems we couldn't foresee, of course. And so we revise the program when we can. It's a little like the guys—in transition, too."

Quovonne is not the first gay in the program. Several have been admitted and at least one other has gone through it, with some conflict. That early client confessed that he kept his fellow residents in front of him, always sitting with his back to a wall or searching behind him on the green after dark. But most residents appeared content merely to tease—tossing out raw, adolescent remarks about gay sex—and by this, charming their anxieties into some repose.

Quovonne, however, incites by parading his slippery status. He dons a pink dress for homecoming at the local high school. He tells Tim that he had his breasts surgically reduced. He borrows Andre's model glue to reaffix one of his long, pink fingernails. Thus derision whispers around him and, on occasion, shouts. Galvin grouses, "This isn't some program for girls!" Yet Quovonne seems unperturbed, either out of some profound serenity—a strong grasp of self—or some intricate delusion.

Now he shakes his hairstyling head at me, a glamorous, dusky black woman's head, which is almost his double except for the tattoo *Miss V* on her throat. We—the three of us—sit under the oak tree, he wearing blue jeans and a red sweatshirt, with a blue and white print bandanna swathing his head. A mauve spaghetti-strap sundress is tossed over his shoulder.

"My hoochy-momma dress," he says, laughing.

He looks at Miss V and says, "My name means 'very powerful, conceited.' My momma's Jamaican, and it comes from that."

He says he's near the younger end of thirty-one children, ages one to forty-six, all but him and his twin sister from the same father.

"They all over this world," he says of his siblings, waving Miss V at the sky. "I met every one of 'em. Some in Jamaica, Haiti. Two brothers in Hawaii. A brother and two sisters in New York. Some in Palm Beach. All us been around. We don't say stepbrothers and sisters, 'cause my mom done raised all of us."

I ask about his brothers. Jen has told me that four of them are drag queens.

Quovonne is enthusiastically matter of fact. "Three of them got the sex change and one, he's like me, only older, and he's ready to get his."

"How can you be so certain," I ask, "at your age? I mean, you just turned seventeen."

"'Cause I know what I like. I know what I want, and that's how I know," he chuckles. "Because I know I'm transgender."

I suggest that perhaps he was unduly influenced by seeing his brothers in drag.

"No, no, my brothers moved out West, and each one got plastic surgery on his face. I was twelve when I met them the first time, but then I already know what I wanted to be. I only saw them dress up like that once, and I was like 'Momma, that's how I wanna dress.' And my momma said, 'no you don', not yet, baby,' 'cause she already knew. I used to tell her everything."

He claims that at five he recognized his desire to be female.

"My daddy used to try to teach all the boys to pee standing up, and I did not wanna learn like that. I wanted to sit down and pee like my momma. And one Christmas my momma and daddy got me all boy toys, and I got mad and cried, and they took them back and got me teddy bears and stuff like that."

"I always liked boys. I'd see a boy and go 'oh, he's so cute,' and I always used to go under him and try to be under him all the time . . . you know, like a child wanting to be with an older person. I used to like Artis, and he was a grown man, and he used to give me candy and stuff, and I used to always be over his house.

"I was always helping Momma, doing cookin' . . . and my twin sister was different. She used to be under my daddy.

"Through the years, I got raped, too. I got raped when I was four, and I got raped again when I was seven, and I got raped again when I was fourteen . . ."

He announces this as though listing the schools he has attended.

"But," he says, "I don't think that changed me inside, or who I was gonna be or . . . who I wanted to be or how I wanted to be."

"Why do you think that?" I ask.

"Because if that's the case, then that woulda changed me against men. Most women when they get raped, who do they go to? Another woman, right? If I got raped, I . . . oh, god, I don't know what I'm trying to say . . . it just didn't change me because I've been feminine all my life."

Quovonne remains clear-eyed, almost casual. He knows I want details. He's told this story before—perhaps to caseworkers or counselors—yet not so often it has become one of the stories he tells. I am mildly repelled by my encroaching sense of voyeurism, so I choose the coward's way to intrusion. I open the door for his memories, but he must invite them in.

"You were four the first time it happened?"

"I remember this man, a Spanish man. His name was Señor Humberto. He stayed in this big old gray house, and we stayed in this big old gray house on the side of him. My momma done knew him for years. He was the type of man who bought kids in the neighborhood candy. He wasn't like no stranger or nothin' like that.

"And we had to have a net thrown over our house, for termites and like that, and we had to stay the night over his house. I remember my sister was in a crib, and I was layin' on the floor. My momma kissed me good-night.

"I can't never lie to you. I don't remember him raping me, but I remember him putting his finger . . . inside my rectum, licking me there and stuff like that. And my stepdad told my momma about it one day, and she was gonna kill that man that did this, but he skipped town. He never got charged for that.

"And when I was seven, I had a flashback that he was in the tub with me again, and I knew someone raped me again 'cause . . . I was cryin' . . . and blood was everywhere. I couldn't never picture this person, though. Every time I do, it always came as my stepdad, and I always told my mom that. I always pretend that he's my stepdaddy."

As Quovonne speaks, his hand crawls slowly, unconsciously from his throat to his chin, then to his cheek, then to his brow. He rubs his eyes, as though exhausted at the end of a long day, as if trying to erase them. His pink fingernails glow, exorbitant, false.

"And when I was fourteen . . . my boyfriend Edward would come over, he was eighteen. And he and my daddy knew each other, but my daddy never think that we was hunching and stuff like that. We didn't do that.

"Well, about one fifty-something A.M., I went to go take out the garbage. My daddy say if I clean up, he give me forty dollars to go to Miami. And Edward came around, and he say come out here. And I say I can't, I ain't got no clothes on. I just got a tee shirt on. He say, just come here, I got something to tell you. He was a step away from the porch, and then the next thing I know I went over right there. He grabbed me by the neck. I started fightin' right back. I said you better let me go. I thought he was playin.' And then I started cryin' and fightin,' and he took me behind the bushes, or wherever. And all of them had sex with me, four of 'em. They tried to make me lick 'em, but I was crying, and I had my mouth closed. And I remember my friend looked out the window and called the police. The next thing I know my momma done beat the boys, almost killed one of them. Every time I'd see the boys, I fight with them or beat them up, 'cause they took from me something I didn't want to give to no one till I was a certain age."

In his lap, Miss V gazes up into his eyes, almost his reflection in the moment's surface. Confidante? Confessor?

Absently, he swoops her up and places her face down on the grass.

"And I didn't have sex with no one after that," he says emphatically. "I wouldn't even call that sex. I wasn't . . . intimate with no one after that . . . till I got with William when I was fourteen and a half. He's the one who took care of me. When I came here, we had a three-bedroom apartment with my daughter and his son."

"Your daughter?"

"Tawna. She's three now."

"Where's her mother?" I try not to sound astonished.

"Linda? She's Spanish. She don't take care of my daughter," he says calmly, "she don't have nothing to do with her, 'cause she was a gay lady and I was gay, and we bop heads to see if it was right for us. She was . . . eighteen and I was fourteen, or whatever. And when we did, we did not like it. She came up pregnant the first time. She was goin' to have an abortion, but nobody believe in that. So she had it, and I raised my child . . . but I haven't seen my child for two months now. Otherwise I raised her . . . and my mom."

"She staying with your mom now?"

"No, she with my sister in New York, 'cause my mom moved out, and there are a lotta problems . . ."

We sit for a moment. A car blaring a hip-hop tune jounces up the street.

"Why," I ask, unaccountably hesitant, "would you have moved into an apartment with William at, what, fourteen or fifteen?"

"'Cause I wasn't getting along with my parents. Jamaican parents say 'you gotta learn things on your own!'

"And William was payin.' He was nineteen. I was just goin' to school and workin.' But then William went to jail 'cause he was selling drugs, and the feds got him . . ."

"That's some heavy stuff," I say, testing the impulse to commiserate.

"Oh, yeah, I've been through a lot . . ." he replies, his voice evaporating, the tone from some matronly reminiscence.

"I came here so I can depend on myself. I never depend on myself. William always bought stuff for me. I want to do everything right and get my daughter and move from outta here. I take things day by day. I hope that in a year maybe me and my lover will have somewhere to go."

"A new lover now, besides William?"

"Yeah," he giggles shyly, "but I can't say who he is."

"Mr. X, eh?"

"Mr. Right . . . I'm not allowed to bring up his name. Staff knows who it is, some staff, but I promised not to say nothin' 'cause he not with it completely yet. He know that we go together and everything, but he don't want everybody to know yet, 'cause . . . he don't want anybody to know."

"Well, you're trying to get your independence. That's good."

"Of course, I'm gonna go to college. I'm gonna be a teacher. All subjects, elementary, or history or science in high school . . . or English. I got a B in English, so I like poems and stuff like that."

"It's a pretty good profession," I offer tepidly, "very satisfying."

"And I think that sometimes I'm gonna be a singer," he says, with inspiration, "'cause I'm always singin.' All I need is someone to help produce me 'cause I don't have no car to get to the studio. I can get the money up . . . "

four

I ASK JEN IF Quovonne's Mr. Right is real, or merely another wish pitted against loneliness.

"Quovonne needs a lot of attention," Jen says.

Later, Quovonne lolls in the chair beside Jen's desk in the office, composing lists of hair-care products he hopes to purchase one day. Returned from morning classes at P-TEC, he leans against the doorjamb, his rucksack tossed on his shoulder, chatting and taunting. He decorates the office walls with construction paper cutouts—pumpkins at Halloween, turkeys and pilgrims at Thanksgiving, and at Christmas a broad evergreen bearing ornaments on which he paints the residents' names. Frequently, he answers the residents' phone in the office vestibule with "this is Quovanna," and Jen rolls her eyes and tells him patiently, again, that it's "Quovonne" as long as he's here. Almost daily, he beseeches her with grievances or puzzlements, though sometimes he simply craves an audience.

"Being with the guys like this is turning out to be part of the job," she tells me somewhat sweetly when I shake my head at how much it seems like elaborate babysitting.

Jen came to Florida in her teens when her family fled the tribal reprisals of small town gossip in Ohio. She exudes courtesy and order. Big-boned, good-girl fortitude. Immaculate complexion. A chin, round and dimpled, which seems always about to quiver, though it never does. Without fail, *she* answers the phone melodically, bearing the respect for decorous forms she would like to instill in the residents: "Transitional Living Program, this is Jen. How may I help you?"

She has worked for two years for the parent organization of the TLP—a nonprofit—mostly as a counselor at the local runaway shelter it operates. Before that, she performed in-home therapeutic interventions as a clinical case manager.

"It was a for-profit agency," she says, "a family-owned operation. That's where I discovered the business end of family dysfunction and mental illness. Eighty-five percent of my hours had to be billed to Medicaid. They logged fake hours and back hours . . . And sometimes the owners paid us with credit cards. The pay was pitiful, really, even worse than here. Everybody who worked there was fresh out of college, so they exploited both workers and clients.

"I left after two years, and the place was eventually closed down. But those poor kids . . . At six, some were already acting out, and many still were with the parents or guardians who were doing things to them, people who sometimes wanted my attention more than their kids did. It was my job to assess the situation and try to build relationships between the families and caregivers . . .

"Sometimes you could get evidence of trouble, like a handprint on an arm or bugs in their food. But just as often you knew something was going on and you couldn't quite get the goods. For instance, bath time might be a problem for a kid—you know, the touching—or a kid starts doing weird sexual stuff with their dolls. I remember one kid, Harold. Even after nine months of contact with me, he could only confide he had something to tell me, but he could never bring himself to do it.

"It can be frustrating, the problems seem so widespread because you mostly come into contact with failure. I remember the guardian *ad litem* for one of the kids. He was almost angry with me. He said, 'Do you have to call in the Child Abuse hotline for *every* bruise you see?'

"What do you say to that? Kids like those become some of our residents . . ."

On another day, lolling in Quovonne's usual seat, I ask Jen—as I ask all the residents and the staff—why she's here.

She leans back in her chair, rolls a pencil down her fingers like a small baton. "During high school, I was a dispatcher for the Treasure Island Police Department. I thought it was cool, learning the codes and such—until I started sending officers out to deal with rapes, or strangulations, or DOAs. But once, there was a schizo guy arrested at St. Petersburg JC for threatening a patrolman. He paced around the holding cell, yelling, his hands fluttering. The toilet was talking to him. There were faces in the wall. I thought, 'That's interesting. I'd like to know more about that reality.'

"But, of course, I'm here now because I got tired of the shelter, and I got the chance to help put the TLP together from scratch. Paul and Frank thought the program should have an all-male staff, but I said, why? And then they realized that it would probably be better this way."

She pauses, nibbles on the pencil's eraser.

"Still, you get tired of being noble. My friends in business say they can't believe I work with *them,* meaning the guys, and it's almost embarrassing. 'Isn't she *good,*' they say. 'What a *good* person.' And I'm not really . . .

"It's a conversation-stopper. 'What do you do?' 'I work at Solomon Brothers.' 'I work at Suntrust.' And then they turn to me: 'I work at Social Services.'

"Silence. Something hangs in the air between us. It's like *Isn't that cute, she works with homeless boys.* Among my conservative friends, what I do is on their tax dollars, and they think it's a drag on the economy.

"Even though it's probably racist to say, I'd like them to see somebody like Tim. He's white, he's clean-cut, but he's still homeless . . ."

Ah, Tim.

He's been at the TLP for nearly a year since Health and Rehabilitative Services removed him, at sixteen, from the custody of abusive foster parents here in St Pete.

"HRS," he says, vituperatively. "It stands for Home Wrecking Service."

He grits his teeth and seethes when his HRS caseworker drives into the parking lot. He grimaces at the mention of her name. She personifies, for him, the clumsy power of structure over individual will, the obtuseness of adults, injustice. Although the TLP—rather than another foster family—assumed guardianship of him, he still sees his caseworker often, too often for his liking, especially since his desire to buy a car has so far been stonewalled by the keepers of state bureaucracy.

His caseworker is also emblematic of the defining event of his life: his mother's death from cancer three years before.

Tim never knew his father. ("I heard his voice on the phone once," he says sourly.) He had no siblings, no relatives with whom he and his mother associated. She, in the neutralizing professional lexicon, suffered from "substance abuse issues" and a "personality disorder." Mother and son ultimately became indigent, tramping through various family shelters and flophouses. Their mutual solitude and dependence, their rage, their resourcefulness, and pity entwined with their poverty, their love. She died seven days after she told Tim she was ill.

Five minutes with Tim and one hears how he despises the motherless world, how it snaps its jaws shut on him over and over without warning. His mother's absence is a force, like that of a collapsed star, and it pulls his own substantial light down within him. It's always with him, as are all his substitutions for grief, and grief itself, patiently awaiting his recognition.

When he first came to the TLP, almost an elfin figure, he dominated the less articulate residents with spat wit and the abrasive quickness of a commodities trader, and he brooded. Evenings, he returned from his shift at a fast food chicken joint, still dressed in the humiliatingly cheerful uniform, cute and pissed, the bill of his company hat low over his eyes. And he would bring out a can of Sterno, say, on which the chicken had been kept warm, light it on the picnic table and pass his hand over the flame as the other residents smoked and bantered. And nearly all would eventually, almost unconsciously follow suit to show they could do it.

Magnetic and aggravated, and inept at close contact with those he drew to himself, Tim slammed many doors, literal and figurative, in those early months. Everything "sucked." And he retreated to his room, remaining almost sealed away there like an immured boy-Pharaoh. Yet he could resurrect himself ten times in an evening to knock on Frank's door, each approach a meager stratagem spurred by the need that bewilders and taunts him. He could also swagger and bully against someone he barely knew, like me, and a minute later, for instance, present for my inspection a container of cottage cheese bearing an expired date.

"Any good, do you think?" he would ask, modestly.

I would sniff and judge it edible, and he would accept this response almost as a directive.

Even now as adult handsomeness begins to shadow his jaw and his frame extends and broadens, he remains boy-rangy and as undulate as a waterspout, his chest little wider than a hand's breadth. And he still sounds misanthropic, though a director of a local art museum has undertaken his mentorship, giving him a job in the gift shop there. Some of the residents embrace the structure of agencies. They relish such systems of clear rewards and punishments, the coordinates by which they chart their position in the cosmos. A few have known nothing else and toil futilely, if at all, to envision existence beyond those minimalist comforts. Tim, however, is not among this number. At some profound level, he resists being a client. And most certainly he will not be a subject—mine or anyone else's—at least not in the

usual way. He is, in this, like the tribesman who refuses to be photographed for fear of losing his spirit to the lens and the human mechanism behind it. There's a part of him that no one is allowed to touch, since he can't touch it.

When I show interest in him, beyond the small talk of the moment, he retreats. I am questions and he, privacy. Maybe he doesn't want to be known, or doesn't know how to be known, or I don't know how to know him. Or, in his eyes, I'm not trustworthy because he believes that once I have his story, I'll abandon him, like everyone who has abandoned him. As if I could get his—or anyone's—story.

Like all who want love, Tim wants it on his own terms. (Why do people think that, simply because someone has suffered, that person would be grateful for any kind of love people are willing, or able, to give?) He never speaks of his mother. He alludes to her, like some oblique reference to God in a sacred text. When she enters his conversation, it is the unpredictable drawing open of a furnace door on the roaring flame within. We sit, for instance, in the office one afternoon, and Mr. Rogers flashes onto the screen as Tim surfs the channels.

"He looks and acts just like some child molester," Tim sneers. "Look at that, a real perv . . ."

I decide that, perhaps, this is an attempt at conversation—and an opportunity to breach the barrier around him—so I play to his obvious intelligence. "Isn't that just some easy MTV irony?" I suggest.

"I get my ideas from growing up with my mother," he replies acidly. "Thank you very much." He returns to the screen. No more eye contact for the rest of the day.

Another time, I enter the office, and he and Jen are framing his GED. He shows me his scores, which are far beyond the minimum to pass.

"I didn't study at all," he says proudly. He slips the document into the frame and points to the slim space between his diploma and the back plate. "You could hide money in there," he observes.

He announces that he'll enroll in the local junior college in the spring. And then he reminisces suddenly, with a note of affection, about a Mr. Green, a counselor, who came from his school to the apartment to tell him about his mother's passing. Mr. Green, who shepherded him through the immediate aftermath, who kept him in school until HRS moved him to the care of the foster family, who followed up after that debacle and helped get him into the TLP.

"You wouldn't believe the people who show up," he says incredulously, "when your mom dies."

He enjoys my company, in company, but flees being alone with me. I happen upon him, for instance, in the laundry room. We force some small talk. He quickly withdraws, heads upstairs toward his room, and stops.

"You're gonna follow me, right?" he says.

Sick with feeling foolish and predatory, I reply, almost angry, "No, I'm not chasing after you. If you want to talk, you'll talk."

Later I tell Jen about it. She's labored to coax from this otherwise vocal soul genuine words about what haunts him.

"Tim needs to feel safe. He'll come around," she says, "He'll talk when he wants you to do something for him."

Later, as I sit under the oak tree with Andre and Salim, Tim marches back and forth along the balcony between his room and Frank's office, as though on business, yet glancing at us, curious.

On another afternoon, in the park nearby, we both happen to take a break from a TLP touch football game, in which he, slight and slow, has fared poorly.

"Just kill me, Don," he says out of nowhere, wiping his brow with the tail of his Brown University tee shirt.

"Are you talking about sports?" I ask.

"Yeah, right."

"Forget about football. Stick to tennis," I try.

"I suck."

"How about racquetball?"

"You mean that '80s game?"

"You don't have to chase the ball as much."

I mention squash, hockey. He looks in the grass.

"Just keep playing," I say.

"Yeah, right," he snorts.

"You gotta try to improve at anything."

We sit quietly for a moment, and he then tells me that he recently went to the symphony with his mentor and "some old people," he says, "who gave money to the museum, people pretty far up the food chain." He hated the Schubert, he tells me, but liked Mozart and Dvorak. "But I don't know anything about it," he says, facing the grass, "I figure that's your stuff."

Tim has seen most of the thirty or so residents admitted to the program thus far, and he's seen many of them go. This passing also impedes his vacillating eagerness to befriend newcomers. His rise to Phase Two, while a triumph, presents him with further challenges, among them increased peer responsibility and an impending arrogance deriving from his success. On his first day at the TLP, for instance, Matt is sent to Tim's room with a blank form so that the latter might advise him on making out a weekly grocery list. The place teems with Salvador Dali paraphernalia—coffee cups, tee shirts—from the museum gift shop. On his bed lies a copy of *The Chants of Maladoror,* which Tim has taken up because Dali—his current fascination—had illustrated an earlier edition of the book. Not knowing what to do with Matt, his new charge, Tim snatches up the book.

"Weird shit," he says, "There's a guy in it with a crab crawling up his ass."

"Lautréamont was an avant-garde writer," I say.

"Yeah, I've heard that term. What's it mean?"

I explain, happy to play the professor. Matt looks on, the blank form for his grocery list in his lap.

"Are there any girls . . . here?" Matt asks, finally.

"None . . . except Quovonne . . . or Quovanna," Tim says.

"Yeah, I saw it," Matt says.

A moment later, Tim has found a way to relate to this stranger with the list who troubles him.

"Ramen noodles, a pound of ground beef." He snaps off the items like a peremptory boss. "Albertson's beef is shit. I go to Kash n' Karry, less fatty . . ."

VH1 emanates soundlessly from the TV. A hip-hop tune on Tim's boom box supplies the audio. Across the screen, a fashion show flows. Tim knows the models by first names.

"There's Linda," he says, pausing in his recitation of necessary comestibles, and "Elle, not bad." He and Matt are stricken by the flicker of a bare breast, or the swivel of tight midriff. Their stares: that stare.

"You gotta make a meal to show them you can," he tells Matt a moment later.

"How about pork brains and eggs?" Matt inquires.

"Dude, did you say brains?"

"Yeah, they're good. My stepdad made them."

Dali's face appears on the TV, and Tim races to turn up the volume.

"Madman, or genius?" the resonant announcer voice asks, "The difference between pathology and art is . . ." But just that fast the camera shifts back to the runway.

"Ah, shit, man," Tim says.

And with that announcer's voice in my head, I'm thinking of Matt and Tim and the rest of the residents: *the difference between independence and deviation, between freedom and anarchy . . ."*

Tim shows both of us a business card from the President's Assistant for Domestic Affairs and a letter of thanks from Bill Clinton for attending a recent election-season conference on homeless and troubled teenagers.

"They had eight of us smart kids and 200 people in business suits," he says. "Dude, we'll see some changes after the election. We told them they need more places like this. Man, you know in Russia, they just throw the homeless kids in jail."

I recall that Frank said Tim returned from the conference with more egotism than esteem, and that he would not be allowed to attend another soon, despite the luster he might bring to the program.

"You want onions and mushrooms?" Tim snaps at Matt.

"Freeze-dried?" Matt supposes.

"Ick, shit. Get fresh. You can keep them in the fridge . . ."

A few days later, a brown chow belonging to a woman in one of the apartments across the sandy alley ventures toward a group of us lounging on the front steps. The dog wants to be petted but hesitates. A step toward us. Another. Matt leans toward the brown, intent stare, and though too far away to touch, he sends out his hand. He gazes at the creature, calls it with a whisper. Finally, he folds down onto his haunches, keeping eye contract. The animal bolts backward.

"That dog is for shit," Tim moans. "It comes and shits in our yard and barks."

"It's been beaten," I say, stating what seems obvious. I'm bored with his constant negation. I've been around him long enough, I decide, to let myself feel this. A pleasing swell.

"That mutt deserves to be beaten," Tim growls.

"You shouldn't stereotype a dog," Matt says, his voice as soft as it was to the chow.

I join in, more brusquely. "You're going to condemn a dog because he shits and barks? What's a dog supposed to do?"

Tim grimaces, leaps and hangs from the metal cross-members supporting the portable basketball hoop. He faces away.

Jen's recent confidence to me somehow shadows this scene: She's talked with her husband about offering to become foster parents to Tim. Her husband is also a social worker—drop-out prevention—and they want a large family, eventually. She believes, it seems, that Tim is different from the rest of the residents, maybe because of his special relationship with HRS, or because his grief brims visibly and makes him seem accessible, more "normal" and "curable."

I think of how eagerly Quovonne chases her mindfulness, how distrustful Tim is of Jen—of all women and most adults—and his inconstant pursuit of Frank's approving presence.

I also remember an incident from one of Jen's home visits as a family interventionist. A filthy child entered the room and asked about the dog chained in the yard, "Mom, do you want me to feed him?"

"No, we fed him yesterday," the mother replied, casually, "Just give him water."

"I never cried about any of the kids I saw in those visits," Jen told me, "but I did about that dog. I guess it was something I didn't have to be professional about."

FIVE

FREQUENTLY, MATT SITS under the live oak, smoking his pipe, his gaze fixed on *Passage to Dawn* or *Elminster,* volumes from the Forgotten Realms series of fantasy novels, of which he possesses many, displaying them proudly.

"Those realms must not be very forgotten," Andre says, after one such showing, "with so many books out."

Matt shrugs, turns his head and spits onto the grass, then returns to his soothing pages and the intricate relations of reluctant mages, time travelers, and heroes laboring to resist buxom succubi. He puffs. To a persisting degree, he resembles my youngest brother at sixteen—which encourages me to imagine a confused good will in his blue eyes, a stricken haplessness. It evokes in me the desire to encourage and perhaps even do for him. Be the big brother. It also evokes some distrust and an old anger that is irrelevant in his presence, perhaps even irrelevant now in my own life. Seeing him like this reminds me that I don't understand.

Matt often talks of the characters in his books—derived from Dungeons and Dragons—as a young Greek might have spoken of Homeric heroes, or a nineteenth-century schoolboy the figures of Arthurian romance. He tells me their stories, one plot imbroglio after another, as though I were as intimate with these elaborate sagas as he. Plunging his imagination into the sheer, floating mountains and spired palaces depicted on the paperback covers, he sometimes starts to spin awkwardly through moves suggestive of tae kwon do. The older boys on the military base where he sometimes lived with his father taught him warrior games with ampguard weapons: staffs, padded on both ends, for striking and blocking. So now he craves knives . . . and swords, begging Frank to let him purchase a samurai model from a Franklin Mint catalog—when he gets a job and some money.

"Not to use, mind you," he says, aware that weapons of any sort are banned from the TLP, "but just for display on my wall."

Tactfully, Frank repeats that no one doubts Matt's responsible intentions but that the passions and proclivities of his neighbors cannot be similarly trusted. Thus, Matt must content himself with lengths of broken broomstick or snapped-off chair arm when impulse commands him to join the Drow warriors of Menzoberranzan in their saber combats.

"I was the designated dweeb in my middle school," he tells me one afternoon, "but I didn't mind. Hey, there were even some people who thought I was gay."

"They were wondering about things like that in middle school?"

He peers at me as though I'm out of it, which I clearly am. To crawl back closer to in, I ask about his long, pointed fingernails, elegant and glossed with clear polish.

"You play guitar?"

"No, I just grew them out. Chicks like them."

"Kind of sensuous looking?" I venture.

"Yeah, they rip," he says, happy for the chance to swagger.

Like a number of the residents at the TLP, Matt is a product of the cleaved household and the liquid excuse. His parents divorced when was seven, and he is a lingering, unfortunate link between them. To his parents—who remain mutually acrimonious—he's apparently a reminder of the bitter former spouse and the choices and dreams of a younger, more presumptuous self, a remaining cause for any contact between them, a damnable vestige, a witness to their suffering, an emissary of their most self-indulgent projections. Whether they dare acknowledge it or not, they want to be rid of him, it seems, especially after the griefs he has contrived for them in recent years. When possible, he tries to turn this and any of their other guilty passions to his favor, even if his actions harm himself most of all.

The drift of school failure, thievery and, finally, homelessness brought him to the TLP. At thirteen, he started breaking into cars and houses—and he was caught, eventually, three times.

"Well, actually, they didn't even catch me one percent of the time," he brags. "I've broken into quite a few cars."

He senses my remote disapproval and puts his book down.

"Like I didn't break in and take stereos or anything like that. But if there was a walkman in there . . . or change, or candy, cigarettes, knives. You know, I've gotten a couple of knives out of cars. Does this sound like a rationalization: It was a lesson to the owners. Besides, I didn't take anything that was very expensive."

He's also broken into houses, some of them on the Air Force base where his father, a career man nearing the twenty years needed for retirement, works as a medical technician.

"They were always unlocked," he says, sincerely. "I never really 'broke' into them."

"Just like you 'borrowed' your sister's car?" I ask, almost chuckling.

He smiles through an expression that pretends to seriousness—surprised that I have paid attention in our previous talks, proud of the camaraderie in this casual investigation of admitted infraction.

"Hey, I've never stolen a car other than from a family member. I borrowed my stepdad's car, and my brother let me drive his van before. And my sister's car . . . well, that was a misunderstanding.

"But I'm pretty much changed now. I haven't broken into a car in quite some time. Once in a while I'll take something, like a pack of cigarettes or something from a store. Because I know I won't get caught."

"Yeah?" I put on my best skeptical countenance, to quell my desire to lecture him.

He doesn't seem possessed of the anger that, he says, shoved his fist through more than one wall or door owned by his distant parents. But something—the Forgotten Realms?—flows even now into that breakage, into the hole in all his stories.

He probably flew through that hole himself when he hopped on his bicycle at his father's house in Texas and, penniless, headed toward his mother in Florida. Three days, and two hundred and fifty miles later, still in Texas, he phoned her from the interstate.

"She started freaking out because every time I call her, I'm always in trouble, even though that's not true."

"But it's generally true?"

"Yeah, sometimes it is true. But I made it specifically clear that I wasn't calling for help. I wasn't calling to ask her to come pick me up or anything like that. I intended to make the trip on my own. I was just calling to let her know what had happened and where I was, though I didn't know the area. And she didn't come pick me up then. I made it to the Sealy exit, or something like that. Then she decided that she was going to come get me. So I waited a day for her to get there."

"Hanging at the Sealy exit?"

"Yeah. I'd slept the night before behind a Wal-Mart. And the night before that I met some guy that was working at a convenience store. I stayed there and I talked to him. And he brought me out a bag of chips that had been slit when the packing box was opened.

"And I helped one guy who had part of his tire with all the cords sticking out and everything. He was trying to get that off and I offered to give him a hand. He said sure and gave me a pair of gloves to put on. And he paid me a couple of bucks. I used that to buy fries and a drink. I found a couple of beers along the road, too. Unopened."

"Yeah?"

"I didn't think to bring any water, and those beers just kind of saved me from thirst. Later, I found some of those Gatorade bottles. You know those little thin ones, with the cap. I rinsed those out real good, and I filled three of them up with water. I rationed it out.

"At the Sealy exit, a bum walked up when I hung up after talking to my mom, and we sat down and started talking. And then he introduced me to a couple of other guys around the area. We got food and everything. They weren't so bad, for bums."

"So were you glad when your mom came?"

"Yeah. I hadn't seen her in about two years."

He suckles thoughtfully on his pipe.

"I came here because she couldn't deal with me either. I ran off, and ran from several of the shelters I ended up in. Boring places."

"Does your dad know you're living here?"

"I doubt it. He doesn't care. He says that he knows me, which isn't true. He's never taken the time to get to know me. The only thing he knows me as is a son and a deviant. That's not all that I am."

He shakes *Homeland* at me—the first volume of the Dark Elf

Trilogy—as though tapping the air, or maybe that enduring hole before him.

"You know, my older sister and brother used to tell me that I was my dad's favorite. It's true. I was always treated better. I wasn't given more per se. I just wasn't punished.

"The whole family was coming to me about that. They would say, 'You get treated better by Dad' and 'Don't worry, you won't get in trouble.' And they'd get pissed at me. And I kind of got tired of it. So I confronted him one time about that.

"I didn't come yelling at him. I just said, 'I wish you wouldn't treat me better than everybody. Either treat me the same or just, you know, don't treat me at all.'

"And he wouldn't hear me. He wouldn't hear any of it at all. I kept going and then he got mad at me. And he packed a sleeping bag and a few other things and bought two cases of beer, and went to Canyon Lake, and passed out drunk in the truck. Even my stepmom got pissed at him about that. He's got a major problem with booze. See this?"

He points to a small scar above his left eyebrow.

"He did this with a seven iron . . . another time when he got drunk and was yelling at me.

"But nobody in the family would help me with committing him into some kind of program. You have to have two family members to commit someone."

A few days later, I find Matt at the picnic table with Galvin. He holds another volume of Forgotten Realms. Groping for an angle into talk, I ask about the story. Galvin, who is usually "thugging" in the company of Andre and Salim, resumes what I later discover is an ongoing theological guerrilla action against Matt.

"What would you fear if there was no God?" he demands,

sponging a little heft from the tone of the prophet. "Money? That's the devil."

"It's worse to worship than to follow the devil," Matt says. His nails, recently painted black for Halloween, are now unpolished and cut short for the job hunt. (Frank had suggested to him that, perhaps, they had undermined his application at the mall shoe store.) He also wears a new yin-yang ring.

"Do you think God created magic?" Galvin asks smugly, searching me for complicity.

"No," Matt replies.

"Where did it come from, then?"

"There is more than one god," Matt says, tamping his pipe calmly.

"What you believe is where you are gonna go," Galvin announces with a sadistic assurance. "If you believe in the devil, that's where you're gonna go. If you believe in nothing, that's where you're gonna go. If you believe you turn into cows, that's where you're gonna go."

"Worshipping God is a selfish act," Matt says.

"Shit," Galvin replies, "I've looked at many religions, Mohammed, Buddhist, Baptist. I'm not just a Christian."

"There are goddesses and gods of murder, beauty, generosity," Matt says, as though reciting the evident. "It's not devil worship. I'll never take the mark of the devil."

"Then why are there spells?"

"To defend a certain sanction of followers . . ."

Galvin scoffs. "That kind of magic I would call wizardry. Fireballs!"

"You can cast fireballs?!" I ask Matt.

"No. I can't cast my own spells. I don't know how. Gods exist but they don't have any power without followers. They just exist."

"What is your goddess, then?" I ask.

"My goddess is . . . mystery."

The goddess of mystery, he explains, is also known as the Wounded Lady in Dungeons and Dragons.

"Shit," Galvin says. He crushes his cigarette and strides off, jealous, I think, of the attention I'm giving Matt.

When Galvin has reached the TLP office, on the far side of the green, I ask about the goddess. I'm serious, but I also hear myself trying to sound serious.

"My life was nothing until nine months ago," Matt says, oddly earnest. "I know this may come off as weird, but I had no point of existence. I had so much reckless behavior . . . I asked God—the old God—to help me, not do it for me . . . and no sign came.

"It took me a long time to see. He's not listening to me. I was a little bit insane with my troubles. If he had heard me at all, I would be dead. He didn't listen, so I started to worship the goddess of mystery.

"I converted at a rough time. My two stepbrothers were going to Oklahoma. I was sleeping on the couch at my dad's house . . .

"When I converted over, things got better. She doesn't speak to me, but I feel her nudge. I have to do things myself, of course."

"How did they get better?"

"I was on restriction with my dad, but two days later, I was off it. I got along better with my steps. It wasn't just a coincidence . . . And so far I've stuck it out. Not everything has been perfect."

"How do you worship her?"

"I believe in her."

"That's it. No ceremony?"

"Ceremonies are for priests and clerics. I'm not a priest. When I need help, I talk to her. I set aside times. Like in the banyan tree at Crescent Lake Park."

"Do you speak?"

"Yeah. I speak to her, like a close friend. Chitchat. Sometimes she doesn't listen, and sometimes she does."

"How do you know?

"I don't. It's important that I speak."

I hesitate and then decide to ask the obvious. "So how does that make her different from the old God?"

"She's never really let me down. She doesn't need to come down in form . . . Sometimes I can feel her presence.

"You have to make a conscious choice, and I don't know if she is the best choice. Maybe the positive thing was in leaving the old God."

SIX

SOMETIMES, DURING A STEAMY afternoon, the TLP resembles a vacated stage set: two floors and one balcony of closed jalousied doors, whitewashed walls and brown tiles lined with pink hibiscus. The only sign of human life is the thumping bass from stereos and radios in the residents' rooms: their separate heartbeats.

Today, however, Salim kicks a slightly deflated basketball around the green. He tries to pop the ball into the air, to catch it, but it squirrels off his toe. He nudges it through the grass, his path drawn by subtler deflections. As he ambles, he stoops a little, as though searching for something lost at his feet.

Slowly, he sits on the ball, almost on his haunches. And Bill stands nearby in his new khaki pants that Jen helped him select at Wal-Mart, the sheen still on them. Affixed to his left breast, an adhesive label announces *Hello, my name is,* with *Bill* scrawled beneath it in Magic Marker. He waits anxiously to go to his new job bagging groceries at the neighborhood Kash n' Karry, more composed than when he first arrived at the TLP, thanks to having resumed his mood medication.

Salim sits on the ball in the sunlight, his elbows on his knees, his hands a doubled fist on which he rests his chin. Thinker. Dreamer. Blank.

Bill orbits lazily around him, hands in his pockets. He lights another cigarette and tries to blow a smoke ring. He snatches a few blades of grass and some dirt and sprinkles them onto the ground like seed.

Despite the elaborate scheduling in Phase One, time at the TLP can devolve to this. The green and the rest of the place—referred to always as "the property"—are surrounded on four sides by a Dairy Queen, a white clapboard house bearing the sign "Study Buddy," a pink Spanish Mediterranean mansion refurbished and renamed The Center for Wellness, and the sandy alley lined by sagging apartments. Beyond this lies the abandoned streets and vagrant venues adjoining the northwest part of downtown. To the east, middle-class Crescent Lake; to the west, six lanes of interstate nowhere. There are gangs, men hunched under freeway bridges, social security taverns, strip malls and mega-malls—as well as shady antebellum lanes and vast glittering pavements under kingly palms.

These surroundings shape a resident's boredom, and much more. With hours such as this, they lean on him like his declared wish to take his place in the adult world and his resentment at having to do it. He admires yet fears the self-creation modestly implied in the program's routine daily demands, such as defining individual responsibilities and goals, envisioning the consequences of one's actions, staking out personal privacy. Dull stuff, when compared to sleeping as you wish or running wide open on some narcotic. The resident is also encircled by memory, that past he brings as a burden to be lifted and yet often wielded as a foolish protection against change. Pliable, pitiable, plentiful memory. Or a vast, provisional erasure of the same.

Einstein, or some such whiz, once said, "Boredom is an excuse for lack of imagination." Yes. But here—when it's not just another of a boy's myriad strategies for "getting over" on whomever's in charge—boredom sometimes seems a fragile repose, maybe the conjuring of some crucial kind of adolescent time, drifty time, heretofore lacking, a mood which the nerves foist on the confused heart for the good in slowing down.

"Do you feel sorry for these guys?" Frank asked me during my first weeks at the TLP. I was then, officially, a new volunteer, and he was trying to measure the extent of Victorian mamahood in me, that sentimentalizing impulse—still widespread, I believe—which tries to see only the innocent among the savage. I couldn't tell him that I felt sorry, not exactly. He approved of this, though we're not so distant in intent from those former do-gooders like Franklin Winslow Johnson, for instance, whose now laughably quaint *Problems of Boyhood, A Course in Ethics for Boys of High-School Age,* circa 1914, was published under the rubric "Constructive Studies."

Six weeks into the program and Salim—like Andre, Quovonne, and Matt—doesn't have a job yet. If he did, no doubt he would not have the opportunity now to be squatting on a semi-deflated globe in the middle of the green. He's applied at the usual fast-food places on 4th Street North. No call backs. Sam says some of those businesses have hired previous TLP residents, but they "haven't worked out," and so the managers look away, courteously. Other enterprises, like the supermarket where the residents are shuttled to buy their weekly groceries, clearly have a no-hire policy, though doubtless they wouldn't acknowledge this. There is also the ubiquitous issue of racism. Occasionally, the Urban League calls the TLP with minimum wage day work—"jobs no one else wants," Sam says—and residents take them. But all the guys claim to be searching for steady employment with more hours and better money. In their first weeks in the program, their inevitable promissory raps featuring fine resolutions and eager compliance are honored as sincere. It's the honeymoon, after all, between staff and resident, and almost every one of the latter takes his chance to sound straight and respectable, sounding out the staff, perhaps, to fathom how much of a line they'll swallow.

"These guys should have a job coach," Sam observes, "someone to train them, socialize them actually, in all they need to know to get and hold a job. Someone to put together an association with local employers."

But there's no money in the budget for such a coach. And mentors with jobs to offer, like Tim's, have not been forthcoming. The guys receive Life Skills training from Jen on interviewing and appearance and language control. In the mornings, she goads them off the property toward the bus stop. Sometimes Sam drives one of them to a specific place to make an application. Jen rolls her eyes at the redundancy of this shepherding: the push, push, as in so many other things—like repeatedly policing the guys about the condition of their rooms, or reminding them about the rules of the laundry. She admits, it sometimes spawns a kind of boredom—in her. She was accustomed to repetition in her work with small children but didn't quite expect the dull, dogged nudging required here, the need to repeat the obvious thirty times, and then thirty-one. She agrees that some of the guys lag purely for the attention in her nagging direction, but that doesn't soothe her much.

"We should have a point system, that would help inspire us," Galvin suggested at one of the weekly house meetings, and there was substantial agreement among the guys. But the staff decided long ago to forgo such a system (a staple of the shelter and group home and other programs familiar to the residents) because they believe it unnecessary.

"We can't force them to do what they ultimately need to do," Frank said to me later, "We're trying to get them to do it on their own, in the face of the usual rewards and punishments of life. That's already a point system, but they don't get that fact . . . or it scares the hell out of them . . ."

So the guys hit the bus stop each day. They step up to counters and desks around the area and ask the party on the other side if there is anything for them. And, upon returning to the TLP, some of them lie to the staff about having asked that question. Some were simply too lazy to inquire. Some, for all their cockiness and survival skills, didn't have the courage to ask. They don't know how. They don't dare.

As I watch Salim, I think of the slowness, the laboriousness that imbues what this place tries to accomplish. Growth. In a more stable "ordinary" childhood and adolescence, the hours of mysterious solitude linger with less overt scrutiny from adults. The texture of being nearby others is thicker. Here, by necessity, one is monitored for progress, however slight. We—America—crave the redemption in this progress. We'll forgive almost anything for that cherished result, even if illusory. Salim sitting with his head in hands, Bill fidgeting with his name tag—not linear enough for us, the observers. In the first months after the TLP opened, one of the local TV stations did a feature on the place. Paul and the more senior administrators welcomed the publicity. Initially, it had been a struggle to convince the neighborhood association that the program was sane and the residents worthy. Good press, the staff reasoned, would strengthen relations. Placed after a report on a teen shooting and statistics showing a five-year rise in juvenile crime in the state, the story focused on a seventeen-year-old resident the newsman called "Ted," with the TLP as a "ray of hope" for troubled teens. Thoroughly middle-class, white, smart and glib, Ted appeared with his back to the camera, tossing a football to Jen. Then, with his face obscured by shadow, he told how bad times began when his mother placed him in a psychiatric hospital for depression when he was ten.

"*Were* you depressed?" the interviewer asked.

"If I was," Ted replied, "I had every right to be."

A voice-over then offered a quick litany of dysfunction and disaster, and then—backed with images of a computer keyboard, Paul in a confident managerial tie, and a key gliding into a door lock—it listed Ted's amazing turnaround at the TLP: his learning how to make a budget, his delivering pizzas part-time, his ascending self-confidence. Each of these personal developments, according to the newscaster's wrap-up, was "one step away from the temptation of crime."

So the TLP looked strong. Ted appeared deserving. And the broadcast had its feel-good segment—which it followed with a story slanted against budget cuts for grade-school gifted programs. All was cool, absolutely.

But Ted was, of course, more complicated than this. He'd first

undergone therapy at age four—when his mother, a teacher, heard her son blame a chair for doing damage rendered by his own misbehavior.

"It had something to do with shadows," Ted told me, resentfully.

"My mother always married fuck-ups," he later explained, "because my dad was a drug user, the other one was an alcoholic, another one was an asshole." He then recited a bloody, dirty chronicle of hospitals, divorce, petty crime . . . and his mother's attempts to deal with him, including "one of those wilderness programs—which I'm going to bomb when I get older."

"Oppositionally defined," Paul said of Ted.

"Happiness pushers," Ted called the shrinks he'd visited.

Three months after the broadcast, Ted was "terminated" from the program. He'd dabbled in reading nonfiction science books, and he'd spoken of studying computer programming at the local college. But generally he relied on a flaccid nihilism to keep himself smiling smugly. I talked about ideas with him—moderately sophisticated freshman intellectualism. He swelled with it, and I fancied I might be having a salutary effect. After all, I was the only adult on the premises without portfolio. I could ask different questions than the staff—which might be refreshing and helpful. I could speak my mind and, maybe, listen to Ted as no one else had. Maybe we'd hear some of his shadows sound out their deeper, real names.

But Ted himself was a shadow. Yes, he shook my hand and joked, with some charm, that he'd just pissed and hadn't bothered washing. And, clumsily, he asserted a mastery of any great thinker I might mention. Freud, Nietzsche—hey, no problem! Still, he worshiped ennui and hugged visions of apocalypse. He spotted our ordinary, adult hypocrisy—the lubricant of civilization—and couldn't get over the pain of this recognition, and the specious power it bestowed on his cowardice. He offered himself to everyone like a vacuum. Why should he have been eager to do otherwise? Everyone, it seemed, found him interesting and yet weirdly unwholesome.

He bagged his job. Eventually, Frank busted him, twice, for smoking pot in his room. No more accommodation could be allowed, so he was made an example to the other residents.

He was the first terminated from the program, and he was luckier than most who washed out. A pair of wispy grandparents arrived in a white Buick and shuttled him to their condo in a retirement village down the coast.

At the time, the staff was very selective in its choice of residents, still trying to define the type most likely to succeed. There was, as yet, no pressure from above to "get the numbers up," fill beds and, thus, justify the outlays for the place. High expectations imbued the screening process. When Ted departed, however, aspirations grew more philosophical.

"It hurt," Jen said. "It was a kind of failure for us. But I've got to get used to the fact there are some kids who are just not right for us. We can't help them. They don't want the help that we can give."

Of course, the local TV station did not return for a follow-up on Ted, and Paul and the rest of senior staff were more or less grateful for this. How could they have explained Ted's shadows in the ray of hope—this boy who is as capable of becoming mayor as a stick-up man?

Salim with Bill, his anxious moon of the moment, will occupy the center of TLP gravity for a minute more, before one saunters to his room and the other to the bus stop. They profess not to like each other, but there they are, dealing, as they must, with presences other than the staff. A resident has his assigned room—as well as access to the group room, the office (if occupied by staff), the basketball hoop in the parking lot, and the green. No resident in Phase One or Two may have guests on the property (aside from immediate family members), though he can come and go as he pleases, provided he fulfills the obligations of his schedule and meets curfew. Thus, when boredom or melancholy or the spurring urge overwhelm him in his free hours, he retreats to his room—a limited stronghold—or he heads out, piercing that invisible membrane between the program and the neighborhood.

The room: a place soon smelling of distraction and dirty socks, fumy naps on couches and young man grease; where TV light eats into the midnight darkness beneath magazine cutouts of Lord Finesse and LL Cool J; where spilled washing powder dusts the carpet and a pair of stepped-out-of jeans; where small chicken bones have been forgotten beside a written reminder from Jen, folded awkwardly into a paper bird, to clean things up. Here, the first house-quiet some of the residents have ever known sometimes creeps and agitates (hence the insistent constancy of thumping bass lines). Here are the few possessions brought along or which they've gathered since arriving: Matt's ascending pyramid of Coke cans; Bill's acoustic guitar with one broken tuning peg; Andre's fuzzy karaoke speaker taped inside a shoe box; Tim's prehistoric computer with external hard drive, its only software, "The Wisdom Program," a list of quotations ranging from Goethe to the *Bhagavad-Gita* without a word of context about the sometimes obscure pronouncements.

And here, also, is the mirror, always. I see Tim glance at it, checking. Quovonne spins before it, checking. Bill, leaning toward it, rakes a comb sluggishly through his hair, then leans closer toward it. That face there, in that other, reflected world: what does each confide to it, if he can confide? That face in the glass which advertises so many secrets. Idol of identity, most-trusted cutthroat. Perhaps each has kissed it once in desperate, intimate hunger. Maybe it's received each one's most grinning and furious *fuck you.*

Beyond the property, among the official destinations, are the skating rink, the St. Pete Pier, Crescent Lake Park, the cineplex. Sometimes the guys pile into the back of Frank's truck and we drop them at the mall for a few hours at evening. There they go, Andre, Salim, and Galvin, for instance, their shorts sagged with impeccable precision. Cruising for pussy, they say, in their best brag. Three kids gawking, it almost seems to me. But not so to mall security, which sometimes demands to see their IDs at the door, and sometimes takes their photograph.

There are also the unofficial destinations, of course, some quite close. For instance, a man named Terry—despite knowing the purpose of the TLP—invited Galvin and Andre several times to smoke dope at his apartment across the sandy alley. Frank couldn't verify that Andre and Galvin were getting high, though their eyes announced it. Rather than bring in the police, Frank remarked to Terry in a friendly way one morning: "You know, these guys are supposed to be drug-free, and we give them pee tests regularly. They sing like little birdies when they get caught. I'd hate to be any adult giving them herb . . ."

After that, no further neighborliness from Terry—unless, of course, more surreptitiously, after curfew. The motel architecture of the TLP, which Frank, Paul, and the others thought might encourage the residents' independence, also allows for the possibility of sneaking off the property late at night, even with Frank living there. One house meeting exploded into exhausting dispute when Frank announced that the staff was considering the installation of motion detectors.

"You want us to trust you!" Tim snarled, arguing against such equipment. "You want us to go through the program. But you don't trust us! You want to turn this place into a prison!"

"We trust you," Jen replied. "But there has to be some means of keeping better tabs on things."

Ultimately, Tim's sentiment prevailed.

Unless a resident tries to hibernate in his room—which some do, until Jen sends them to the bus stop—he leaves the property when he can. He may first arrive at the TLP knowing no one, but soon some "friend" from the surrounding blocks makes his acquaintance and appears at the property line like a wooing suitor. Snagger, who might pass for a shabby D'Artagnan, is one such. He hangs with whomever's available among his musketeers: Salim, Galvin, Andre.

"You know they're doing all of the above," Frank says, "but as long as they're following the program regulations—and not clashing with the law—it's their business."

The only phone for residents rings in the bottom floor office vestibule, jangles across the green. For many months after the TLP first filled up, it rang and rang all day—until Paul requisitioned an answering machine. The messages are mostly from girls—met in detox or at a shelter; at the skating rink or the mall. And messages from girls in the neighborhood. These "hood rats," as Salim calls the last group of three or four, often stroll in pairs, up the sandy alley, usually at evening. Thirteen or fourteen years old, with that infant skin snug around the early womanly curves, they swing past in tight styles, midriffs bared, eyes shocked into lures by fashion magazine makeup tips. Daughters of troubled homes or apparently fine homes—maybe even proud households in the neighborhood association—they're testing their look, wishing to be desired by these "older men" at the picnic table under the live oak.

"I know that number," Jen says. "I gave my parents a lot of problems because I was attracted to guys like these, guys I thought were dangerous . . . and sexy." She laughs at the prospect of an Andre or Matt as sex object but then sobers a little. "It was one of the reasons why my family moved to Florida, to get me away from them."

For all the muttering derision the guys level at the "rats," they notice the parade. The phone rings.

"It was Karen," Bill explains, "Her and Salim are sleeping together."

"I thought she was blowing Galvin," I say, trying to seem apprised. "Now she's with Salim?"

I've seen Karen at the Dairy Queen, lean in a tight white tee shirt. She's maybe fourteen. Several times she has appeared on her bike at the end of the sandy alley, almost like Snagger.

"She just slept with Galvin twice," Bill says.

"So, does she come around and do each new boy at the TLP?" I ask. "Is that what she does?"

"She wouldn't do me," Bill says, mournfully.

A few weeks before, another girl from the neighborhood had invited him to her house.

"A date," he'd bragged.

But Jen had suspected this. Since Bill had resumed his medication after coming into the program, much of the truculence in his Popeye squint had ebbed to a flat, slightly ironic stare. He'd abandoned his rants about construction work and acquired his job at a local supermarket. He scrawled his poems—with lines like "I'd be better off shooting myself in the head"—in a gray notebook and bummed smokes from Matt, who sometimes kept him around to deride. He no longer yelled or punched walls about his mother, a lesbian who had given birth to him through artificial insemination but who would not have him back again, not after all the tangled violence between them. His hair cut to look like a pelt on a shaved head, his torso thick and round like a plumb bob, he lumbered unattractively and tried to sound as cool as he imagined everyone around him was. But he was too much himself.

"I'll never forget my first kiss," he said one day, hoping to boast, "how her lips first tasted."

"How?" asked Salim, somewhat sneeringly.

"They tasted minty."

"That's it," Salim said, appalled, rising from the table, "I'm outta here."

"Why, am I weird?" Bill asked, clawing at the edge of another sudden cliff he'd tripped over.

Jen had fished around and learned from Tim and Matt that the girl who had asked Bill over to her house was planning to have her boyfriend pound him when he arrived, maybe for fun. Somehow Jen had convinced Bill not to go.

The residents' phone rings. But on occasion its power lies in silence, in possibility. Andre sits one afternoon with his back against the steps to the balcony, looking off, thinking about a woman he met on the bus that morning.

"Twenty-one," he says, deeply, "and she has a kid and all that. She gave me her number."

"Are you going to call her?" I ask.

"My momma used to tell me: 'You can always get a girlfriend. They's all around.' That's why I'm worryin' now about gettin' a job and money, and like that . . ."

But he gazes at the number from the woman as it shimmies before him in the pavement heat.

Matt has also been discovered by a twenty-one-year-old woman, Randi, who dances at a nude bar on the causeway near Tampa. He claims that he met her at the St. Pete pier and that she lives with relatives nearby. He swears he's sneaked her into his room only once. ("You won't tell anybody, will you?") Usually, they go to the "balling room" up in the branches of the vast banyan tree at Crescent Lake.

"She's moving so fast," he says. "She tells me she's falling in love with me, and I don't know what to do about it. All my other relationships have bonds. After some of the luster wears off . . . maybe it will stop."

"Yeah?" I say, doubtful.

"I was engaged once," he declares solemnly. "I'd planned a long engagement. A job, a home. I thought it should be stable . . . But she broke it off. She wanted her necklace back, too. 'You keep the rings,' I told her. I kept the necklace, for spite, I guess, but then my stepmom took it. I've never really put Marisa out of my mind, even though I haven't seen her in two years."

He shows me a photo from his wallet: a girl's orderly smile framed by dark curls lit in a small-town portrait studio.

"What do you think Randi sees in you?"

"She says I act older than my age . . . I tell her once in a while, it's just good to sit there. No sex. I'm not a machine. I can't just perform duties."

"Uh-huh," I say, folding my arms and nodding hugely.

"No, really," he explains, "*Love* is caring and stuff like that. I love Randi. But *in love,* that's when you're totally there for a lifetime. It's what you need for a long-lasting marriage. *In love* is more in depth, at the spiritual level."

One evening, a shadowy figure appears under the streetlight at the end of the sandy alley, and Matt rises wordlessly among his levels and strides toward it. The goddess of mystery?

"Matt and his witch woman," Galvin scoffs, indignant, "Liars! Wackos!"

SEVEN

A BOY HIDES UNDER a parked car. How long has he been there? Two minutes? Ten? He doesn't know. Panting with dread, he scans the surroundings for signs of those chasing him. He hears the first sirens of the squad cars and ambulances, which, according to the neighborhood, always come more slowly to this section of Philadelphia—because the cops fear the possibility of meeting a riot. He's not thinking about the convenience store he and his gang were on their way to stick up. Nor the rival gang they happened upon in the park instead. Nor how one of his boys, Horace, had whipped one of theirs a couple of weeks before, and now they had some mutual diplomacy and then bang bang, and everybody was running, except Horace, who'd taken it in the chest.

He's not thinking of how Horace saved his ass once, getting him out of a broken-into house before the cops showed, or how Horace ripped off his new tape deck to hock for weed. He's not wondering what good having big balls did for Horace.

No, the converging wails seem to introduce the boy to the cool pain in his left calf. He realizes for the first time that his shoe brims with blood. Already, a stickiness encrusts the leather and denim.

He cranes his neck to eye the wound, but no such luck in this confined space. He sobs *fuck fuck fuck* . . . and the faint odor of motor oil envelops him.

He ends up in a hospital emergency room. He doesn't ask about Horace. Too chancy. His own wound, it turns out, is a bullet graze.

"Minor," says the nurse.

But it isn't exactly minor.

Two days later he learns that Horace is dead. A hole in the chest. And he's staying with Elma and Treat again.

He doesn't tell his parents about Horace, or anything. His mother is busy at the Baptist church, as usual. His father sits with his Torah, the leukemia percolating through him, his rheumy eyes—somehow wearied by seeing each of his ten children grow up—long ago almost blind to the boy, his youngest, the one he couldn't handle even at twelve. And the boy doesn't tell his sisters or three older brothers—brothers who say Allah is more important than family . . .

What are they gonna care? he thinks.

Elma cooks dinner for the boy. She doesn't preach like she did in those days when he first became best friends with her grandson Treat and she would read to them, and whip him too when she whipped Treat for acting up.

And Treat says he accepts the boy back as his best friend, though he hasn't seen him very much in the last year, since the boy started running with Horace and the gang that he and everybody called the "family."

They eat a good dinner, a silent dinner. And some time not long afterward, the old woman sits the boy down and tells him softly but firmly that he must join the service.

"It's the only way," she says, "before something else happens."

The boy thinks even more surely than before that he remembers a surprised look on Horace's face at the instant the gun popped its little pop. He's seeing that surprised face a lot these days and feeling that sticky effusion of his own blood and its smell like something worn out and dumped from a crankcase. He can see, too, that Treat is just being nice to him, that he's busy with what he's busy with now, and it isn't being best friends. He can see he himself is starting to get busy with how things aren't like they used to be. More of that oily blood.

The Air Force recruiter listens and listens to his sixteen-and-a-half-year-old life and is doubtful, but the boy talks and talks. Soon enough he's begging, willing to do whatever.

His parents sign the emancipation papers. Emancipation. And the recruiter takes him in. Says the military will make a man of him. Elma smiles and hugs the boy, and Treat shakes his hand. And Horace, he's fucking forever surprised.

A second boy runs through the woods not far from his house in suburban Pittsburgh, runs from a man and two women. Gone for two months, his mother has come back now. She sits in the van in the driveway with his five rounded-up siblings, waiting for the man and two women to catch her middle son so that they can all leave the place for good. Leave it to her husband, leave him alone, with nothing, the bastard, teach him a lesson about getting even.

The boy dodges and dips through the brush. He knows it well from years of play. He hides, he skitters. The man and the two women are shouting for him, winded already, he can tell, but close. Sticks jab him and branches whip his face; he ducks and trips once. He gets up panting. He sees the woman's bright red slacks through the green. He heads toward the big sinkhole, into the heavier woods. His heart pounds in his mouth.

Down into the sink, he slides, into the cooler, darker green, the abrasive leaves raking his back, the itch.

He crouches beside a tree trunk and listens. He hears them calling his name. They're at the lip of the sink, not willing to scrabble down it without clear a sign of him. He sits quietly and listens. Eventually, their voices fade. He sits a long time, sniffling in the shades.

Finally, he claws back to the lip and then creeps through the woods. He finds the van gone from the driveway. The house is empty. His old man will be home from the office in a few hours.

At least I didn't ditch him, he thinks.

He goes to the liquor cabinet and sneaks a pull on the old man's bottle of Wild Turkey, and then he wonders if it's sneaking, really, when no one is around to catch you.

For the next couple of years, he doesn't know where his siblings are. The old man works long hours as a top sales rep at the rubber manufacturing company, kissing the martinis. When he comes home at night, the boy brings him in from the car, the old man like a drooping, fleshy cross draped across the boy's back. On the nights the old man comes home sober, he says, "C'mon, let's go to the bar." And at the bar, the boy plays the bowling machines and chats with the waitresses.

Junior high rolls around. When the old man passes out, the boy lifts some cash from his wallet. He takes the old man's car out. There is a standing account at the local market, so in the mornings, the boy and his friend Spook charge food for the day. A beer distributor–friend drops a couple of cases at the house regularly. The boy and Spook do a twelve-pack a day, watching the tube. Maybe some people stopping at the house, buying some herb.

The old man drinks with most of the boy's teachers at the bar—regulars, too—so they pass his son along.

At some point, the boy starts tripping. He sits with Spook on the lip of the sinkhole in the cooler, darker woods and drifts down into those beautiful shades, and forgets. It all makes elegant sense, a perfect relief.

He takes the old man's car out.

He breaks and enters.

He's nailed, more than once.

By sixteen, he has his own lawyer, he knows his rights, and he's out in twenty minutes.

He violates more than one probation.

And one winter night, he's unbolting a battery from a car in an apartment complex. He hears a click and feels the security guard's .357 Magnum against his skull. A security guard carrying a .357!

With his record, they charge him with grand theft auto. For a freakin' battery! He's looking at five years in prison.

He and his father approach the owner of the car. How much to forget the whole thing?

"How much are you willing to pay?" the man asks.

"Let's say, $300?"

"Hey," the man says, laughing sarcastically, "I missed a day of work. I'll take . . . $700."

The old man writes the check, though he says later to the boy, "That guy could be in the can just as easily as you."

One of his father's friends from the bar, a cop, comes to court on the day of the hearing. He vouches for the kid. Since the plaintiff hasn't shown, the judge lets the boy off.

Five years in jail. So close to a different life. $700 close. What a trip!

These two boys, Sam the former, Frank the latter, sit on each side of me in Frank's pickup on the weekly trip to the supermarket. The residents sway in the back, whooping or staring out across the passing lawns like stolid, wind-blown hounds. House-buying is our topic. My wife Lisa and I have been looking half-heartedly, considering ownership, that alliance with place. Frank, too, is mulling it. The commercial lawn business he started on the side two years ago is expanding. (Daily, he mows and landscapes from dawn until early afternoon, sometimes now employing Andre for a little quick cash and encouragement.) At thirty-eight, he's decided to marry again, and, this time, start a family—which means that, eventually, he'll move out of the TLP staff apartment next to the office on the second floor.

"I bought my house in North Tampa," Sam says, "from some folks in financial trouble. That's the way to go. I offered them a rock bottom price. They needed the money. My place even has a pool."

"Yeah," Frank says, "but you're way the hell out. What, forty minutes from the base and an hour from here?"

As their words cross before me, I keep thinking of the boy beneath the car and the boy in the sinkhole. How did they became these men?

"I was looking for love," Sam told me some weeks earlier, as we talked about Horace. "I was looking for someone to watch my back side. But nobody's really your friend in those kinds of situations."

He stood two steps above me on the stairs leading to the second-floor of the TLP. He rubbed his jaw and peered directly at me. The vessels jagged up and over the surface of his vast inner bicep and forearm, beneath flesh smooth and matte-finished like fine black leather. When I'd met him three years ago at the runaway shelter (he'd worked weekends there), he'd . . . well . . . he'd unsettled me, a gold stud in his ear and those muscles lapped onto him as if by a deific trowel. Nonetheless, he'd crushed my hand warmly and introduced me to the kids there that day; he'd sat through the entire writing session, composing poems with the kids, spurring them to read their work aloud by going first.

"I was arrested twice during my first two years in the service," he went on. "Essentially, I was still a thug. But I learned to be more responsible. Eventually, I got a promotion. I had people I was responsible for and people I was working for. That's how I learned. I found out that the only way people would respect me was if I respected myself."

He moved slowly past me, down the steps, and then turned and looked up.

"Horace was carrying a gun for me to use that night at the robbery. I hadn't ever held a gun before. I just know I wouldn't have used it, I know it. But one of the other guys would have. We were going to that store to harm people and instead we got hurt. It was a message from God. All of it."

On another afternoon, alone in the office, Frank recalled, "After that scrape with the battery, I said, 'I'll never do that again.' But I forgot about it after a while. I didn't have anybody watching for me. I thought I was invincible."

He sat back in his chair and the spring beneath him creaked, like the winding of some mechanism. He wore the expression of a hardware store man assuring me that the parts in question will work, as they have worked for a thousand other Handy Dans. We'd known each other almost a year and a half, and he—like Sam—had rarely spoken of his past, and almost never to the residents, except to inform them that he'd forgotten more than they knew about bad behavior.

"Of course, I was arrested again. I knew what I was doing was wrong. And I never denied it. I would say, 'Okay I'll take the punishment.'

"I felt guilty every time I did it. But I needed money, for drugs, or whatever. I always felt guilty about it. I'd feel so bad I'd have to get high to escape."

He laughed, delighted at the irony, maybe at the distance.

"In those days, downers were my favorite, but I was pretty much a garbage truck. I'd get up in the morning, start drinking and getting high. I used to work in restaurants. I'd drink cooking wine by the gallon. I'd pick up my buddy in the morning—like five o'clock—and I'd be drinking a beer, and I'd have a beer for him. I'd have some herb twisted up and we'd smoke that. We'd get to downtown Pittsburgh and you could always find a sleaze-ball bar that was open, and have some more beer. Then we'd go to work and have some heroin—a lot of guys who lived up on the Hill brought it in. The Hill was a bad neighborhood.

"We'd snort it. People weren't doing it much that way then, but now it's big time. More people snort heroin now than shoot it.

"The wait staff and the chefs would stash a case of wine and a couple of cases of beer in the office, and we'd have an eight ball of coke in, and we'd say, 'all right, let's go to work.'

"We'd have like 2,000 people for a banquet that night. We'd do all the preparation, put it all together, take a break, do the coke and beer, and then go out and serve. Back then, an eight ball would last me about a day. I was taking all kinds of things. I had an open script for Xanax. I did speed and downers, switching gears."

He laughed and the chair creaked. It seemed impossible that he could, with such a history, appear as he did, moderately large, the planes in his jaw and brow charged with an angular handsomeness, dimpled. When I'd first met him he'd looked—in his requisite surfer tee shirt and zories—like a wayward beach boy at the age when he must finally decide to pitch it and get the degree, the job, or remain in the sun. He flashed a bleached blond mohawk. Tan. I guessed late twenties. Maybe thirty. Even after the mohawk went, he seemed strong and young.

"By the end of the week," he went on, "I'd be taking ten hits to stay awake. People would have Quaaludes. I'd be having thirteen, fourteen of them. People would be falling all around on a half of one. I'd be working. For a while, I used to run the glasses at a bar . . ." He shook his head and laughed, "Doing fourteen Quaaludes . . . I'd have a handful of glasses, breaking them . . . and the bartender feeding me beer and shots . . ."

Sam planted his elbows on the picnic table and crowed, "Twelve years in the service. Eight more to go and then I'm retired. Retired at thirty-six and a half."

I asked him if he might return to Philadelphia, to the old neighborhood.

"I went back about a year ago, to see my folks. Most of my old friends there are either dead or just a little older. Nothing's much changed. It seemed like time had stopped. They go to the same hangouts, the same clubs."

He leaned forward and with some import, said, "But I have nephews and nieces growing up in gangs, and I have something to do there."

He groped toward a vision of saving these kids, of starting a program in the old neighborhood, maybe a shelter or something like the TLP. I wondered if this possibility drove him to work so hard for this organization. His job at the base—where he was a noncom in charge of a hundred or more people—was full-time. Yet here, as "contract labor," one of the gap-fillers, his time card brimmed with hours. He was on call to the TLP, it seemed, twenty-four/seven. He watched over the place on holidays, on weekends—cutting some of the guys' hair, tossing the football. I wondered, as did Frank, when he had time for his girlfriend Andrea, or the other women he'd claimed to date.

"I don't need much sleep," he'd explained when I'd asked, teasing. "I can rest at the base."

He had even applied for a full-time position at the shelter and then at the TLP when they had come open. He didn't get either job, he said, because they told him he didn't have the qualifications. He smelled racism, however, and brooded about it when we were alone. Each time a new position opened, he swore to me that if he didn't get it, he was going to quit, just walk away from the TLP. Then what would they do without their pack mule?

"I'm not ready to go back to the neighborhood yet," he told me at the picnic table, almost whispering. "I'm not afraid of death. I was in the Persian Gulf. But I think if I do go back, I won't last long, because somebody will want to get rid of me."

"Why?" I asked.

"Because my old friends, when I talk to them on the phone, when they're alone with me, they show me an interesting respect, almost an envy. They say, 'If I'd gone into the military like you, I'd be gettin' closer to retirement. I'd have something. It's good that you did that. I wish I had.' But when they see me in person, or in a group, they condemn me. They focus on all the things I did that were criminal before I went into the military. All the things I was never caught or punished for. They don't pay any attention to the good you do. The good is quickly forgotten. They want to show you that you are the same as them, run-down, like them.

"If I went back somebody would probably kill me, just to get rid of me, because I'd be a reminder of all the things that happened to them and all the things they didn't do. They talk about being your friends. But the bottom line is always: what can you do for me now? what can you do for me now? what can you do for me now?

"They don't care about what you did for them yesterday or last week or a year ago. They care about getting through today, getting over on whatever it is they need. So the memory is short."

"I remember a guy blowing his head off playing Russian roulette at a party," Frank said, as we sat over beans and rice one evening in his apartment.

"Another guy committed suicide. Another guy got into a fight two days after his marriage and got killed. One New Year's Eve four of my friends were killed in a car wreck. I lost a lot of friends to car wrecks. Also fires, guys falling asleep with a burning cigarette. Not too many people survive the kind of shit we were doing. It was depressing."

He explained that he was often so strapped for drug money that he would buy appliances—"gifts"—for his wife on a credit card, and then either return them for cash or hock them.

"She'd come downstairs for breakfast," he said, stroking his bottom lip with his thumbnail, almost grinning, "and she'd hunt around and then she'd ask, 'Didn't we have a toaster?'

"When I finally started to come to and clean up, we both knew the marriage was over . . . Luckily, there were no kids involved . . .

"I'm six feet one, and I weighed 130 pounds then. The detox people wanted me to go to the hospital because they thought I might die from the seizures I was going to have once I started coming down. But I told them: you have to take me now, because if I walk away, I'll never come back. And so I signed away all liability, and they said okay. I was there thirty-five days, fourteen in detox and twenty-one in rehab. And then I went through the twelve-step program. At first, I went to meetings three, four, five times a day.

"That was nine years ago."

"Now," I said, "you're an upstanding member of SO-si-e-TEE."

We laughed, and he swigged from his jug of mineral water, a constant companion.

"Well," he said, looking down, partly proud and partly shy, "I don't know about that. Standing, maybe . . ."

"What made you do it?" I asked. "I mean, what made you check in and stay with it?"

"I woke up one day, just after New Year's and didn't remember what had happened since Christmas. And my wife wasn't speaking a word to me . . ." He smiled wryly. "So I knew it wasn't good.

"To this day nobody will tell me what I did. I've got no idea."

I sit between Sam and Frank in the pickup. We move along a main drag where no one lives but certain kinds of business occur—cars sold, chain restaurant food served. Anywhere ugly U.S.A. With Frank's lawn business logo on the doors, and the guys in back, we might pass for a crew at the end of a workday.

Still on the subject of houses, Sam tells of his new neighbors from India, who called the law when his friends came for a party—so many cars full of black people! They even harass him about his garbage cans and his lawn, any and every little thing. The aggravation reminds him of another house he had wanted to buy before the one he currently owns.

"I'd been approved for a mortgage from the VA, and I'd made an offer, and they were interested. Until they saw my face. Then they withdrew the house from sale."

He sits in resentful silence.

I try to allay it. "Why would they want to do that?" I ask, stupidly.

"They didn't want me in the neighborhood," he says, bitterly. That croup in his voice grinds the words.

More awkwardness and silence. A gelatinous liberal angst trembles in me, makes me reverentially dumb.

"Well," says Frank, coolly, piercing this solemnity, "I wouldn't want you in my neighborhood, either."

EIGHT

AT ABOUT THIS TIME, Miss V sees something which isn't all of it but enough. She's the only one who sees this much, no doubt. She gazes, most likely, from her usual place on Quovonne's dresser, lit by the blue flush of the television set, the sound turned down on the infomercials and ads for 900 numbers. It's after curfew: the junk-food-eating, lonely-staring, what-is-this-life-that's-supposedly-mine hour. There, she sees her twin, Quovonne, square-shouldered in his spaghetti strap dress, his made-up face rubbed and buffed. Prom lovely. Dance club doable.

She sees Quovonne caressing Mr. Right's bare back, so lightly—more lightly than any girl has. Quovonne's hands—half cat whisker, half silk scarf—fan out along Mr. Right's sides, tripping the thousand springs wound tight in the nerves there, trying to convince Mr. Right that he *is* Mr. Right and wise to have let himself sneak into this moment.

She sees Mr. Right check a shiver as the whisker-scarves circle to his chest. So many past impulses have led him without a thought. But here he's not ready to capitulate yet, even to himself.

Maybe he's diving into the depth of his gangsta sangfroid for the pearl of permission to feel the way he's feeling. That pearl: a lucent tear of mute separation.

Maybe he's reckoning that Quovonne has a girl's heart, so Quovonne is a girl. Girl enough.

Or maybe his body simply astonishes him, like the first time-lapse film of blossoming.

Miss V sees her twin putting on a power. An ancient ache there, too.

She watches Mr. Right turn, at last, and Quovonne kiss him before he can think otherwise. A long, winding kiss.

Miss V can keep a secret.

But Mr. Right will return to this secret, more recklessly, until one afternoon the door opens after a quick knock and Frank joins Miss V witnessing its kiss.

Now, however, Quovonne kneels, and Mr. Right raises his face to the ceiling, maybe thinking *just this once.* Maybe thinking nothing at all. Only sinking into the glory of being Mr. Right—until he surfaces, gasping and bearing pearls, and he is Andre again.

NINE

TERRI, A YOUNG INDIAN woman who runs Life Skills at the runaway shelter, is guest speaker at the weekly group session.

"What is culture?" she asks.

Shrugs.

A recent university graduate, she's notecard-anxious, prim . . . "Webster defines it as 'improvement of mind' . . ."

The guys stare off.

". . . more than a period of time. It's a collage of different things, just like the culture of the TLP."

"You mean like Florida is different from New York," Quovonne says. The guys settle behind this observation.

"So," Terri says, "how would you define discrimination?"

"Judging you by your culture?" replies Galvin.

"Can you discriminate apart from culture?" Terri asks. "You know, Webster says it is 'to show partiality and prejudice.' Is there a difference between prejudice and discrimination?"

"Prejudice is the white man's car that runs over your foot," Quovonne says.

"Have you suffered prejudice?" Terri asks.

"You go through it every day," says Quovonne. "It happened the other day when I got on the bus to go to P-TEC. An old woman got on, and I got up and let her have my seat, and I went to the back of the bus, and she said, 'That's where you belong.'"

"It's painful, isn't it?" Terri says. "I remember being followed around stores at the mall by the clerks, who thought just because I was young-looking that I was there to shoplift."

"I go through it every day," Quovonne says, "as a black person and gay . . ."

Andre slumps, his chin plowing deep into the number 4 on the front of his Notre Dame jersey. Since Frank walked in on him and Quovonne last week, he's not made eye contact. He flicks himself away, vanishes like a deer in thick woods. Discreetly, Frank met with him and Quovonne separately and together, and explained that he was bending the regulations by offering them a second chance. They agreed to keep their hands off each other. Officially, only the staff knows what happened, but the underground channels of peer intuition seem active with dawning awareness. Andre senses the world's inquisitorial glare—but it's mostly his own harsh gaze on himself. Not even a whisper of rap has chittered from him for a week.

Terri and the others drift onto the subject of bloodlines. She offers more definitions from Webster and asks, "When did you first see anyone of a different race or color?"

"I've got mixed blood," Quovonne announces brightly, "Chinese, Japanese, Somali blood. My dad sat us down when we were little and explained it."

"I saw a black man and a white lady on the base," Matt says, "and my father explained it to me."

"I didn't see anybody white until I went to school," says Quovonne. "I remember Mr. Quigley, my fifth-grade teacher. He told us blacks come from the jungle."

"I was raised in India until I was five," Terri says, feeling a small bond with Quovonne, "and I didn't see a white person until I was on the plane coming to the States."

"You Cherokee?" Quovonne asks.

Terri pauses, puzzlement crinkling her brow. "No, I'm from India."

Quovonne smiles emptily at her, embarrassed but not able to ascertain precisely his *faux pas*. Galvin sighs at Quovonne's miscue, as though it is further evidence of the inferiority of gays.

"What do you write on applications in the blank marked 'race'?" Terri asks, changing directions.

"Other," Andre intones. It's the first time he's spoken. He still looks at the floor.

"Why?" Terri asks.

"I could be born a white man," Andre says, raising his face toward hers at last, "a white man who just stood out too long in the sun."

Shifting again, Terri asks, "What image would a white man represent, say, in the '20s?"

"Power," Matt says.

"What about blacks?"

"Slaves," says Quovonne.

"There weren't any slaves in America in the '20s," Salim says, shaking his head.

"No?" Quovonne replies, astonished. "How was it that Martin Luther King was settin' the slaves free?"

Galvin sighs derisively.

Terri asks about other cultural images. Gangsters. White and black women in the '50s. Movies of the '60s and '70s. John Shaft. Cheech and Chong.

"What about the '80s?" she asks.

"That's when rap came on," Andre says.

She mentions an interview she read with rapper Tupac Shakur, recently gunned down by rival gang members. Andre smiles at the mention of Tupac and, animated for the first time in days, summarizes a song in which his idol compares race relations in America to a sumptuous party attended only by whites; hungry for admission to these delights, a black man knocks on the door but is denied, so he bangs harder and harder—until he must break down the barrier.

"People were talkin' about the violence in his lyrics," Andre concludes, "but that's the way things is. We're gonna have to use some more violence to get what we're gonna get."

"I think prejudice is gonna come back with the Muslims," Quovonne observes.

"Most of them don't realize that Malcolm went to Africa and had a bigger view," Terri says. Everyone sits a moment with this, then she asks, "What do we need to fight prejudice?"

"We get it all from our parents," Tim says, a tone of fatality trailing his words.

"My daddy would go with white women," Quovonne says, "but he would say that a white man doesn't want to see a black man make it. I learned about prejudice and tolerance from my mom. I guess takin' a ride in the white car might help."

Salim breaks in, "Galvin is more like a black person . . ."

"I've heard people say that people like Galvin are wrong to act black," Terri offers, "that it's a kind of lie."

"It's just the way you carry yourself," Andre says.

I jump in. "But don't you and I and Quovonne share more than you two share with Africans?"

I go on to relate that the Chinese make the distinction between Chinese and non-Chinese, insiders and outsiders . . . and how they think all Westerners look more or less alike.

"My neighbor in Changchun used to say, 'Western babies are so cute, except that they grow up to have such big noses.'"

Terri picks up the theme of similarity and difference. "Cannibals believe it's awful to eat anything lower than a human because you take on the characteristics of the thing you eat."

Andre, intrigued by this, asks, "So how would the neighborhood of cannibals work? Somebody down the street dies and everybody comes for a cookout?"

"They go for roadkill," Tim jokes.

"Cannibals don't have streets," Terri says, "so no roadkill."

Andre and Tim ponder people without streets.

"So, let's say Grandpa dies," Andre says. "Who gets to eat first?"

The following week, the guys gather, as usual, in the office for group. Jen announces another "special guest": Reverend Platt, from the local Episcopal Church.

Earlier, she'd expressed trepidation to me about allowing him on the property. He'd called twice and was emphatic that he only wanted to announce an Annual Breakfast for Men and Boys, and perhaps say a few words about the residency program for troubled youth sponsored by his congregation. But Jen didn't want him proselytizing. On the other hand, she thought that his visit might yield some benefit, given the religious disputes between Galvin and Matt.

Jen opens the door. A middle-aged black man in a blue shirt and clerical collar enters, accompanied, "as the diocese prescribes," he says, by Mr. Gumbs, also black, old and severely vertical, with tufts of white hair, like stranded milkweed seeds, inside his ears.

Reverend Platt invites the residents to the Annual Breakfast and passes around a ring binder on the congregation's residency program: mostly photocopied snapshots of humble outbuildings and young boys "ready" to serve, their destinies elevated and their hopes renewed by this aspiration. He invites everyone to Sunday services, and then distributes, only to the residents, metal fish—for their key chains—inscribed with "God is Love."

The door opens and Andre enters, panting. A billed cap dips low over his eyes. He scans for a seat, the only one available between myself and Quovonne, and he throws himself into it. Since his exchange with Terri last week, he has said little. Jen thinks he might be getting high and trying to conceal the glaze.

Standing on the edge of the circle, Reverend Platt measures the mood of the group and then honors his impulse to plumb these possible apostles. He addresses Tim, who's opposite him. "What would you say if asked: Who are you?"

Tim shrugs. "My name, I guess . . ."

He points at Tim and asks Matt, "Do you respect him?"

"Yes." Matt replies automatically.

"Do you love him? Would you die for him?"

Matt pauses. Discomfort zone. "Uh . . ."

"What do you believe in?" the Reverend asks.

Back on easier turf. "The goddess of mystery."

"That's good," says the minister, almost backing away. "That's good. You thought I would condemn you . . . No."

But Reverend Platt is puzzled, not quite sure how to proceed.

"I was involved in the church once," Salim says. "I was looking for guidance and help, and it never came. That's why I gave it up."

He has, however, slipped his fish onto his key chain. Matt, too, has attached his fish to the key chain around his neck.

"If I could prove to you that the Lord lives," says Reverend Platt, regaining his momentum, "would you follow him?"

"Yes, but you can prove it?" Salim asks.

"Does one and one equal two?"

"Well, yes."

"Well . . ." says Reverend Platt, pausing for drama, "that's the Bible."

"Huh?" Salim replies, searching other faces in the circle, shaking his head as if to clear it.

"That's the truth," Reverend Platt declares.

"There's no God," Salim says, toeing the carpet. "People aren't going to be controlled by beliefs like that."

"You say people aren't controlling people, people like the devil?"

"Yeah."

"What about the people dealing dope?"

Salim smiles. He's been had, but he just shakes his head.

Reverend Platt says, again, that he won't take up any more time—all the while glancing at Jen for her permission to go on. He takes out a dollar bill. He holds it before his face but doesn't seem to notice it's upside down.

"How much does this control you?" he asks the room.

"Everybody needs money," Matt says.

"Yes, I like money, too," the minister says, acting as though he has foreseen all retorts.

Mr. Gumbs, seated on the couch, stares into a distance as remote from the scene as Bill, who, beside him, is stupefied today by his medication.

"People all over are in the power of this," Reverend Platt asserts of the dollar bill. "They are full of the darkness of—"

He then thinks better of it and puts the bill away.

"Are you trying to throw these riddles at us to snag us?" Tim snarls.

Politely, he drops his fish into Reverend Platt's palm and leaves the room.

Reverend Platt invites us to hold hands for a prayer. Some, like Quovonne, bow their heads and comply. But Andre draws the bill of his cap farther down over his eyes and folds his arms. In the corner, Jen sighs. Matt looks up and grins goofily at me.

As Reverend Platt and Mr. Gumbs depart, the minister surprises Salim by shaking his hand three ways, all soul ways—maybe trying to cover all the ways he knows of the soul.

TEN

I CROSS TAMPA BAY, to the TLP, via the Howard Franklin Bridge, once nicknamed "the Frankenstein" for its monstrous traffic snarls, until it was replaced by a higher, wider, more accommodating incarnation. It arcs and stretches over shimmering shoals and emerald coves, and the bluer reaches which shudder to a darker hue as fingerlings scatter en masse from a hungry maw. In all directions, summer cumulus and cumulonimbus dollop up through the ether and descend to the horizon with the curvature of the earth, and at night the surrounding metro sprawl glitters like artful embroidery.

As I cross, I find myself scanning the faces in other cars, or in sport fishing boats lolling in the shadows of pilings. I wonder about them, and about the pilots of the airliners swooping over the bridge on final approaches to the airport, and about the flight attendants. I begin to wonder about the deejay on the radio, the talk show host, the singer of the new hit or the reader of books on tape. It's a creeping wonder, and after awhile, it advances toward the office parks lining the shore, toward the personnel there—all that human resource.

More to the point, I wonder about their children. Where are they now? Are they well? Have they been loved? Has that man at the wheel of the sedan given up—in fear—on his son? Has that woman in the step van betrayed her daughter? How many missing parents file and close the deal and make appointments on the twelfth floor there? What shouting or blows have sprung from that pilot now coolly noting the local time, or what punishing silence from that passenger in 14F, gazing down on our placid estuaries? A beautiful day to fly, to fly away.

I have no right to such questions, of course. Not in these instances . . . and not because I'm childless. My "creeping wonder"—and its futile, interrogative blaming—reveals the urge to connect the residents with the parents in their stories, people who may hardly resemble, physically or emotionally, their narrative counterparts. Since the opening of the program, I've seen only one parent: Bill's mother, who drops off an occasional carton of cigarettes for her son. Parents rarely, if ever, visit the TLP, and when they do it's usually only one of the pair—who, if pressed, blames the absent partner for all the ills. Most often, they are voices on the phone, signatures on forms. Just as often, they are complete nonpresences, replaced by a guardian frequently indifferent, exasperated, or belligerent.

I remember one early resident, Alan, who was jumped on his way to sign up for GED classes at the local high school. At 7:30 A.M., in a drugstore parking lot, three thugs pounded him. Rush hour traffic swirled past the scene, yet no one dialed a cell phone to the police. These thugs were most likely part of a gang that had viciously beaten two other young men in the area, stealing their basketball shoes, just as they had stolen Alan's. They broke Alan's jaw in four places and severely bruised the rest of him. As Frank said, "They were trying to kill him, but they just got tired. There's a lot of rage out there."

Alan dragged himself the mile from the parking lot back to the TLP. Jen said that when he staggered into the doorway, she thought he had been knifed there was so much blood. His face swelled so that he looked like a disfigured infant. His throat and jaw expanded like the neck of a bullfrog. Huge contusions wormed around his right eye, which had become a milky button pressed deep into the flesh. That first day after he'd slept off the sedatives, he wandered gingerly around the place in brown socks, shoeless for the moment, his jaw wired shut.

When called about the matter, his only nearby relative, an uncle, said, "Well, if he hadn't been getting into trouble up here so that he had to go to your place, none of that would have happened to him, now would it?" He offered no assistance.

"If it's between an adult and a kid," Salim says, "they always take the adult's side." Hanging with the residents encourages one to agree, given our innumerable rationalizations and broad powers over the young. We are "they." Yet being with these same guys also affirms most doubts about them, as well. After some reflection, Jen recalled that Alan was wearing a jacket when he stood bloodied in the doorway, unnecessary in Florida at that time of year, except late at night. He also retained the $40 check for his GED application. Why hadn't the attackers stolen it? Most important, his face had already swollen considerably by the time he had supposedly returned to the TLP. Was it possible that he had sneaked out after curfew, maybe gotten high and mouthed off to the party who battered him, and only later—upon coming to—returned to the TLP, slipped the GED check into his pocket, and told a more amenable tale? Absolutely. In this instance, given Alan's sufferings, Jen did not further investigate the likelihood.

Being with the residents also nags my sensibility in another way. I see future residents, everywhere, it seems. A small girl, for instance, sits alone in a car at a roadside tavern, the windows rolled up tight on an August night as stifling as a sweatshirt pulled tight against a face. A well-dressed woman in a department store draws her three children impatiently along; unable to keep up, the smallest falls, and the woman snatches the toddler by the arm and yanks him; the child does not cry out because he knows that to cry would summon greater fury. Near midnight, on Christmas, a boy of ten or eleven shoots baskets in the driveway of his empty house, alone.

Crossing the water on the former Frankenstein, I'm reminded, too, how much simpler are things than people. A bridge is re-engineered and loses its "monstrous" identification. But an Andre? A Galvin? Sometimes I leave the TLP for home, elated with what has occurred there. (Usually, this results from some incident where I believe I've been of help.) Sometimes, on the way to the place, a sickly weight of futility and foreboding presses on me. I drive into a resistance to going "there" again, feeling foolish and extraneous. I remember Tim testing my motives, with "you're just writing this book because you want to get rid of your guilt."

No.

But crossing the Bay is as much a psychic as physical journey. The waters separate my life in Tampa from the life of the TLP, and they are only one of many questionable "protective" barriers. Andre, for instance, comes from Tampa as well. (His transfer to the TLP was his first trip to the other side of the Bay.) In Tampa, however, a freeway substantially divides my neighborhood in the south end of town from his in the north-central. It's a rampart, in essence, in which "urban renewal" drove through a once-thriving black business district a few decades ago.

Yet Andre told me he played basketball regularly at the park down the street from my home while he was kept at Beach Place, a facility for troubled teens. I was surprised Andre could be so close by—even under supervision—this kid with a growing record. The south end, bordered by water, is just about the only pretty place to live in Tampa proper. Its most splendid avenues—refurbished by the cash boom of the '80s and nostalgia for early-twentieth-century architecture—are desirable, expensive, and bestowed with the inflated prestige of the better section of a provincial center. Long porches and sweet lawns flow there beneath children with advantages that make the visitor's heart soften, for a moment, with hope for the world.

These streets, however, often adjoin grittier, peeling or weary areas, jealous of their proximity, awaiting their booms. Streets like the one where I rent. Home seventy years ago to black domestics employed in the dynastic houses along the Bayshore, my neighborhood is perhaps two-thirds white, incipiently gentrifying, separated from "others" yet near them. Entangled. A city councilman, for instance, lives two doors down from me. Two blocks away, however, on Kennedy Boulevard, a boy prostitute lingers on the evening corner, gazing frankly, almost accusingly at drivers as they pass. There are three law offices, a Montessori school, and two crack houses, these last two often retired from service. Day and night, poorer whites and blacks from the ramshackle blocks abutting the freeway stroll past my porch on the way to the new supermarket south of us, some of the kids bearing angry, rude boom boxes. Over the past five years, as the neighborhood has gone "up" from its decades of urban decline, there have been two shootings—a drug dealer and then a bicyclist who happened upon the scene. (The gun's *pop! . . . pop!* out my window now suggests the sound of Horace's death, though here neither victim was killed.) On another night, through that same window, a whoosh boomed from the alley, where a car had been nestled purposefully against the porch of an apartment and set afire. In that same alley, I've encountered various men—and one woman with a small boy—foraging in the trash. Indigents, black and white, have rung my doorbell—usually in winter—sometimes asking for work, or trying to sell personal goods, or simply begging for a few dollars.

I mention these things because as neighborhoods go, this one is pretty good. Despite moments of mayhem, it's generally quiet. House pride spurs most of the owners along the street. Property values are rising; new upscale shops and cafes open weekly. Expensive yuppie apartments were recently constructed along the nearby railroad track. At that location, a commuter stop was installed but was removed shortly thereafter—most likely because those in the more influential streets farther east and south didn't want that kind of vulnerability. After all, they live in Old Hyde Park, where cops cruise in golf carts and iron lamp posts are festooned with red ribbons at Christmas, where the historic preservation association monitors all refurbishing, and a small, tony shopping center hosts busloads of tourists in the cleanliness of a Weimar. We're near them and getting nearer—our own transitional living program. The organizers of our new neighborhood association bear petitions for me to sign, and I do, mostly. They hold meetings, and I've gone, feeling like a silly trooper—a symptom of my weak civic musculature, no doubt.

My renting neighbors next door reflect the changes of the street. Among them, there was a family of indeterminate constitution, but with a "daughter" who one day called to two young boom boxers sauntering along. Somehow they knew she wanted to buy weed, and they cut the trade there on the curb. After this, Sara moved in, a single mother who'd come to Tampa from Hawaii to start life again with a small house painting business. She hired a man who eventually became a semi-boyfriend—until he started to get drunk regularly, shouting and threatening her. Now the place houses newlyweds in their late twenties—he of the ponytail and serious mien, a computer specialist; she ambitious and firm of tone, the manager of apartment complexes along the water: both of them concerned about crime prevention and now owners of a boxer pup, Roadie, future watch dog.

Sara's departure has grown more troubling since I've come to know the TLP residents. She'd moved in one afternoon with her adolescent daughter, Janie, and within a couple of days, they stood on our porch, short, pudgy and lucent as milk, the mother proud, the daughter shy, a pair of mutually orbiting galaxies, with an understanding and a history, I think now, driven by exigency. Sara flattered Lisa and me by declaring that our proximity could not but elevate the quality of her daughter's life. She wanted us to read some of Janie's wonderful writing. Janie swiveled politely, her hands clasped demurely behind her back. We exchanged phone numbers and assured each other that we could call if there was anything we might need. Then mother and daughter returned to the extensive sprucing of their new place.

In the following weeks, from my study window, I sometimes heard Sara and Janie shouting over the television, sometimes singing a cappella, sometimes laughing, and I began to notice that Janie seemed to stay home from school most of the time. Then one night, Sarah, splattered with white paint, smelling faintly of liquor, came over and asked if Lisa or I had seen anyone strange around her house during the day. She said she'd hired some undependable people for her business—methadone users—and she had already fired one of them and he had threatened her. She'd come home to discover the aloe plant missing from her porch but apparently nothing else touched. We'd seen no one and told her so.

A month later, angry and suspicious, she asked if we had reported her to HRS. Evidently, someone else had noticed Janie home alone all day.

"Those men who come to my house are just my employees," she said harshly, as if peeling back a layer of skin.

We replied that she didn't need to explain. It was her concern.

Gone thereafter was her friendly wave, and the "hi" over the back fence. Instead, the grimace and the set shoulders of the embattled. And flaunted silence.

Finally, I said to her at the trash cans, "Sara, we didn't call HRS on you. Believe me. Your business is your business."

She gritted her teeth and shook her head and marched away.

So we had been convicted by accusation—as I suppose she felt she had been convicted by the unknown caller. The arrogant respectability which she imputed to us has always repelled me. Yet we, she had decided, were that kind. We could set the wheels of the state spinning against her. We could believe we were capable of judging someone like her. As if we knew. Yes, we were that kind.

The matter reminded me of a time I approached a woman in a parked car to ask directions. Just as I tried to speak, she rolled up her window. Hey! I thought, you don't have to do that, I'm a good person!

But what did that woman recognize in me?

In Sara's case, of course, the fear lay in her perpetual vulnerability to familiar uncontrollable forces rather than a possible "threat" from a stranger. She, like all the other Saras, could be hassled, investigated. Her decency could be questioned, her means of support easily injured. I remember her revving her ancient car in the morning, over and over, trying to get it to idle long enough so that she could put it into gear and go to a job. It panted and died, panted and died, body and frame rattling like pebbles in a coffee can. The rhythm of the loosening hold. The melody of unaffordable repair. To trouble her further, and maybe banish her exhaust, all somebody had to do was pick up the phone.

Within the month, she and Janie had vacated the house for another new life. She reminds me now of those neighbor women from my childhood who seemed to stray into one of the small rental houses on our blue collar street, stay for a while, and then move on. Mrs. Calvin, for instance, with three children. I played with her oldest son Ronny. She seemed to yell as she spoke in the bedroom Ronny shared with one of his sisters, a room dimmed into blueness by homemade curtains fashioned from old bath towels. For dinner—the only one I had at their place—she served us spaghetti, the sauce thinned, no doubt, by short funds into a vapid, peach-hued broth. Even as a child, I saw something raw and hopeless in her—a woman in the same situation as Tim's mother—and I was appalled by it, fearful.

When the Calvins moved on, to Salt Lake City, I imagined Ronny among gleaming spires and sun-spangled pavements, a better place than where they had lived near us. But the presence now of those boy prostitutes on Kennedy Boulevard several blocks from my current home contest that childhood vision. Mrs. Calvin and the proximity of the Mormon faith and the remoteness of the desert may have cultivated in Ronny the desire to labor by the rules and to respect himself as well as others, and maybe even to come to know irony well enough not to be surprised by it or dependent on it for the survival of his very earthly soul. Who knows? That time—thirty years ago—was easier, we are told, simpler. Not as many drugs and guns on the streets. Not as much consumerism. Not as many adults willing to jettison their progeny or exploit hapless youth. Not as many fathers gone. Still, I recall schoolmates in my adolescence, some quite respectable, who sniffed glue and dropped acid. I remember the syringe lying on the pumped vein it fed with its phantasms, the arm outstretched and draped across a rebel boy's lap at lunch hour behind the storage shed next to the junior high school track. It was supposed to be a glamorous piercing, there in our ordinary corner of Des Moines. It was the sort of seed that flowered into the recurring admission these days that family "dysfunction" and preempted childhood are as commonplace now as two-car garages and 401K plans.

Semi-poverty, of several varieties, could hardly have eased away from the Calvins out west. I couldn't understand this then. My mother did, however, intuiting her own housewife metaphysic from the blueness of the Calvins' rooms. That's why she would not leave my father and their failed marriage, and take her five children into the world—even at their occasional urging. She would stay, like many mothers did, hoping that economic stability would hold us sanely together despite all other shocks and lures from without and within. She had that choice.

Maybe Sara should have been reported. Certainly, Janie should have been in school, though their situation seemed more benign to me, foolishly, because music and laughter often spilled from their open windows, and they were both female. Occasionally now, from a rental house across the street, the shouting of a certain kind of "strong" male bludgeons the evening. That voice splits the ground beneath me, sounding from the substrata of my own childhood. I know that voice. It's my father in his fury at my mother, at us children, in that "simpler" time when far fewer dared dial up Social Services for help. It's also my own enraged voice. I listen to it, surprised by it, ashamed of its helpless savagery. Is it time to pick up the phone? Report my father, who, in many ways, was an exceptionally good man? Report on myself?

Before the TLP opened, I spent several months around the runaway shelter operated by the TLP's "parent" organization, conducting poetry workshops and, later, simply volunteering. Nearly all of the TLP residents have spent time in places like this, triage operations which seek to reunite the runaway with family or to provide drug treatment or other types of counseling. There were, of course, lurid and pathetic, even sensational, cases, nearly the stuff of the local newscast. But as I read the pages in the milieu log and sat in family sessions and simply talked with kids, I came to realize that many of the clients had fled families more like mine than I thought possible. I began to see my family—my generation and the ones preceding and succeeding it—through their eyes. We had been a two-car family with a lake house in the country, snug within that post–World War II, blue-collar prosperity which has since faded with weakened labor unions and the exportation of manufacturing jobs to venues abroad. Catholic school. Music lessons. Chores and values. We were enriched and drilled. But there was still my father's alcoholism, and the chaos it sowed. And there is now one of my brothers, aged thirty-three—a father of four kids who are currently living with their widowed grandmother—who has just been returned to jail, having violated his probation by taking more drugs and then trying to pass his urine tests by substituting a sample from his four-year-old son.

Along Bayshore Boulevard on the weekend custody days, the fathers skate with their sons. Sometimes they stop to watch a great blue heron perched on a crab trap at low tide ponder how to remove the captive crustaceans. Some are the same men—accountants and lawyers and other quite responsibly captive folk—jogging along on other days, wearing tee shirts declaiming, "No Rules!" As if they, or anyone, really would crave such a thing. As if it were possible. But some sons are too literal or idealistic or cynical to bear such contradictions as these in their fathers, and such contradiction is ubiquitous.

Myriad theories about the problems of the residents hover around them, in no sustained order:

- They blame anyone and anything but themselves.
- They blame only themselves, to the point of inertia.
- Their parents have blamed everyone and everything but themselves, including their children.
- They're grieving for the loss of their parents.
- They've seen their parents siphon off the water from the

neighbor's line, or tap the cable for free, or lie in a thousand small, insidious ways.

- They've been hurt, dramatically, and now want to be excused.
- They're afraid to fail and yet want to fail, so that they can be relieved of their fear. But when they fail, their fear of failure only deepens.
- They've learned fear at home and refined that knowledge on the street, where you can't show fear. They mistake this condition for personal power, so they cling to the street.
- They're afraid—like some old people—of change, especially of changing themselves.
- They're afraid of change because they've never had any stability.
- They're spoiled and cowardly.
- They're a concoction of cruel hard-wiring and bad narratives.
- They're . . .

After I'd left home for good, I lived in an apartment in a phlegmy, slack-jawed town in upstate New York. Broke, weeping over my failed poems, involved in a destructive sexual friendship, I lived amid boxes of books stacked in the shape of furniture covered with blankets—a "chair" here, a "couch" there. I slept on a foam pad on the floor beside a "closet" constructed of grocery store cartons stacked on their sides. It was the year I'd learn to drink alone, watching the downpouring star-flecked void through my back screen door.

One night on the foam, I dreamed that I rode a bicycle with a broken goose neck, around and around, at the foot of my home street. Some distance away, my father appeared.

"You come back here," he commanded flatly, pointing to the spot in front him. "You come back here."

"No," I replied, my tone almost childish.

I kept on peddling the bike, trying to steer, the front wheel sometimes swinging in the opposite direction from the handlebars, sometimes turning as I wished.

"You come back here."

"No."

Around and around.

I was older than the guys when I had this dream, fortunate, perhaps, to be possessed by such a home, and luckier still to have it until I was able to begin the long, clumsy steering away from it. As I cross the Bay now, and the former Frankenstein rises above the water, I think more and more about—for lack of a better word—the "trajectory" of the residents' lives, of all our lives. That arc of each being's achievement—spiritual, cultural, economic. I've seen that arc beginning to reveal (or establish?) itself in the behavior of fourth and fifth grade boys—some already convinced, for whatever reason, that school is useless and life is boring. In *Society Without the Father,* the psychologist Mitscherlich quotes his colleague Luxemburger: "Heredity is not fate, but the threat of fate." The same might be said of the class system in America, though we seem less willing to acknowledge its existence, since it offers so many examples of exceptions to its pacifying rule. By class, I mean the level of a person's awareness of multiple possibilities and ambitions in life, and the autonomy and advantage such a worldview offers. Whatever their economic backgrounds and intelligence, the guys possess little of this awareness. They fantasize about wealth and fame and the other conventional destinies of the beleaguered and impotent. But they don't much realize that they could go beyond the customs and habits of their little island life, their personal barbarism. They haven't had the crucial privilege of that vision—which would not be a privilege in a more just world.

George Eliot once wrote that it's never too late to become the person we were meant to be. Choosing to perceive such an assertion optimistically, I make blues tapes for Andre and Quovonne; I offer books to Matt . . . Maybe I've turned to the guys for the excitement of transformation—the great potential of their youth. It is, after all, our cultural narcotic, our great uncontrolled substance. It's as though I didn't have more transforming ahead, as though I was not still challenged by reality and desire. I'm not naive in the way the guys are. No, I'm naive differently, in the way one is who believes he is no longer innocent. I cross the former Frankenstein—the bridge which links and separates—accompanied by my creeping wonder, staring at the fellow traffic, maybe staring, dear reader, at you.

ELEVEN

IN THE BACK of Frank's truck heading down one of the main boulevards of St. Petersburg, Quovonne says indignantly to Tim, "Why do you think you're so high? You shouldn't do that."

"Low self-esteem," Matt mutters to me, in an aside.

"You almost made your point," Tim replies sourly to Quovonne.

"You shouldn't be that way," says Quovonne. "Why are you so mighty? You need to learn—"

"Shaddup!" Tim shouts.

Matt says, in another aside, "I don't have high esteem or low esteem. Just none." He smiles.

"I have high," says Quovonne. "I am the best. There is no one like me. Everyone is unique. They all high."

At the stoplight, the woman behind the wheel of the city bus beside us waves at Quovonne and smiles in obvious delight. He waves back. He knows her, he says, from his daily rides to P-TEC.

Matt tells me of unscrewing bolts from the floor of a school bus and throwing them out the window, breaking the windshield of a car.

"It was a good school," he says. "Cool."

I ask him why he didn't stay. He seems surprised by the question.

"They threw me out because I didn't do enough," he explains. "I could have done the stuff they wanted."

At the next stoplight, he suddenly peers over my shoulder. Across the street behind me, a drug deal is unfolding. Two young men stick greenbacks through the wrought iron door of a moldy, cinder block apartment complex, and two older men on the other side shove the goods into their customers' hands.

"What's going down, there?" Matt mutters in a tone from beyond the bars of his usual decorum, cocky, conspiratorial. A smile slithers out across his face. Almost a leer.

At present, everyone but Andre has managed to find at least a part-time job. Salim takes pizza orders, Quovonne makes doughnuts, Bill bags groceries, and Galvin—overcoming the white spaces in his employment history—assembles circuit boards full time at a small computer plant. So the guys are rarely all together except in the late evenings and on group days like this. (Andre still works for Frank occasionally. He did receive a phone message from the manager of a supermarket where he had applied, but when he returned the call, excited, anxious, he found that the manager had not tried to get in touch with him at all. It was, Andre figured later, a practical joke hatched by Snagger or another of the neighborhood crew.)

Matt was hired by a sandwich shop on 4th Street North. He returned from his first day, bounding, outfitted in the company visor and a shirt that announced, with the usual employee relations rah-rah, *Sandwich Artist*. The man who had hired him, Matt bragged, was so impressed that he suggested that he might make Matt assistant manager by the end of the week.

Matt's wormy smile at the drug deal hooks into me now. In that moment, his face assumes a new intimacy between us. I glimpse a smugness and vigor, a wholly opposite character from the genial, slightly feckless charm-boy I usually encounter. That new face vanishes as the traffic light changes and Frank's truck rumbles onward. Again, as usual, Matt somewhat resembles my younger brother at sixteen—my brother now more than twice that age and back in jail. The one we all tried to help—until we surrendered. I know, of course, that I'm not really talking to my brother—or to our past—when Matt and I spin into one of our long, evening dialogues. I know I'm not getting any closer to that boy my brother was and still is, and to the anger I bear at him for his failures. But such possible connections spur me, sometimes, to listen differently to Matt than to the other residents.

"I'm not against excelling in school," Matt told me one night under the oak. "It's that they *expect* you to get a good grade. I have a problem with that. If somebody asks me to do something or wants me to do something, that's fine. But if they expect me to do it, that's not. I shouldn't be expected to do anything. It's a free country. Everybody's their own person. They should be able to do what they want to do. I figure that I've learned enough in school. I mean, enough to survive. I'm not saying that I'm going to have some major job or anything like that."

"Why not?" I replied, the eager proponent of education. "You seem to be very interested in having your freedom. Isn't there more freedom in having lots of different options? Lots of different ways you could go in life?"

"Well," he said, leaning back with his hands on his knees, "I plan on opening my own business. And I'm not going to spread it world wide or anything, though it may get that way some day. You see, I don't want to be like Scrooge. I just want to live comfortably with enough money to do the things I want and have the things I need.

And besides, I don't even want to have everything that I want because then that leaves nothing to hope for."

He paused and then looked up into the leaves. "You could be the stupidest person in the world, but if that piece of paper says you have a degree in anything, people respect you. I think that's really ignorant, because of all the smart people in the world who don't have a college degree because they don't want one . . . And, besides, you learn a lot from any type of books you read, and I read a lot. I read science fiction, creature fantasy, regular fiction. You learn a lot vocabulary-wise, and you learn a lot about life situations, just as you would learn from a history book."

He lit one of his cherry-flavor cigarillos. "Most of the problems I have are with people expecting me to do things. Like here at the TLP, it doesn't matter how much I like a place, or how much I'm getting along in the place, they *expect* me to do something."

"So you don't like authority," I said.

"Authority? Well, if they tell me to do something, that's fine. But I still have that choice of whether I can not do it and get in trouble. Say they ask me to just mow this area." His hand swept across the green. "I wouldn't have a problem with that. But if they told me to do it and they expected me to do it no matter what, I wouldn't do it. See, I know the difference between when somebody tells me to do something, or asks me to do something, or wants me to do something . . . and when they expect me to do it."

"Why are expectations so bad?"

"Because I don't expect anybody to do anything. I don't expect anything. No matter how much I want something, I don't expect it. And I don't expect anything from myself. If I think I'm going to do something, I don't expect myself to do it. And if I don't do it, I didn't expect it happen."

"Sounds like expecting things is one way people are connected," I said. "Like in a real love relationship, people expect people to do things. They expect them to be there. They expect them to love and care for them."

"I don't believe that," he said, spewing honeyed smoke and spitting into the grass. "If I was married and my wife said she was going to be home at a certain time, I wouldn't expect her to be home at that time. No . . . I wouldn't even expect my wife to call and tell me. Because she's a free and different person, like everybody else. No one's a part of me. They're not connected to me in any physical way. So, I have no control over them, so I don't expect anything."

Approximately a week before the sandwich shop hired him, Matt had been caught shoplifting at one of the mall department stores. Frank and Jen and Sam conferred with him in the office for over an hour, hoping to fashion some disciplinary action that might encourage in him a more enlightened approach to laws and limits. Later, Matt steamed and fulminated.

"One of my philosophies," he declared, as we sat on the stoop in front of his room, "is 'Rules were meant to be broken.' When they're made, they're expected to be broken, or else people wouldn't have law enforcement. I don't break the rules on purpose. Let me make that clear. But I'll break rules, and I can accept the consequences. As long as they're not blown out of proportion, like this meeting with Jen and Frank, and this waiting for a punishment. At my parents' house, I'd be grounded for a week and that's that."

"But you're not at your parents' house," I replied.

"Nowhere else I've been have I had to *discuss* the punishment. Frank and Jen have spent two or three days trying to figure out *what* they're going to do. Hey, they're not my parents, but basically they're kind of a parent figure."

"You mean the one you're supposed to resist?"

"No, not exactly resist. I don't try to resist anybody, really, unless—"

"I don't believe that," I said, tired of his usual line. "I know enough of your story from your own mouth, to know that's not true."

He laughed. "OK, so it's not all the way true. But I just won't outright—"

"My view is that you do what you want to do most of the time—"

"Pretty much—"

"And if you don't get into trouble, it's only because you've decided that you didn't want to do that troublesome thing. It doesn't have anything to do with you towing the line—"

"Ah . . . yeah," he said, wincing. "I try not to get into trouble. But if something comes up and *I'm* gonna do it, I'll just try to do it when they don't see—"

"Of course!" I said. "It's like your B&Es, a rationalization for saying 'fuck it, I'll do what I want to do.'"

"I can understand that I have to follow certain rules," he said solemnly.

"So, how do you determine the difference between a rule that you need to follow and a rule that doesn't matter?"

He propped his elbows on his knees. "There's not really ones that can broken and ones that have to be followed. It's just . . . there are some rules I ignore because they have nothing to do with me. Like the rule against fighting on the property. I ignore that because I don't fight. I mean I typically will stay out of fight. If one comes up, if it's out of my control, I'll fight if I have to. But otherwise, I just ignore that rule. It doesn't apply."

"It doesn't cause you any pain to follow that rule."

He laughed. "I guess you could put it that way."

We sat silent for a few moments, and then, still bothered, he again complained about not having yet received his punishment. I asked him if he understood that Frank and Jen might not trust him.

"I don't understand why," he sighed incredulously. "I didn't say I was going to follow all the rules. I never promised that."

"You made that agreement when you came in here."

"No, I made an agreement to do my *best* to follow the rules. In the contract it doesn't say: You *will* follow the rules or you *will* be thrown out."

"They're bending the rules right now to keep you," I lectured. "If they had been following the letter of the law, you'd be out of here right now. I mean, how trustworthy are you if you're shoplifting?"

He laughed and tossed back some ice cubes from his glass. "OK," he said, crunching, "in some ways, you may not be able to trust me to *follow* every rule to the exact letter. You may not be able to trust me to . . . not shoplift, whatever. But . . ." He paused. "You could trust my word."

Now I laughed. "How? Face it. You're suspect. It's like your pick-up strategy with girls: I'll pretend my come-on line is a joke, so it doesn't seem real, but if the girl responds, then I'll snap her up."

"Yeeaahh," he said, stretching out his reluctant assent. "But I'm trustworthy in a relationship. I won't steal from a girl. I won't lie to a girl. Never have. Never will." This last sentiment lifted his chin slightly.

"Those are good things," I said. "But do you know how you sound otherwise?"

"OK," he said, tossing back more ice. "By nature I'm a thief. Most of the time I can't suppress it. My whole point of going into that store was to take something . . . All I really planned to get were earrings. A pair of stud earrings, 'cause I didn't have any. But I was walking around. I *saw the wallet*. I always wanted a chain wallet. It's a nice one, like thirty-something bucks. Way too expensive to buy. Well, I said, let's see. I probably could have gotten away with it. I delayed. I thought too much. That was my downfall, 'cause I stopped to talk to some old lady near the door. As soon as I started to walk away they said, 'Excuse me, sir.' I thought, 'Aw man, I'm screwed now.'"

He bit down on a particularly hard chunk of ice.

"Well, I tried to run, I tried to get away. I mean, almost did. The guy was a little bigger than me . . ." He shook his head. "A little faster, too. He just kind of picked me up and slammed me down. My arm hurt, but I lived with it. It's one of the things you've got to expect when you're a thief."

For a moment, I considered pointing out that he'd just admitted to having an expectation.

"So why are you a thief?" I asked.

"I can't help it?" Again his interrogative tone reached toward me, an antenna.

"Right," I said, sarcastically, "I'm a killer. I can't help it. I'm a wife abuser. I can't help it. I'm an alcoholic. I can't help it."

"It's true," he pleaded. "It doesn't make it any better. Even when I was little. I was five and I used to steal from the 7-Eleven on base. I'd take little candies. It was thievery. But I didn't take things from family members and friends."

He paused, the antenna reaching again. "Okay," he admitted, "it *spread a little* and I took money from my parents' business . . ."

We sat for a minute. "So," I said, finally, "you have an interesting and complex relationship to the truth. You're pretty good at telling yourself lies."

"Not exactly," he said. "I'll tell the truth," his voice again rose at the end of the sentence, almost curling into a question mark, "just not the whole truth."

I rolled my eyes. "How can partial truth be the truth?

"Okay," he said, "Suppose I got in a fight because I stole something from somebody. Let's say the principal or a cop wanted to know what happened, and I said, 'This guy came up to me, started yelling and lashed out at me.' Now that's the truth."

"No, that's really just a deception."

"There's a difference between a deception and lying."

"Yeah?"

"A lie is outright. That example of the fight story wasn't an outright lie. It was a deception. A lie is saying something that didn't *even* happen."

"The half-truth is the most effective lie."

"It's not a lie. It's a deception. It's not a lie because you're telling the truth."

"Listen to what you're saying!" I exclaimed, exasperated. "You're being a sophist. In classical times a sophist was a debater who didn't care about the truth, he just wanted to sound credible. If the audience believed him, that was all that mattered. Sophists were early advertising executives, really."

"Basically like a lawyer."

"Yeah," I replied. "So now we're talking about the truth, and you're arguing that the deception is honest."

"The deception isn't *honest,*" he insisted. "But it's *not a lie, either.* It's something right in between."

"It's an untruth!"

"It's an untruth but not all the way false."

"You're protecting yourself."

"Why would I need to protect myself?" he asked, again incredulous. He paused. "Okay, I'll admit that I'm not very bright."

"No," I replied with some weight. "I'd say you're very bright. I'd also say the person you lie to most often is *you*."

"Hey," he said. "I *have* a conscience." He tossed back more ice. "To a certain extent."

I laugh to myself, recalling Matt's protestations. Then I remember the wormy smile and wonder what extent of conscience lies behind it. That smile which shoves away my presumptions about "getting to" him or to any further understanding of my brother. That smile which may, in fact, be the attribute through which he and my brother most resemble one another.

Frank's truck rocks to a stop at Crescent Lake Park, and we all tumble out and spread across a grassy zone between the tennis courts and the baseball diamond. Andre whips the football to Galvin, an elegant feathery flick. Galvin snags it and heaves, and the ball, almost tumbling in its flight, plows into Andre's hands. Galvin then dashes long. As he suddenly zags right, Andre slings a tight spiral to Galvin's left. It arrives just as Galvin zags to his left and turns. A leaf alighting on the fingertips. Completion.

They worked out these pass patterns on the green, and one day afterward drafted me as their hapless defensive back. I tried, without success, to intercept Andre's pinpoint deliveries.

"You move a lot," Galvin told me, proud of his teamwork with Andre and his superiority over me. "But you don't seem to be going anywhere."

I conceded that he was right but didn't give him what he most wanted from this exchange: my praise. I didn't realize until later that he had lingered at the end of his words, hoping there beside me with that sidelong gaze, spinning the football up and down and up between his hands. As a teacher, I encourage and laud almost by reflex. As a man with this younger man, I just didn't give. Had not comprehended, or, worse, had maybe withheld my approval out of some competitive hardness. In this place of all places.

With a full-time job now, Galvin doesn't sit as often under the oak with Andre and bitch to the ground between his soles. He's cooled a bit to Andre, as well, partly as his arrogance—formerly subdued by his circumstances on arrival at the TLP—has again arisen on his ascending confidence. Also, he senses the extra tension between Andre and Quovonne.

"When you go around with someone and they're your friend," he complains to me repeatedly, wanting me to confirm his fears, "and they go behind your back, and they're having a relationship, and they deny it over and over, then it stinks."

For now, however, Galvin goes long one more time and hauls in Andre's pass, their exclusive contact.

The group finally divides up for a game of touch football. Galvin, Andre, Frank, and Tim versus Matt, Bill, Salim, Sam, and me.

Quovonne, wearing turquoise shorts and a matching sleeveless top, his hair gelled down like a flapper, smoothes a bedspread under a tree at the sideline and pulls his school books from a pack.

"I'm a cheerleader, not a football player," he announces brightly to the group.

"Jeezuz!" Tim mutters, annoyed, as he heads down the field with his team to receive the kickoff.

The game begins, and it isn't long before sweat, grass stain, the amazing catch, and the perfect taunt draw us into their harmony. Often Andre has lamented that the excitement in life for him ended when he became too old for Little League football. After that, he didn't know where to turn for the joy of physical solidarity which glows in him now: suddenly Mr. Eye Contact, Sir Grin. In fact, most of the guys seem soothed by the play—though some, like Salim and Bill, are clearly out of shape. They pull off their tee shirts and reveal middle-aged frontage still baby-fat fresh but gleaned from long lounges among industrial starches.

After a few touchdowns, I take a break—to even the teams—and slump down beside Quovonne in the shade. A blond girl of, perhaps, six sits beside him.

"Jilly Duncan," she says, tossing, from hand to hand, a baseball with the cover ripped off. She says she found it in the bushes near the diamond—where the teenage recruits for the new pro team in town sometimes practice. Her parents seem nowhere in sight.

A sheaf of writing paper lies in Quovonne's lap. He's etched a paragraph and, forehead in hand, studies the likelihood of carving out more words. At last he looks up, slightly dazed as though a deep sleep had mashed his face into a pillow.

"I'm supposed to write an essay for school," he says, "on, 'What are the problems high schools face today in the education system?' But I don't know what else to say."

He shows me his opening passage: the usual bland generalities—gangs, drugs, overcrowding, racism—in a barely literate tangle. This uninspired subject wearies him, but he's determined to do what the teacher requests. He doesn't admit to his boredom until I mention the possibility. Then I urge him to probe his own experience, commandeer the subject. He wrestles down a few words and offers me his baffled eye.

"Tell what you know about gangs," I say, hoping to help him fire some flesh into this void of abstraction.

He lays down his pencil and stares off beyond Jilly Duncan, toward the lake.

"Have you had any experience with gangs?" I ask.

"Sure," he says, finally, turning back toward me. "My sister. She was my twin. When she was seven, she got shot by a gang here and here and here." He touches his shoulder, chest, and forehead.

I ask him what happened. He, his sister and father were walking down the street in their Miami neighborhood. A passing car slowed. Shots.

"She was wild like me," he says and watches Jilly and her ball. A moment later, he shuffles his papers into his bag.

"I'm gonna ask for an extension," he says.

The game halts for a water break. While the guys rest in the shade, Quovonne demonstrates a few cheerleading routines for Jilly, who tries to follow his lead. Afterward, he scoops up the football. When Jilly saunters past me to play catch with him, she taps me on the top of the head—to let me know she's not afraid of anything?

Tim rags on Quovonne for throwing "like a girl." Tim, seaweed arm.

"I can play as good as anybody," Quovonne says. "Wooo!" He hops as he lobs the ball to Jilly, who—fearless—almost catches it. In displays such as the cheerleading and now this repartee, Quovonne moves, like some women, to fill the surrounding male eyes. In their gazes captive or averted, he tests the premise of himself as female, seeking a confirmation, a power, or sounding for a limit. Yet he can't suppress his square-shouldered, muscular maleness. He maintains a stereotype of female gesture and manner—until he has cause to run or shout in happy excitement or anger. Then his body immediately shatters the diminutive aspect, thickens, strengthens. It commits itself to space with a new velocity, confidence, and ease—if only for a few seconds. Now I can only wonder if that woman he wishes to be, the one in which he immures himself only to resurrect in moments of unconsciousness—is that not the dead twin sister?

"If you're so athletic," Frank says to Quovonne. "C'mon. Into the game."

Quovonne demurs but stays on the field, and the teams fan out to resume play. At times, he veers from the pushing and blocking. At other times, he races and laughs and plunges. He even catches a pass from Matt, though Andre is supposed to be covering him on that play and is clearly laying off.

A half hour later, we leave Jilly at the park. ("I live across the street," she says.) Frank drives us to the Dairy Queen near the TLP and springs for a round of cones with sprinkles. We sprawl at long tables beside the building. In the window is a black-and-white photo of the Dairy Queen. In every regard it appears the same as the current surroundings. Above the image, someone has written *1955*. I point out the picture to the guys. Galvin studies it in genuine wonder. Matt notes the photographer's position while taking the shot.

"Once you go black, you never go back," Quovonne sings out to Frank, who is licking a chocolate ice cream cone. Quovonne sounding for a little transgression.

"Not true," Frank says, suavely, "My last girlfriend was black."

Quovonne giggles, surprised at the notion.

Frank leans over and whispers into Quovonne's ear. Quovonne's mouth racks into a huge "O" and then he bellows.

The good will carries us along. For the first time since Miss V witnessed Quovonne with Mr. Right, Andre and Frank resume their old one-upmanship brag fest. Andre rides Frank about changing sides for the second half of the game and then losing.

Frank holds his hands up as if ready for frisking. "It's my job," he announces in mock sobriety, "to make you guys feel good, to build your self-esteem. That's why I let you win."

"That's the first time you've done your job then," Tim says, laughing.

Later, back at the TLP, this energy lingers. As the guys wander off to their rooms, Quovonne sprays Tim and then Frank with the garden hose. Getting soaked in the process, Frank marches toward Quovonne, who abandons his position. Frank pursues and finally captures Quovonne. He drags him, howling and laughing, within range of the hose. Tim blasts them both, also revenging himself, no doubt, on Quovonne for his earlier remarks about Tim's insolence.

Drenched and dripping, Tim lunges to hug me, and I scamper off.

The second time he approaches, I say, "Go ahead," sweat-soaked anyway.

But he backs off, grinning. Pointless to him now, since I'm willing. Besides, he'd have to touch me.

TWELVE

A FEW DAYS LATER, as Frank and I linger in the driveway after curfew, Les steps out of the darkness at the edge of the property. Terminated nearly a year ago, he's come to Jen twice to beg for readmittance to the program.

Frank stiffens slightly. He folds his arms. No handshakes.

Les is surprisingly thin, his hair shorn of the huge, dry, flangey locks. After meeting Frank's flat hello and some cold chat, he snatches the beeper clipped to his belt, shakes it, and asserts that he gets innumerable calls. He was one of the first batch at the TLP. He wore the same tee shirt every day—black with a lightning bolt slashing across the chest—until Frank took him aside and instructed him about laundry. A thick chain draped from his wallet to his belt loop. He was the kind who tried to cheat at board games but wasn't quick enough. Muscular yet rounded by fat, a coward and blowhard, he fancied himself an athlete and a man's man. Forbidden like all the other residents to smoke after curfew, he told me that he once craved nicotine so much, he woke in the middle of the night, ground some butts into a glass of water and drank it.

He was terminated for repeatedly breaking curfew and for "not moving ahead" with the program. Jen was only slightly regretful.

"He was a liar," she said, "but there was something about him I liked."

Yet few of the residents were displeased. A vast, almost wholly unacknowledged association with violence, as victim and victimizer, hovered over him like a sky that had fallen and would fall again. Anyone could see it in the "playful" slugs in the shoulder he exchanged with another resident at the time, Craig—the increasing force in each of his blows until Craig realized there was no end for Les and so declined to escalate and continue the contest.

Now trying to warm up the scene, Les begins to tell about us about Chase, his girlfriend.

"She's bisexual and—"

"Don't want to go with you there," Frank says, cutting him off.

After eviction from the TLP, Les wandered and eventually ended up at the Refuge, a religiously affiliated soup kitchen–shelter near the freeway overpass. There he met Chase and, despite the segregation of the sleeping quarters, got her pregnant. Tim told me that he'd encountered Les begging a dinner for Chase in front of a KFC.

"Idiot!" Tim said.

In a week, Les had spent his $190 in food stamps and so was broke.

"I could go through all the Phases now with no problem," Les says, inching back to his motive for this visit.

"You know you're not supposed to be on the property," Frank says quietly. "The other guys will want unauthorized visitors . . ."

Les says he has only two dollars in food stamps.

"Ah, that makes for tough times," Frank says, his arms still folded

Les acknowledges once more that he squandered his opportunities at the TLP. He says that when he encounters one of the current residents, he counsels them not to be so foolish.

"I could do all the Phases," he says again, looking away from us both.

Frank leans over and picks a blossom from one of the hibiscus bushes he'd planted along the driveway just before the TLP opened—bushes that Les always claimed were killed by a winter freeze during his time there.

"Here," Frank says, "give this to Chase."

Les's brief return resurrected the memory of an incident that occurred not long after his departure and before the admission of Andre, Quovonne, Salim, Bill, and Galvin—a time, for these latter residents, analogous to what happens in the house before you are born. Events possibly crucial to you, and yet unknown to you.

One day in group, Carlos, a quiet, spectacled gangbanger, brought up the subject of the crying baby in the apartments next door to the TLP.

"What are we going to do?" he asked. "For the last few nights, it sounds like they must be beating it to death."

"If anyone wants to inquire about it," Jen said, "come to me and we'll investigate."

"No!" Tim shouted. "I've heard the sounds, too. But, man, if we call, they'll bring in HRS. When I was a kid HRS took me away, and two weeks later someone broke my nose. Christ! Everybody judges us, and then they beat their kids. We didn't put the apartments there. It's just part of our home. Cabbage Patch, Snoopy—people who beat their kids."

"Tim, anyone can have the option of looking into this if they want to," Jen said.

"Dude, I would never touch my child like that," Carlos said.

"We'll call the HRS hotline," Jen suggested.

"Oh, the kid will just get more abuse," Tim moaned. "We'll call HRS. That'll make a hit with the neighborhood." He pounded on the arm of the chair. "I was abducted in the middle of the night by HRS. My nose was broken and it's still sensitive!"

"My old lady hit with an extension cord," Carlos said. "You get hit because you turn off too many lights, or you drink out of the milk container, or something like that. I know where you're coming from."

"Right, I had it easy," Tim said sarcastically. "I was hit with knives and forks . . ."

He sat for a moment in the sudden quiet.

"It's such a hard judgment call," Tim continued. "Lots of kids are raised by smacks and come out all right. It's the ultimate insult, someone like HRS comes into your house and tells you how to raise your kids."

Jen then invited Paul into the group room to mediate.

"I hear the crying once or twice a night," Carlos said.

"We'll do the hotline," Paul said. "It'll be anonymous."

Carlos and Tim and the rest then decided suddenly to scale back their investigation, agreeing to wait until they heard the crying again and then call the police.

"Okay, elect someone to go to Frank and make the call when it's time," Jen said. "It would probably be better if it was happening in the morning. And it would probably be best to be anonymous. We don't want to start a neighbor war."

No call was ever made. No mention of the crying baby recurred. Frank asserted to me that his windows, too, opened onto those apartments, and he hadn't heard a thing. Jen speculated that Carlos and

Tim might have made up the story or imagined the beating, so volatile were their feelings about their own past sufferings. So proud they were of them and so ashamed. Thus: they as the crying baby next door.

Still, I listened two or three times at evening from Carlos's back windows, and I thought I heard a baby, though it was laughing.

The feared "neighbor war" did not manifest, but a different crisis reawakened the neighborhood's anxiety about the program and tested its trust.

A month after the debate about the crying baby, Carlos, Jason, Ralph, and Zachariah (a brief TLP resident) broke into a house several blocks from the TLP, tied up the sole resident, and threatened to kill him if he didn't give them the correct ATM numbers for his card. He capitulated and they went to a bank machine. When they found the numbers were false, they actually returned to the scene of the crime. By then, the man had escaped his bonds. The police were present to apprehend all but Zachariah, who managed somehow to elude capture.

Carlos, the only legal adult in the group, was remanded to the county jail and was charged with home invasion—a crime which would qualify him, if convicted, for thirty-one to fifty-eight years in prison. Jason spent a few weeks in juvenile detention and was released to his parents until the hearing. Ralph, only weeks from the age of majority, sat in jail for a few days. During that time someone added something to his shampoo that caused his hair to fall out. Ultimately, he was released on the condition that he leave the state. For almost a week thereafter, he rode a bicycle back and forth in front of the TLP several times a day, and then he disappeared.

Zachariah had not yet been arrested, though the police knew who he was and where he could be found.

Carlos claimed that they had not broken into the house, that they had met the victim at the St. Pete Pier, and he had invited them to his place for drinks. Only when he had made sexual advances had they tied him up—simply to defend themselves . . .

Frank and Paul conjectured about the authorities' new get-tough policy regarding home invasions. In the previous months, local newspapers had seethed with terrorizing tales of murderous incursions on suburban man. Opportunistic legislators had chimed in with calls for righteous ruthlessness.

"They're probably going to make an example of him," Paul said, staring into his computer screen, "him and the next one hundred guys."

So Carlos sat in the county jail, awaiting his hearing, the weeks—and then months—passing.

Though cool, Paul took the whole matter personally, as a devastating betrayal. He believed in the Phases, the forms, the levels of order. He had helped design them, after all. He believed, also, in the virtue and power of reason: anyone who was offered help would be crazy not to accept it sooner or later, and make the most of it—even someone who, like the guys, had been thrown away. This faith imbued his confidence in those months before the TLP opened, when he and the staff defeated a handful of bigots and fear mongers for the support of the neighborhood association. The program *would* work, provided the residents were the kind for whom it had been created. And who was that? The young man, for instance, who had been the first candidate for admission? He'd needed a safe place to live, perhaps only for six months. He had applied for admission to the University of Miami and had real hopes of getting in. Eventually, he'd found other living arrangements.

Paul had given himself to the TLP and, then, to the guys. With the arrest, he reached a tipping point. Not long afterward, he took a job managing a cleaning crew of seventy for a hospital in Mississippi. Better money, he said, and better benefits.

Tim, too, struggled with the arrest. He confessed to Jen that he knew—or at least he *thought* he knew—beforehand that Carlos and the rest were up for perpetration on the night in question. He'd kept this information, or intuition—whichever it was—to himself. He was scrupulous about allegiances, formal or not, with his peers.

"Staff guilt-tripped me," he said later, "totally overboard." He laughed. "But things were most fun when Carlos and those guys were around. They were always up to some shit. I remember Carlos dropped me on the ground once, and my neck's hurt ever since. I think of him every morning."

The police awakened Frank at 3 A.M. on the night of the arrest, and he went down to the station. The whole matter agitated him, though he didn't share Paul's idealism. He knew the guys "were no angels." Yet, as Paul stared dejectedly into the computer screen, perhaps deciding to put his résumé in the mail, Frank murmured, almost to himself, "You stick up for them because people are condemning them from the git-go, and they're buying into all this anyway, trying to live up to the negative image they have of being misfits and losers . . . They fuck up and we defend them. Why?"

THIRTEEN

THE BOY, PERHAPS THIRTEEN, fidgeted through my poetry-writing session at the runaway shelter one Saturday afternoon. He refused to do any writing exercises, doodling instead or, occasionally, tormenting the other kids around the table, bragging about bourbon highs taken neat from a tall glass. Now and again, from beneath the bill of his ball cap, he tossed me an odd, rude eye. As the session wore on, my patience with him ebbed. While everyone was working, I finally leaned over the table at him and slid some white bond under his face down-turned and obscured by the hat.

"I want to hear something from you," I commanded.

He didn't look up. "You said we weren't required to do anything."

"That's true," I replied, my frustration rising. "You're such a tough guy. Write about that."

He stared at the paper. "Well, what if I ain't tough?"

"That's *interesting,*" I said, ire coiling up through my throat. "Write about *that.*"

He tipped his head back, as though he was hoping to appear menacing—or, perhaps, he was afraid he was about to be struck.

"Well, what if I'm both?" he asked.

At last, I understood the source of his strange, hard looks: both of his eyes were swollen. The left one, slightly more puckered and purpled, nestled on a faint, green quarter moon.

That chin thrust out. And that extra gleam in the blackened eye. There I leaned over him—like the bullying father—and he peered up at me as though at some portentous sky. To see now what that sky had in mind.

"Well, what if I tell you I'm not gonna do anything?" he asked.

"That's okay with me," I said, retreating, ashamed. "That's just fine."

Eventually, the boy settled himself on one of the exercises and easily spun out some doggerel which jarred loose a laugh from the table. Grateful for this opportunity, I praised him. At the end of the session, he insisted that I follow him to the back of the shelter where a small arts and crafts workshop had been set up for clients. He opened a closet door.

"There," he said, dragging out a large pine toolbox. "I made it."

His skill was evident, all lines true and each corner snugged by dove-tail joints. I praised him again, even more grateful for the gift of his craft and his thirst for attention, his willingness to show what mattered to him, even if it further implicated me in the deeper gleam of the eye with the green quarter moon.

"Had Narcissus himself seen his own face when he had been angry," wrote the seventeenth-century English clergyman Thomas Fuller, "he never would have fallen in love with himself." Those words now accompany my memory of the boy eager to be proud of himself and worthy, and the man I was while standing over him—capable, it seemed, of a fury the boy knew too well. A fury I knew, as a boy, too well. A fury which, even as a teenager, had terrified me with the possibility that I might one day raise a hand against wife or child. *Never,* I'd vowed, pleading with my puzzled heart. Me, ugly man.

I think of those words, too, when I see Andre skulk across the green, a few weeks after the football game at Crescent Lake Park, the bill of his hat pulled low against what Miss V has seen him do again. No job has materialized for him yet, and this has begun to zero out the confidence that working part time for Frank has engendered. Andre has begun to float, perhaps to float away, and Frank has begun, ever so slightly, to loosen his hopeful grip on Andre's string.

That troubling, deeper gleam. It emanates from behind the eye-slit of the taken-up dance mask, from the deep center of the iris, back where the twisting gods of night chase a young man through his vision quest. It's the knowing pebble beneath the clear, sun-banged stream. Arcturus in the personal void no one else is allowed to touch. Rage. Shame. Fear. Strength. Ignorance. Confusion. Incapacity. Gem of many facets.

It lives in the face of Galvin's father, which Galvin claims appeared to him in a dream in the form of a boxing glove. It lives in Galvin slugging Tim one afternoon and Tim saying nothing to staff about it.

It imbues the fact that Matt was not promoted to assistant manager at the sandwich shop but was fired for general lassitude; that Bill was sacked by the grocery store for an outburst against the assistant manager.

It spurs Quovonne's bitter monologues about the alleged rapes of female Army recruits by their male superiors at the Aberdeen Proving Ground (something to deflect him from his own problems). It permits Salim's pat claim that he's "society's child."

It riles group meetings and suffuses the coolness of a secret tear and the blunt skepticism of the tender believer betrayed. It asserts, "My momma spoiled me. She shoulda slapped me more." It laughs at the poster in the TLP office, detailing a hundred ways to handle stress ("stop worrying, start enjoying") and the poster of Andrew Carnegie declaring, "You cannot push anyone up a ladder unless he is willing to climb a little."

It presides as Sam and Galvin sit under the oak, talking about extremist black Muslims, "the five percenters," as they call them.

"There were a bunch of them in my barracks in the Job Corps," Galvin says, "tough and wild. They were always prayin' all night."

"Two of my brothers tried to get me into that stuff back in the old neighborhood," Sam says. "They're fanatics. Nuts." He doesn't tell Galvin, as he has told me, that his brothers have slain several people in what they call their "holy war."

Later the gleam reflects on Sam and the old man from one of the apartments across the sandy alley who each day combs the dumpsters for returnable cans, his legs bowed like some toy cowboy detached from the back of his stallion, but thin and wrapped with ace bandages. Sam and the man mimic friendliness as they chat in the alley, but the man has called the police several times on the guys. Once, he claimed that a resident ran past his wife and ripped a bottle of liquor from her hand—a boy from Room 3. At the time, no one was staying in Room 3. On another occasion, someone smeared feces on the man's steps and hanging laundry and drew a Star of David in feces on his door. (Sam thinks that whoever did the latter was trying to draw a pentagram but didn't know how.)

"The cops told us we needed to have someone watching our guys twenty-four/seven," Sam says as we walk back to the office. "I told them that they had no proof, and that they've got problems in this neighborhood, and it's easier to blame these kids than deal with the problems, which are harder to solve."

Those problems—another reflection of the gleam—manifested most recently not more than fifteen blocks south of the TLP. Two white police officers—one male and one female—stopped a car after an alleged high-speed chase. The driver of the car refused to roll down his windows at the command of the officers. Since the windows were heavily tinted, the patrolman stepped in front of the car to get a better view of the driver, and the female officer used a baton to knock out the driver's side window. Apparently, the car lurched forward, "like when you take your foot off the brake," one witness said.

The patrolman drew his pistol and fired several rounds into the car, killing the driver, a black male just a month past his eighteenth birthday. That night, rioters angry about what they saw as a clear act of institutional racism, burst upon a twenty-five-block area, throwing rocks, wrecking cars, and setting fire to at least twenty-eight buildings, burning several to the ground. The television played it as a local version of the LA riots of 1992: as a reopening of old, unhealed wounds; as an advertisement for more central control; and—without daring to actually say it—as a sign that St. Pete was perhaps not such a somnolent backwater but a real city accruing some of the poignant glamour of metropolitan social problems. One report about the shooting concluded with the image of the female officer's baton beneath the front wheel of the blasted car. Flame billowed through the riot footage, much of it shot from above, focusing on property damage.

In the succeeding days and weeks, a local—some would say radical—black organization held meetings and "convicted" the patrolman who fired the shots, and the police chief, of murder. Eventually, city authorities saw the group as a menace and prevented its members from gathering. At the height of the tensions, President Clinton's apparatus mentioned that he might visit St. Pete. Instead, Henry Cisneros, head of HUD, came and lamented the tragic pervasiveness of black-on-black violence. Newspaper editorials called for calm and better social service solutions and respect for the rule of law. Several city forums were convened, the ancient agonies of race in America again articulated. A grand jury reviewed the case and found no grounds to indict the officer who fired the shots, though he was suspended for two months without pay for putting himself in harm's way by walking in front of a stopped car with an unknown driver.

The dead teenager turned out to have a lengthy rap sheet. Also, the car happened to be stolen, which the officers did not know at the time. Neither detail, of course, aided the case of those outraged. Later reports narrated the usual details of blighted, black male adolescence—feckless and absent adults, drug dealing, an obsession with the "nihilistic lyrics of gangsta rappers"—and one article recounted the teenager's divagations through at least four juvenile facilities over six years. It all sounded like Andre, down to the hip fashion gear.

Why had these programs—some like the TLP—failed the dead boy? Why, as one writer asked, had he not been arrested when he had failed to show up for mandatory counseling sessions?

"The obvious one," said the head of the state's Department of Juvenile Justice, "is that intensive aftercare was not in place."

"He stood up on his own," said his older brother, "never needed any group of guys to boost him."

From the green of the TLP, several of us watched police choppers rake spotlights over the riot area.

"That's what Tupac was talkin' about," Andre said, his first social remark in days.

Tim also bore the gleam—most recently when Paul left just a few weeks after Andre, Salim, Bill, Quovonne, and Matt arrived at the TLP. The latter group did not understand the impact of his departure, though it would affect them all. For Tim, however, it was an act of abandonment, another betrayal, since Paul often treated him well and always at Tim's convenience. In addition to this disappointment, Jen and Frank wondered uneasily about how the new manager would change the system, which they had helped design, and Sam grumbled, to me, about getting a boss, at last, who would hire him full time. After several weeks, the central administration asked David to "step up," as he described it, and temporarily oversee matters.

In his mid-thirties, married with one son—and trying to finish his dissertation—David already had plenty to do besides his usual counseling work, which involved a juvenile caseload that extended in all directions from the TLP's parent organization. Still, he undertook what he imagined to be Paul's job. Repeatedly, he told the guys, "I'm clearing my decks and then I'll be available full time." But the weeks elapsed, and he still spent most of his day in meetings elsewhere. Finally, he issued a memo listing the hours he would be at the TLP. He also wrote a memo which told the residents they could leave a voice mail message if they wanted to talk with him. Generally, when he was around, he sat in the office, though he instituted an "open door" policy, actually leaving the door ajar. None of guys passed through it uninvited, however.

"He's clueless," Tim said, a veteran of the weekly group therapy sessions David ran just after the TLP opened.

David in his tie and horn-rimmed glasses. With his academic asides and parentheticals, his titter-titter chuckle-chuckle. With his memos and his door ajar.

One day, he "elevated" Bill, pushing him to the edge of anxiety, and then over the edge. Bill ranted and stalked, and Jen, frustrated with David but subordinate to him, tried to calm Bill in his room. David said his actions were necessary, to help Bill, whose medication was still not right.

On another day, he called Matt into the office. He was worried, he said, about Matt's reading—too much fantasy. They talked, and he declared that they now saw eye to eye. Each agreed to read a novel chosen by the other. Matt selected *Elminster.* David, *Shoeless Joe.*

In the office now, David holds a bicycle tire pump that looks like an old-fashioned insecticide sprayer, the type Grandpa would pump over his garden. He studies its long needle.

"I can't say I've heard many wonderful things about you," he says to me. "I don't mention those things unless I do. But I haven't heard any negatives about you, and those things usually pop up quickly. So you must be doing something with the guys."

Later, talking of angry clients and his role in deciding whether or not a person should be forcibly incarcerated for psychiatric evaluation, he leans back in the chair. He pumps the sprayer.

"It's a big responsibility," he says. "There's so much power in being able to Baker Act people. You know, putting people away, even for few hours, with just your signature."

On a group outing, at an arcade near the beach, Salim and I stand side by side, clutching our .357 Magnums. We blast bank robbers and paramilitary ninjas—as well as a few bank tellers and hapless pedestrians—who scurry from behind desks and alley dumpsters, or pop up in the back seats of getaway cars and chopper cockpits. We hardly aim. No time.

"Reload!" a panicked drone voice commands when we've emptied a clip, "Reload! Reload!" And we slap the appropriate button.

We blast until our trigger fingers are sore and we can't hold our arms out in front of us any longer.

After a short break, Frank and I play air hockey, out of a sidelong nostalgia for our early twenties, when the game became a staple of neighborhood bars across the country. Frank flips the puck onto the table and we begin, and suddenly we're both twenty at the Great Plains Saloon, the Licorice Stick Lounge, the Stumble Inn. I slap the puck straight into Frank's goal. He pulls it out, and I do it again, and again. I can't hit them any other way, it seems, though I try some off-speed stuff and some angles. It's been too long since I last played to control the thing, really. No skill on my part. I'm simply quicker and too odd for him, a southpaw. And Frank smiles and slips another token into the slot, and we hammer again. *Gonna get you this time.* But he doesn't. He can't. I don't even know how to slow my shots down just enough to help him win respectably, and I don't want him to win, anyway. He's faster than I am on the football field, a better shot on the basketball court. Kid's stuff, and we know it. But his edginess leans on the table as he trains his will on the puck. *Gonna get you this time.* Until, at last, he chooses grace and shakes us both free after a half dozen games—a choice neither of us would have made at twenty.

On the way back to the TLP, Salim sits alone in the far back seat of the step van. He rests his chin on the top of the seat and stares out, baleful as a Labrador puppy, at the encroaching loneliness in the passing neon of tourist tee shirt shops and raw bars. Maybe he wants to be seen in this apparent sadness. Maybe this is how he appears most of the time, when alone. His right eye suddenly squints shut, just as it did when we blasted with our Magnums and he sometimes tried, futilely, to aim at his nemeses and shoot before they killed him. All around us the machines screamed and exploded and flashed, like an exhausting, repetitive passion, a psychic funland that empties the soul's pockets. It seems now that the room brimmed with its own odd version of the gleam, as though sunlight banked, in a thousand angles, from bowls of multicolored fluid. As though we were inside the gleam.

"Quovonne'd like to pull that 'poor little black boy' stuff on me," Sam says, "but it's not gonna work. Even being gay. He has to get over being the victim. He's not the first to suffer prejudice, Lord knows.

"I've been studying some of this material on transsexuals. I'm not bothered by his homosexuality, but I am worried about some other things."

Sam says that Quovonne invents tales about people, and he worries that Quovonne might make up things about him, as he has about other staff members. His fear, it seems, is justified. Quovonne, for instance, has several times asserted that he smelled whiskey on Frank's breath.

Sam says that Quovonne left his room unlocked, so he went into it, searching for something to filch—to teach Quovonne a lesson about leaving his place open. Sam found a letter to Andre—or about Andre—which Quovonne later read to Jen in the office, striking out Andre's name and inserting "my special one."

"Quovonne wants everyone to be interested in his passion," Sam says. "And I can understand Andre's problems. Quovonne can look like a girl, and act like a girl, and Andre can see that. There are times when I refer to Quovonne as a she. It's almost unconscious."

In the office the next day, Jen confesses, "I'm working as much as possible with Quovonne and Andre, but there are limits to how much help I can give. Quovonne wants Andre dependent on him, I think, just like his baby, as a kind of substitute for his child. Andre may be gay. He may not be gay. But right now he's mostly just hungry for love. He doesn't know what to do. He packed his bag the other night and was going down the alley, but he came back.

"We have to face it. The program's therapeutic component needs to be larger."

I mention the situation at the TLP to a friend of mine, a top manager of a national nonprofit organization, who describes himself as a "midwestern striver." I recount the guys' difficulties in getting and keeping jobs, and the many needs of the gleam.

"There's overemployment in the U.S.," Striver says. "Been to any fast-food restaurants lately? Look at many of the people in service sector jobs near the bottom end. These are people who aren't really competent and shouldn't really be there, but those businesses need the bodies. Those businesses are in trouble, of course."

He sighs, this man raised by a single mother in a humble section of a small town. He takes in a long breath.

"There's a large sorting process that goes on at a certain level," he says with a tone of angular rationality, "and it's mostly a matter of cash flow—"

"Demographics," I say.

"And don't forget psychometrics. Most of the staff at this place you're talking about is near the bottom of the sorting process. They've made it through college, or they've been to college, at least. Some of the clients are just below this, and most of them will get sorted to the bottom. They never really had much of a chance, some of them, anyway. And of course, the rest below that never even got as high as the sorting process.

"Often, people further down the decision-making chain in nonprofits are less results-oriented, partly because they have genuinely noble motives. They look for general goodwill or general improvements—which are usually vague and mostly wishful thinking. Organizations like the one you describe don't usually hire the best team to get the job done, anyway. They don't have the money. And there's no real longitudinal base for measuring success in this particular business. How long before you can be sure each of these guys will live reasonably productive lives? Ten years? Maybe. But only then would you give your shrinks and your staff bonuses for turning a guy around.

"And all this is predicated on having a good idea for getting the job done. Finding a good idea among all the bullshit ideas and then bringing it into reality is nearly impossible."

What to do with the gleam?

David makes out new contracts for the guys to sign. He calls them in one by one.

At a fast-food joint, Sam orders a super cheeseburger and fries. Matt and Bill cast him a look that asks: *Aren't you gonna get us burgers, too?*

"Buy your own, boys," Sam says. "Get a job."

One afternoon in Quovonne's room, VHI gleams on the TV: a Madonna video, with lyrics from her song "Express Yourself" flowing in bright captions beneath scenes mooched from Fritz Lang's "Metropolis." To the sampled rap rhythm track popping from his boom box tape, Quovonne punches himself through a choreographed routine. He stares at the TV as he braces for his solo, then delivers "Check Me Out," a song he says he wrote with Andre.

As he works through it, I try to pin down his words but can't. Too garbled by his fuzzy microphone. I glance at the lyrics he has copied out meticulously for me.

It's my time, the fly
time to make a new
rhyme.
So Yall niggaz grab a
sit and check out me.
I'm just a new fly honey.
For all you hoes got beef
for this sexy mommie

He folds into his performance, spinning. His features flare out and then squinch. He works into the microphone, mingling his moves with those learned lip-synching songs from Queen Latifa, Yo Yo,

Heather B. The chair beside him brims with stuffed clowns, rabbits, bears, Sesame Street characters, Cabbage Patch puppets. In wall posters, J. Sragga Benz, L'Son, Kriss Kross glare down at the scene, some of them grabbing their crotches. Thumbtacked beside them hangs a Christmas card from last year, imprinted with John 1:4, "It was his life, and his life was the light of men."

And all you brothers that
think you the Lnanee
you messed a round with
them dumb mommie,
and you niggaz be acting
Funny I'm the kind of female
will take a niggar money,
And for you fool be talking
that moashi turn around Bitch
I'll make you eat this black pussy.

A new video comes on the TV. Scenes: a black man gunned down, a black man grieving, a black man doing push-ups in a jail cell, black-and-white women bent over and shaking it into the camera.

Behind the set, at the far end of the room, Andre burrows into a sports magazine like a stereotypical TV husband withdrawn from a stereotypical nagging wife—except that he is desperate to be here, almost sounding out the lyric under his breath.

I got a Bomb as click something
Bitch you can get hook on
I'm not down to
suck a nigger dick but

I don't mind riding that shit
I'll leave a suck ass niggaz
hanging in the "96"

Quovonne gyrates and hefts with such conviction, with such razor-fussy gesture and intense sensuality, that I'm impressed, almost embarrassed. Like the toolbox of the boy with the quarter moon eye, the song is their crucial expression now. It echoes with the hunger to give significant form to the jumble without and within—a form which declares: I'm here, I can do this, I matter. And Quovonne and Andre are not alone in this. Occasionally, Bill chops out chords on his acoustic guitar and snaps off fashionably affectless bullet-through-the-brain anthems he wrote for a band he says he once led called "Political Rape." Matt writes a few pages of his own fantasy novel—a scene where the hero murders his brother—partially cribbed, he admits, from a book he just finished reading.

If not entirely artful, these works exhibit the desire that can lead to art—though art's no answer in itself for the question posed by the gleam in the lives that spawned them. Each of the guys imitates, and imitation—or "modeling," as the psychologists would say—lies at the center of learning how to shape a work of art or a life. It's where we start. It's often the place to which we return, with the hope of being more conscious than before. Frank, Jen, Sam, and David want to model responsible behavior. But, of course, they're competing with all the other possible personal fictions now surrounding each ego—some dangerous or stupid, some wise and greatly more liberating, many merely generated by sophistical marketing; options that populate our so-called "post-modern" landscape, our exhilarated and anxious moment. Plato foresaw the situation when he banished poets from his perfect republic because their poems misrepresented the reality he cherished and, among other sins, would make soldiers question the likelihood that their glorious deaths in battle would result in sweet, eternal life among the shades. He also wrote: "A change to a new type of music is something to beware of as a hazard of all our fortunes. For the modes of music are never disturbed without unsettling of the most fundamental political and social conventions . . ."

More poets, more views—though not all of us have access to them all. And how worthy the claim of music billed as "new"? To the extent the guys, or anyone, can choose, which of the available defining expressions does one adopt or adapt? Why?

Quovonne finishes the song and sings it a second time, slowing the beat to the haunted, rubbery, narcotic trudge that originated among tinted-window low riders in the Tampa projects. Afterward, he announces he has more songs to write, among them, "Glamorous," "Daddy's Little Girl," "My Gangsta Life."

"What do you think 'Check Me Out' is about?" he asks suddenly.

Surprised by the question, I look at him and then at Andre, who still bores into his magazine.

"Independence, sex, power?" I say, groping.

"That's right," he replies, his amazement mounting into some personal confirmation. "That's right."

The next day, Frank tells me that $300 is missing from the office safe.

"All of it is residents' money," he says, "cash Tim was saving for a car, and some we'd convinced Salim and Bill to tuck away. Only staff had the combination."

"So who do you think did it?"

"Not Jen," he replies, "Miss Polly Purebred."

"Sam?" I ask, "Why? He's military, responsible and all—"

"Who knows if his stories are true," Frank says, "He lied about buying a house. He lives with his aunt. He's so full of shit most of the time . . ."

I think of Sam sneaking two loaves of day-old white bread from the emergency cupboard in the office and giving them to Les when he came begging once.

"Anyway," Frank says, "all the staff's going in for lie detector tests." He pauses. "Keep it cool, if you don't mind. The company will replace the cash. We're not telling the guys."

Had Narcissus seen his own face when . . . Well, what if I'm both? . . . And don't forget psychometrics . . . The therapeutic component needs to be . . . Time to make a new rhyme . . . Reload! Reload!

FOURTEEN

"C'MON," MATT SAYS. "Step across."

We stand in the big banyan tree beside Crescent Lake. Easily twenty or more feet in diameter, the banyan is so riddled with nooks and clefts, and so layered—its branches and roots twining and swirling thickly from leaves to the ground—that it could pass for a home to Tolkienesque gnomes or a mystical forest from the cover of one of Matt's fantasy books.

Matt centers himself on one arm of a vast V of branch running nearly parallel to the ground. I brace myself on the opposing arm. The only way to get to his side is to grab the knob of bark protruding from the trunk between us and swing across the drop. Twenty or more feet below, Bill—not a climber and chary of heights—stares indifferently at swans near the shore and sucks a cigarette which Matt sold to him for ten cents. Lately, Matt has allowed Bill sidekick flunky status, and Bill—his manner thickened by Mellaril and Prozac—seems content to endure Matt's superior attitude, the occasional sadistic policing and ridicule. He follows. He hangs. He offers an occasional word.

I survey the drop, the knob of bark, Matt on the far arm. We've crawled up through the narrows, past a small platform cradling a few crushed beer cans, and then on around a minute balcony that overlooks the lake. We've toured the "balling room," the eye of the tree—where Matt says he meets Randi, the nude dancer, the "witch woman" for whom he may have been trying to shoplift that wallet from the department store. Any laying there, it seems, could occur only while standing.

"It's actually pretty easy," Matt observed. "Once you get in the right spot, there's quite a bit of room. A *lot* of people have been up here."

In the center of the eye is a charred pit where small fires have clawed.

On my side of the branch, I wonder why I'm even contemplating this next step, though I did ask Matt and Bill to show me the tree. I peer down at Bill, at the jagged roots and rocks along the shore. I suddenly feel brittle: adventurer morphing into actuary. And Matt suddenly straightens and rests his fists on his hips, creepily confident.

"C'mon," he says, coaxing me to trust him. Now, the wormy smile, the wet-rimmed eyes. "Just swing out."

Later, in the ebbing afternoon sun, the three of us loaf at the edge of a concrete culvert leading into the lake. The banyan looms beside us, covered with spray-painted and carved graffiti. Bill says he despises the writing. Matt defends it. Soon, I shove my way into his monologue.

"You write on a piece of paper," I say, "and somebody can read it or not. But when you write on a wall or tree, everybody has to see."

"Okay," Matt replies, "but . . . but some things take on that role. They have that story that they tell. Usually it's those things that go on for centuries and centuries."

"So," I reply, "because something's old, like this tree, you get to carve on it?"

"Everybody's gotta do something to leave their mark," Matt continues, "whether you're famous and you're in the papers or in the history books or you're just a . . . common folk . . . because there's always one tree in the neighborhood that's more populated than the rest. You don't see all these trees around here like this, not just in form, but in their . . . character. Because this tree, for one, is the hang-out spot. This a good place. You can go up inside it and play around. And everyone comes to it and leaves their mark and that lives on during the centuries of the tree. And usually it's the oldest trees, the ones that live the longest, that have that character."

"Aren't there better ways to leave a mark than just to carve it on a tree, if you want to be remembered?" I ask. "That's where your imagination needs to come into play."

"Not everybody can leave their mark all in one way," Matt explains. "Some people leave their mark just by changing the physical characteristic of the tree, not just by the carving. Like with the cutting." He points to a square notch below. "Somebody cut that piece out. And that added that . . . *spot* . . . to the character of the tree."

"Or we could say that they defaced the tree," I reply, "changed the tree from what it originally was."

Matt lies back on the grass. "People come to this tree. They say: *Hey, they fixed up a little sit down spot*. It's those types of things that give character. You add, but you take some with you. You take that memory, but you leave your memory behind also, so that everybody else knows."

"Yeah," I say. "I see that. As a writer, you're carving on the tree when you carve on the page, though it's a different kind of tree you're carving on."

"But writing in the book," Matt says, "I may not leave my mark. My writing may not . . . make it to publishing."

"And even if it's published, it can be forgotten pretty easily."

"There's a lotta books out there," Matt says. "Like *Uncle Tom's Cabin*. That one's for the most part a forgotten book. Not a lotta people read it."

"Not read often," I offer, now the English prof, "but not entirely forgotten. The grade school in the neighborhood where I grew up was named after Harriet Beecher Stowe, who wrote *Uncle Tom's Cabin*."

"I saw the movie," Matt says. "About slavery. You know that twenty-four-hour movie?"

"I've watched it about three or four times. I'll watch it all day, tape after tape, and then the next day, the same thing. Usually I get through it in two, maybe three days. . . ."

We watch swans, pairs, cruising through sunset glitter. We light smokes from Matt's Zippo, which is so new he won't let anyone handle it yet.

"I've never had a lot of places that I was attached to," he announces suddenly. "Like when I lived in Pensacola. That was the longest place, the first seven years of my life . . . But when you live somewhere and find that place where you feel alive, then you feel comfortable there. Like up in the tree. That becomes your spot—whether or not other people go there."

"That makes sense," I say.

"All those carvings. I can't say the tree doesn't mind, but . . . they won't kill the tree. Even if the whole outer shell, every space on the outer shell was carved on, it wouldn't kill the tree."

"Actually, if you carve a ring around the tree, it kills it," I say. "The ring stops the flow of matter up through the bark. It stops the circulation, and the tree dies. But if you just carve your name, the circulation will flow around it."

Matt contemplates this news for a moment, picking up a stick.

"This tree would be a lot bigger," he says, "if the county and state didn't decide that they want to keep it under control."

He taps the concrete with the stick.

"That's probably true," I say. "It's been whacked on all the ends."

He points the stick toward one of the lopped branches. "See that one right there? It just goes out, then *wham*—"

"Huge," Bill says.

"It just stops, man! Stops!"

"Well," I say, mustering my Father Time tone, "this was once probably all pasture land, too . . . or wetlands . . . a hundred years ago. There may not have been a lake here. It has that man-made look."

"Maybe they put those palms trees in," Bill speculates.

"But you couldn't put a tree here like this banyan," I add. "It's something that can't be moved. It can be chopped down, killed. You were talking about moving around, but this tree is about the most settled thing you could find."

"There's not a lot in the world that hasn't changed," Matt says with the confident resonance of a TV pitchman. "But this tree is here. Always. If the county decided it didn't want it here, I'd be out petitioning against that because, even if a tree doesn't have any major significance, it shouldn't be cut down. This tree didn't have any choice to be here." He pauses. "I know people may say that things don't have feelings, but see this right here?" He scoops up a stone from the shore. "You may not realize it, but a rock is a living thing, *in a way*."

"Yeah?" I ask, coaxing.

He knocks the rock against the concrete culvert.

"This may not hurt the rock. A sledgehammer hitting it may not hurt it, but the rock sees. It just doesn't see things as we see them."

Bill chortles at the conceit.

"During the time you've been standing there," Matt continues, "it barely notices stuff, because a rock is . . . always there. It's one of those unchanging things, one of those unyielding things. And whether it's a natural rock that you find in the ground or one that was man-made, it's, in a sense, a living thing. If there were a way that you could talk to it, you could probably talk to a tree. Because people talk to animals. It's the same thing." His bottom lip curls over, an assured blossom. "Especially with trees, because trees don't have mouths. They don't have ears. They just exist. They're in their own world, and their communications are either so primitive or so totally different than ours. They don't *sound,* they don't need *thought*. If the tree talked, think of things it could say. It could speak and speak, about all the things its roots come into contact with."

"Those roots may go all the way over to the other side of the park," Bill says.

"Common human error is to think we rule," Matt says, flying. "We don't. Nature shows us that time and time again. Think of hurricanes. A hurricane is . . . a kind of an extra plane . . . an entity. Its body *is* the wind. Like a tornado. That's why tornadoes are so unpredictable. That's why they can jump around like that. You ever seen a gust of wind go like this?"

He hops up and swivels, and then dervishes madly.

"It moves that way because of mood," he says, stopping suddenly, "because it wants to move that way. This way and this way and this way and this way."

"That's an incredible theory," I say, trying to thrust some admiration into my words. A calm in my voice, however, suggests that I'm watching a performance, some foreign rite, for which I'm trying to show respect out of good manners.

"It's elemental," Matt says. "Not in the same sense as a D&D type of thing. Wind can't solidify into a human form . . . but it's like, you know, the theory that we all once communicated telepathically. We didn't need words."

"You mean like a common language beneath, or before, language?" I ask.

"The separateness," he says, picking up the stone he'd knocked against the culvert and hurling it into the lake. "That's what gets me. Sometimes I wonder what it would be like if I was in another body, if I wasn't me but somebody else. I walk through the park and wonder about some guy sitting on the bench. You know, what if I was him? But you can't say that kind of thing to people."

"Hey, dude," Bill asks the chilly evening air. "What's life like for you?"

FIFTEEN

I CROSS THE FORMER Frankenstein to the TLP with three white chairs in my car trunk. On the radio, the announcer reports that surveillance satellites and reconnaissance planes have, at last, located 700,000 Rwandan refugees lost for some days in the bush on their flight from recent ethnic violence.

700,000 . . . lost?

To the monitors and the aid programmers, that is. And lost to our understanding. All of that life an abstraction of words and images—except to each neuron firing there, each individual lease on the mortal coil.

A trait of our time: that we can be the voyeurs of such grand suffering and such chaos . . . yet we are supposed to be assured by an announcer that the lost have been found, the order restored.

Thus, a moral crux: what do I do about what I'm told and shown of the wider world; it is so little about so much, and so immensely constant . . .

"You want to invent a language of compassion," a friend once observed to me, "but compassion is a silent art."

Yes, but . . .

Jen's mother died of cancer yesterday. She was diagnosed six weeks ago. Inoperable. Jen said her mother and father gathered the immediate family around the kitchen table to discuss the future—just as they had gathered their children years ago to announce the move from Ohio to Florida.

On this night, however, her mother stated her wishes for the funeral. There was weeping. They found themselves taking snapshots.

The news of her mother's illness raced through the TLP. Tim identified immediately, almost envious of Jen's allotted time to prepare for this loss, using it a little to approach how one might say good-bye if given the chance. For Jen, he buffed the burrs from his tone. He even grew solicitous. Jen and her husband had decided several months before not to approach Tim about adoption—because they were too young, she said—but she retained the notion that Tim was different from the rest of the guys. His new warmth pleased her—such a break from his usual misogynistic spouts.

On the morning after Halloween, confused and grieving about her mother's worsening condition, she told me, "Everyone here but Tim has hurt somebody in their life outside of this place. Sometimes they come in and talk about it. Just the other day, Andre said he's amazed when he thinks of having robbed people. But when he was doing it, he said, it just seemed normal. I think that if we had a complete record of what these guys have done, we wouldn't want them here. I'm thinking, too, about those trick-or-treaters who came to my door last night. I'm wondering if, maybe, I shouldn't go back to dealing with little kids."

So, the chin of resolution has begun to quiver.

During these events, Sam arrived at the TLP, wearing suspenders and a tie. He announced that he had just come from a meeting where he'd received orders to select forty troops under his command for a larger airlift to Zaire. Again, the Rwanda catastrophe. He cut Andre's hair, since Andre—though he has returned to school, intermittently—still had no job and, thus, no money for a serious style. He pressed Bill's pants and scrounged a tie for Bill from the back office closet, so that Bill—pacing and yet nearly catatonic with trepidation—would be squared away on his first day bagging at another grocery store. He debated with Quovonne about the merits of the latter using deodorant, Quovonne insisting that before he came to the TLP he did not need such a thing, since he was never "musky" but always smelled "floral fresh, like a girl."

As he worked, Sam mused now and then on who he would choose for the Zaire assignment, trying to restrain the exhilaration spawned by his new orders. He was far, it seemed, from the hole in his old friend Horace's chest—this man who, like Frank, is able to insist that he loves at least one of his parents. I imagined the $300 in his fancy pocket, then discarded the thought. I didn't like how it made me feel.

"He just purchased a video game for Salim," Frank told me later, when I mentioned this. "It was something like seventy bucks. Where'd he get the money for that generosity?"

As the days flowed over the oak, I received my first playful punches from Tim. It occurred, one afternoon, before he realized what he was doing. Only fourteen months for him to loosen enough for that shadow boxing.

And Quovonne comforted Bill like a tender-handed mother after Bill was fired from that second bagging job—his temper, again. He sat with Bill until long after dark, assuring him that he could get another job, a better job, just wait, you'll see. Quovonne also made

Thanksgiving dinner for the guys—featuring collard greens, sweet potato pie—and as he said, beaming, "they tore into it." Afterward, Quovonne and Salim shot baskets at the portable hoop in the parking lot—Quovonne wearing a burgundy pants suit and Salim a tee shirt that advised, *Eat Your Parents!* Twice, Quovonne sank clumsy-girl heaves, and Salim matched him with graceful swishes. Then Salim started taking longer and longer shots—until the distance became too great for Quovonne's phony femme style. Confident of his power, then, and able to be courtly, Salim edged closer to the basket and shot. But Quovonne, suddenly more awkward and playing a subtextual game as well, missed on purpose several times in a row, drawing him further in.

Courtshipping. At evening, a few of the guys usually idled under the net. One of them would jump and hang on the backboard bar, do pull-ups or spins. Then drop. Or another would grab one of the vertical bars and try to extend himself out, parallel to the ground. Then nearly everyone would try to do it. That kind of sudden energy. And there was unaccountable reminiscence—about the double Dutch style of jumping rope, seesaws fulcrummed by parking lot curbs, baseball cards clipped to bike frames, revving, as you pumped the pedals, like a real engine.

Kid time mingled with adult time. Andre juggled driveway pebbles. Reverend Platt's fish again appeared on Salim and Matt's key chains. Tim rubbed the steering wheel of Sam's Monte Carlo, sitting in the midst of his desire, exploring it, probing and stretching, trying it on. Under the net, Quovonne said that his twin sister once had a toy gun that looked so real the police might stop you to check it. A week before she was shot, she whipped it out at a middle-aged man. "Freeze, Haitian!" she shouted, through her brother's memory, his two-handed grip on the remembered pistol lifted from cop shows. The man trembled in fear, or maybe he was only playing along? Quovonne rolled with laughter as he concluded, a coldness remote from the sleepy grief in his expression when, on that day in the park, he told of her death.

And in the office, Jen and Clark (visiting from the South Shelter) grew nostalgic for their childhood streets. Jen said that when she was thirteen, she tried to sneak off and smoke a cigarette secretly, but she couldn't find a place where she was unknown.

Clark recalled a day he struck a neighbor boy who had kicked his dog, just as the boy's mother strode into view. She swatted Clark with a small branch from a tree, and he cursed her and swatted her back. She sent him home, and before he could explain to his mother what had happened, his mother sent him to his room. Somehow she already knew what had transpired. As the denouement approached, Clark's features bore the child's astonishment before the organized dominion of parents.

He also recounted the time he decided to run away. Through an almost mythic post-war American suburb, his mother drove him to the bus depot, dropped him off, and drove away. He began to sob, just as she came around the block. "Don't you ever threaten to run away again," she said, giving him the hard, lip-buttoning eye as he climbed into the car, and he never did. Though one time, he opened his upstairs bedroom window and pushed a chest of drawers against it, thinking that his mother would believe he had fallen from the window and disappeared. He hid in the bushes below, assuming she would weep for him missing. But she merely came along, closed the window, and hefted the chest back to its usual spot.

Seated beneath a poster declaring *No Fear!* he said that his extensive work in group homes had taught him that if places like the TLP are to succeed, they must provide their residents with experiences they've never had before.

"We need to celebrate the kind of men we want these boys to become," he said, with his usual inspired shininess. "The TLP must give them a place to be different than they are in the outside world. It must give them permission to be different. We adults have to retrain ourselves because we don't give kids the praise they need. We don't give ourselves the support we need. The adult world trains us to be fairly destructive to ourselves . . .

"And we need to provide models for intimacy. Quovonne, for instance, needs to see that he is making choices about who he is and how he appears to others. Some of the guys who've left here early may have gone because they were getting close to success. Someone was trusting them for the first time, and for no reason, and they couldn't handle that . . ."

Time. The first time. The only time. Another time . . .

Galvin was promoted to Phase Two—mainly for his steady work at the circuit board plant. The announcement came during the weekly group session and drew sparse applause, that slapping like the last fat raindrops on a plastic awning. Three new guys were also admitted to the program, their presence partly intended to prod Andre, Bill, Quovonne, Matt, and Salim, all still in Phase I six months after admission.

The staff has also begun to resent David (and the uppity-ups at the central office) partly out of personal dislike for the former but more out of animosity toward directionless central authority. Though a few candidates have been interviewed for Paul's position, no replacement appears in sight, and Frank and Jen worry about drift, wondering about the commitment of "the company" to the TLP, given some of its recent problems. As a consequence, we dwell increasingly on the need to surround the guys with more structure—how much more and of what kind? There are the shopping list forms. There is the posted weekly chore schedule: laundry room and office clean-up, A/C filters changed, sweeping. *All chores must be done by 3:00 P.M. Virtually no excuses will be accepted for not accepting your chore.* We mull bromides about the need for some guys to "hit bottom" before they commit to change. We let the sweet draw of the punitive impulse touch the tongue, but we make no such suggestions. Creatures of the current cultural Panopticon, we're not as vexed as the residents are by curtailed freedoms. We only wonder how we—or anybody—might better teach them responsibility in a world where establishing "deniability" is standard procedure in positions of authority. Where even a Pol Pot can shrug off accountability for the slaughter of millions, though he might allow that certain political opponents had to be eliminated.

In the front row of a nearly empty theater, I sat between Salim and Matt as James Spader ripped away a lusty Teri Hatcher's underclothes in *Two Days in the Valley* and, later—after Hatcher's been gutshot in a cat fight with another woman and is clearly dying—Spader offers to put her out of her misery with a pistol shot to the heart. I wonder how much useful irony brimmed in the guys' wide, devouring eyes turned up toward the screen. Are they same eyes turned toward the choppers over St. Pete, or toward the mirror? The guys often wear a little emotional badge that pleads *Excuse me*. Maybe it's one way to flee the cool comfort offered by the surveillance satellite and the assured announcer. A flight when childhood has disappeared from the surroundings. Childhood: that commendable invention of a benevolent sentimentality.

Us and the guys: conventional adherents to opposing worldviews? Not quite. But something close to that. Imbued as we are with cliché.

A *Newsweek* cover article declared that the black gangsta ethos undermines black culture because the young gangstas are not working for the cause of black liberation but for what they can get. (An accurate critique? Or merely an argument for keeping young black men on the cultural plantation with the work of "raising the race"?)

A *Time* magazine article related that when mature male elephants were removed from their herds—either by poachers or through a "relocation program"—the younger males began to roam in violent, delinquent packs, even attacking rhinos. Only the return of the mature male elephants curbed this destruction. The sociology lesson was implied but clear. Beyond it lay another: Be wary of metaphor.

"God will make you *suffer!*" Quovonne proclaimed in one of his theological struggle sessions with Matt. "It says it in the Bible!"

And Matt replied, "No. God only withholds things. And, anyway, what's behind God, anyway? There's always the next thing."

I told Jen I must go deeper. And she nodded with a practiced gesture of comprehension. Deeper for what? I drop my weighted line, strain at my sonar to fathom life just below the surface of the unfolding scene and in the currents below. I circle and circle the meanings. Waves. Whitecaps. Nothing.

I'm nagged, on occasion now, by the intimate assertion that cowardice has kept me from having—or even wanting—children. Somewhere in adolescence, I must have decided that I would become my parents *if* I had children. And once I had become them, I would never possess the time—kid or adult—to sort the sorting that lay before me. I would never mature into the fully grown man I guessed I wanted to be, since existence seemed especially pointless and absurd without that attempt. Of course, I could have chosen to believe that fatherhood would ripen me well. But a part of the thing we call self was entranced by the former discovery, and it became fixed. So I haul its rigid, questionable form with other such articles through the modest frauds of adulthood, toward age. And those parents who ditch their progeny for the glorious American second chance, who choose the new, ruthless spouse or a lunge at personal resurrection over their obligation to difficult sons; or those unable from the start to tame their own dire proclivities, uncertified, answerless, filtered out of the money train, fed on glamorous idiocy; or those truncated by toil, or slapped together by success; or even those frightened by the unaccountable gleam in the gaze of their own birthed flesh; these as well as the good and lucky, pitched toward pride and the grace of becoming fondly remembered ancestors: what do they haul? All of us from the bitten, sizzling core of individualism, among the wide variety of human fruit in the seeds of that precious, rusting apple.

And now the white chairs in my car trunk. Uniform stackable plastic. On my front porch, I've sat in them, listening to friends crow about their kids' music lessons or bitch about the office, arguing about this or that cultural phenomenon . . . or maybe swapping the latest news from Tom, a mutual acquaintance. In Rwanda now, he is transporting supplies for a relief agency—maybe, at this moment, humping sacked grain to those 700,000 just found. His e-mail from there bears startling understatement. How much of this is his adherence to official censorship we don't know. In the white chairs, my friends and I have shrugged at each other—thinking of news magazine pictures—and assumed he's witnessed unspeakable woe, the fly on the wide dead eye of abjection. There, he has seen something that has drawn him. He left Rwanda a year ago and then signed for a second tour—just as he had gone to Kenya years before, in the Peace Corps, and then come home, only to return to Africa after a brief estrangement. He gives his money away—the latest recipient a Kenyan woman whose college tuition he paid. We guessed he was in love, but he says nothing of the matter. Unlike the radio announcer, he has no assurances, this white Florida boy who went off into the wound of the far world as his answer to the question of what to do.

I haul my small cache to the TLP because the last of the white wooden chairs usually reserved for the shade of the oak were demolished two days ago. Suddenly, Andre and Quovonne were shouting at each other on the green. Both snatched up chairs like battle axes and swung into each other. Somewhere between them hung—along with Mr. Right and Quovonne's baby—the subject of Tamika, a girl Andre met in a shelter in Valrico before coming to the TLP. Several times, she had given Andre bus fare, and he had crossed the water to meet her for an afternoon at one of the malls. He'd just returned from such a date.

Wood shattered, and Frank separated Andre and Quovonne, sending them to their rooms to cool.

"I think one of them should go," he told Jen in the office afterward. David had suggested "termination" some time before, but Jen and Frank had been reluctant. They wanted the guys to have every chance, and they wanted to keep the TLP numbers up. Bureaucratically, they didn't need further failure.

They spoke to Andre and Quovonne separately. The former shrugged the fight off on Quovonne. Agitated blandness. His chatty wit had vanished, his usual murmuring rap sunk inward. Frank warned Andre that he was "on thin ice." He said he hoped this warning was clear. He stared fully, and with finality, at Andre. On occasion, he still had taken Andre along on certain jobs for his lawn maintenance business—and had paid him more than Andre was really worth as a worker.

The talk with Quovonne fell like a series of transparencies, each one overlaying all those preceding it, the general picture they produced gaining a detail here and there with each layer, new information sometimes unintentionally given. The picture? Frank frustrated, having hoped that previous talks with Andre and Quovonne—and their promises to abide by the house rules—would ensure domestic peace. Quovonne claiming that he was struck first and then retaliated, "just like my momma told me to do." Quovonne repeatedly declaring that things are "okay" now, that word a personal spell which is supposed to banish further encroachments on his view of reality, conjuring the door he shuts on the world when, at last, he feels relieved or absolved of his actions in question. Jen invoking Ghandi and Martin Luther King to encourage Quovonne to consider more spiritual and ingenious responses to anger, but Quovonne—trapped at a familiar, elemental level—insisting that King was violent, Ghandi was violent. Things are okay now. Okay. Okay.

Outside, on the green, Matt and Tim, who witnessed the fight, toyed with pieces of the chairs. Matt flipped a couple of broken legs like numchucks, showing, he claimed, some ninja moves learned from his ampguard combats. Tim shredded this posturing with a laugh and examined the snapped-off back. The fight had not been the first between Andre and Quovonne, but it had been the most spectacular. Tim and Matt recounted each blow, exhilarated by it all.

Tim toed the chair, still usable for sitting but wounded and now somehow vulnerable to him.

"Think we can break it?" he asked Matt.

And stomping, twisting, slamming, bit by bit—dreamy, laughing, enthusiastic, unregarding, curious, fleetingly vengeful, almost ritualistic—they did. They turned it into bones.

I place the three white plastic chairs under the oak, and, not many days after this, Galvin, Andre, and I sit in them. Andre and Galvin have spent more time together lately, though it's a jagged intimacy. We don't say much until Quovonne appears on the balcony on the other side of the green and strolls toward the office.

"Hey Andre," Galvin says, "Why don't you wrestle Quovonne?"

"Huh?" Andre replies. "Why? I don't like wrestling."

"Go wrestle that man walking down the street," Galvin says.

Andre looks away from him. "I don't like wrestling."

"Go jump in front of a car or something."

"Why?" Andre asks.

"I don't know," Galvin says. "You ask *me* stupid questions."

A single engine aircraft passes over, towing an advertisement for happy hour at one of the local beach bars.

"I love bein' sarcastic," Galvin says, finally, a shine in his tone. "I love bein' an asshole . . . *sometimes* . . . only when people try to be assholes to me."

We sit silent for a moment, then Andre rises and leaves.

"He's aggravated with me," Galvin mutters, as Andre disappears in his room, "because he knows that I think he messes around with Quovonne."

"Have you confronted him about it?"

"Once, but he ended up . . . *lyin'*."

He slaps the word down like a trump card.

"He lies about everything, even about little questions. He lies about an incident that happened when there's no reason to lie. When I tell him what he's tryin' to do, he lies about that, too. So he's lyin' on top of a lie . . . about lyin.' And then he wonders why I don't hang out with him."

"You look like you've been hanging out with him. You, Salim, and Andre look like a trio . . . What's wrong with him being gay?"

"*I'm* not gay," Galvin says. "If you hang out with a bunch of assholes, you're an asshole. If you hang out with a bunch of people that do their responsibilities, then you do your responsibilities. If you hang out with a bunch of thieves, you're gonna thieve. You hang out with gay people, you must be gay. Isn't that how it goes?"

"There's some truth in that, but you could make a few more distinctions."

"What's the difference?"

"Why should sexual preference be the only thing that defines who a person is? What if somebody said: 'You're a guy with a nose ring.' And you were then judged only on your having a nose ring. You're a guy who works on circuit boards, so you're nothing else."

"Call me a nerd. I know I ain't a nerd."

"There's more to you, of course."

"You associate with people you want to be like."

"Does that mean if you hung around married people, you'd want to be married?"

He leans back and looks at me as though his eyelids are struggling against sunlight. "I'd probably be a hopeless romantic," he says.

"What if you grew up with somebody, a friend, and he turned out to be gay?"

"Then . . . that's where the line drops. All the times we hung out and I thought he was so straight, he coulda been thinking, 'Oh, I like him.' I don't like that. They don't know how to reproduce with another sex. Gay people can't have sex, except the booty hole, and that is disgusting, or oral sex. What's so wonderful about that? And girls . . . they play with toys or have oral sex. It ain't real sex."

I'm in a stalking mood. "Oral sex between genders—is that fake sex, too?"

"All I know is that society is starting to get used to it, and I'm a rebel because if society gets used to gay people, we're gonna think it's normal, and kids are gonna grow up thinking it's okay to be . . . gay, and when something happens at school where people make fun of a kid or say 'oh, he's gay,' he's gonna start thinking, 'maybe I am gay. There's so many people who are gay. Yeah, I probably am gay.'"

"Do you think people choose to be gay?"

"Yeah."

"Why would anyone choose to be gay?"

"Something might have happened in their life. Even though they were born feminine . . . You shoulda seen me when I was young. I talked real high. I had a lot of *s*'s in my speech . . . a—what do they call it?—a lisp . . . which made me sound like I was gay, and I was called gay a lot, but it never made me change. But some people's words can change a person."

"Yeah?"

"Society starts thinkin' it's okay, and then somebody says 'you're gay,' and then you think you are, and then they start looking at the gay people, and then there's the lust involved with it. That's all it is is lust. Gay people who have sex, it's lust. Then natural attraction comes in. Then they start liking it a lot, which is basically taking it down to an *animal instinct*."

The italics leap and shout in his sentences.

"Animals," he goes on, "try to have sex with anything, male or female, until they find out that it's male—"

"So why don't heterosexuals try to have sex with males and females until they find out that they want to be with the opposite sex?"

"Heterosexual? What is that?"

"That's straight."

"Okay, say a man and a girl, married, have a baby, and they split up, and the baby's only three months old . . ." He pauses, and I wonder if he's thinking of himself. "And the father gets custody," he continues, "and then society says he's able to marry the same sex, so he marries his boyfriend that he liked all this time. And then the baby grows up around two guys that kiss, you know . . . and the baby grows knowing that his dad is *gay*. And your parents are your figures of life that you're gonna learn from as you get old, so if you grow up in a gay atmosphere, eventually you're gonna turn gay. If you grow up in a rough atmosphere, eventually you're gonna grow up rough."

"Yeah," I reply, "but the gay people I know say they had their feelings from earliest childhood. Why would anyone choose to be gay? Many people hate gays. They're afraid of them. Why would somebody choose to be something people feared or hated?"

"Maybe it's a problem, a chemical imbalance that made them like boys."

"Maybe it's not a problem. Maybe it's nature."

"Nature," he says, "is sort of takin' a toll on itself."

"What if there's a gene for it?"

"If there's a gene for it, it's because of past tense people screwin' around and being nasty and psychotic. In the early AD or BC, in the Bible, there was a whole city where everybody was always thievin' and robbin.'"

"Sodom."

"God said, 'If you don't stop that, I'll destroy your town, and I shall not let nothin' grow there.'"

"So if Andre turns to you and says, 'Yeah, I'm gay, and I've been fooling around with Quovonne,' what would you do?"

"I would say, 'You're a fucking liar, and I don't want to ever want to talk to you again.'"

"Even if he tells you the truth!"

"Yeah, he's done lied to me so many times . . ."

"So he's in a no-win situation with you . . ."

"Yeah, he done *fucked up*." He slaps the words. "If he woulda told when I asked him, then . . ."

"What would you have done?"

"I would have said, 'We can't hang out.'"

"So he would have lost anyway." I pause to let this settle on him. "You wanted him to tell you the truth, so you could punish him."

"There's no punishing there."

"He loses your friendship."

"He knew how I felt . . . and he hid it." He taps the ashtray aimlesslessly, nervously on the picnic table.

"He cared enough about your friendship to hide it from you."

We sit for a moment, the tapping between us.

"He must like it," Galvin declares. "And I don't want to be around people to where we become real good friends . . . I don't want to be in that situation, no matter what. And I make sure I let it be known." A pause, more tapping, as if trying to break through to level below. "I can't even associate with gays. It's bad . . . well . . . except for Clark. He's a gay person that don't try to impress or try to startle . . . He doesn't try to talk gay or act gay."

"How do you know Clark's gay? Did you ask him?"

"I made fun of him a *long* time ago. Like six years ago when I was a runaway at the south shelter."

"Why did he tell you?"

"I don't know but I found out. He held it from me . . . I guess it's . . . personal."

"Your mom is dead," Andre says to Jen, a couple of days after she returns from bereavement leave, "so you know how it is. But my mom is alive gone."

Later, fending off the sting in the memory of this remark, she says to me, "We don't know what it's like for them out there." And I think of Tom in the far "out there" with the 700,000 Rwandan refugees.

Matt ran away, to the local "out there," but returned after two nights. Immediately, David wanted him put on meds. Sam told me, "Matt's an intelligent guy, not violent. He made a mistake when he mentioned that he'd been on medication before. Now that's all David can think about. To my mind, Matt is just acting the way he is because he's getting a free ride."

I stop at the DQ before heading back across the old Frankenstein. There, I find Matt sitting with a girl on the white benches beneath the corrugated awning.

"Hi!" Matt says. The girl—a pale sliver—shakes my hand.

"Lex," she says briskly. "Nice ring." She holds it up with my finger through it.

"It was my father's," I explain, "from his high school graduation." Suddenly, I feel protective of the ring. No one has ever remarked on it. My mother gave it to me after his death.

But now Lex is peering at the wedding band on my other hand. Awkward beneath her lingering gaze—Is this the pickpocket's eye?—I accept a second compliment and excuse myself.

"It's what's on the inside that counts," she says, assured, it seems, of our mutual understanding.

SIXTEEN

As I ENTER THE MUSEUM only a mile or so from the TLP, I remember one of the docents tapping what looked like a snapped-off auto antenna on the glass of one of the master's early works.

"Now Dali," the docent declared to his tour group, "He's not like you or me. He was a genius!"

Certainly Dali was a genius of marketing, and the groves of his inspiration still bear ample fruit. The museum shop, bedecked for the Christmas holidays, teems with posters, books, stationery, gewgaws of every price—all brushed with the consoling radiance of a better department store.

I've come to buy perfume for my wife and—without warning—to see Tim in action. For several months, since he was "adopted" by the manager of the museum, he has worked here, initially in the stock room and now at the counter.

He spots me first, smiling a little as though found out. In a black shirt and narrow tie, he appears even thinner than usual. He is eager to help me, though clumsy. He tries to tease. And I realize, finally, why I find this gracelessness in him attractive: it resembles my own attempts, over a lifetime, at suavity, aplomb, poise—at *self-possession*—and my failures. All of our failures to reach the cool we imagine just beyond us.

It's the first time Tim and I have encountered each other outside the prescribed roles of the TLP. As public creatures, salesman and customer, we're somewhat like travelers sharing a seat on some bus in a foreign land—strangers to each other and the surroundings yet with a sense of common purpose, perhaps even a common interest. On one of the early group trips to the mall, Frank and I browsed in a surf shop after releasing the guys to their wanderings. A clerk of about seventeen talked with Frank about boards and wax and waves, his devotion to the older man's expertise and enthusiasm growing with each swapped opinion. I watched it all, wondering what exactly made this boy "fit in." His dress quoted gangsta/rebel fashion. But the edginess and anger in it had been smoothed away by the decision to punch a time clock and maybe save up for new stereo speakers. Like white male yuppies in their Beemers, blasting rap on a Saturday afternoon, his transgressions would be articulated within the confines of consumption or managed as one more among the secrets of the outwardly adhering. He personified what our guys lack in manner or intention. Life skills of another sort.

But now here is Tim, fitting in, nearly. A kind of progress. A reason for Frank and Jen's whispered pride.

I ask for the perfume by name. A Christmas gift. I examine different size bottles and linger over the possibilities, perhaps because some of that whispered pride in Tim—though unearned on my part—goads me to stretch this encounter. I want to ask him how it feels to appear ordinary and, thus, a sensational success. But that's not quite the question either. I sniff the perfume and think of my high school weekends working in the men's department at Sears, puffed up and, at times, world-weary behind my tie, laying *Can I help you?* on the moms and wives and girlfriends in a quandary over which print to choose for their apparently indifferent males. Each day, minutes before the store opened, a recorded woman swept onto the PA and announced with synthetic cheer, "Good morning, it's a wonderful day to be alive and working for Sears," and I sneered with the requisite irony. But my deeper nature was sounded one Saturday when I returned from break to find Mr. Burns, the manager, waiting for me. He asked me to come to the stockroom and there explained that I had vacated the floor and left no one in my stead. This was true, since the person who was supposed to relieve me had overstayed his time on break. I had gone off, assuming that trouble would snag him for his tardiness. In a terrifyingly soft voice, Mr. Burns explained that he knew it was only a mistake on my part. I had shown much initiative on the job, and that was a worthy trait. But rules were rules. And so on and so forth, at length. He hovered over me in his expensive suit, and I thought he was going to fire me. But he concluded his sermon by asserting that he had a great deal of faith in me. Oh, how I lapped at that faith! My head hung low for it. Gratitude for not being fired, for not being shamed.

Maybe it's that desperate gratitude—even when unarticulated—that has helped Tim advance here. It can substitute for trust, his scarcest resource. Once, in western North Carolina, I spent a summer afternoon with a friend and his daughters at the swimming pool run by the Jewish Community Center—an organization of friends and families known to each other in the area. A stranger, I swam and played with my friend's daughters and with other children—all wholly unafraid of me, or, rather, unafraid of adults. Children accustomed to trusting adults, in this context, at least. Children assuming that adults knew best and meant well. And this conception had been carefully cultivated and maintained by the organization—by a community, really—whose adult members know how varied are the motives of others.

One day, Galvin, Andre, and Salim sat under the oak and complained that Tim didn't trust them. Andre said that he had loaned Tim CDs, but that Tim would not reciprocate. Salim and Galvin claimed that Tim would not let them visit his room, though Tim would knock on their doors in the middle of the night when he needed to talk.

"We're all family here," Salim declared, "and if you can't trust family, who can you trust?"

I put aside their own histories as both victims and perpetrators of petty thievery and asked, "How well do you trust the family you came from? How well do you even understand your own family, let alone somebody like Tim, who's almost a stranger?"

The exchange reminds me of a time I accompanied a group of runaways from the south shelter on a field trip to the county courthouse. We sat through an hour of miscreants before the bench—presumably to discourage our group from the lure of lawlessness—and then we toured county offices, especially the motor vehicle division. There, among the maze of desks and partitioned spaces, the mostly gray-bouffed lady typists and their round, male managers doted on our band—assuming that we were from the local middle school. They smiled and tossed a quip. One staffer demonstrated to a girl who had been repeatedly assaulted by her stepbrother how to call up a file. Another explained to a boy who regularly huffed air conditioning gas the protocols for accessing all the registrations on his street. Those kids grinned with some interest and some incomprehension that anyone could care about such things . . . all day and for a lifetime. How would the file maker have reacted had she known about this girl's occasional, expedient prostitution? Or the producer of protocols were she to learn that the street name her young visitor had given as his home actually ran past the shelter, his residence only for the previous few days? Yet the kids apparently seemed normal, even ordinary, to these people—which maybe says something about the way adults see adolescents now. Or don't see them.

I study the perfume bottle in Tim's hand—its surrealist parabolas pitched atop a comic pair of starlet lips. A jumble, like Tim's darker passions about women, the new—and yet old—strangers in his life. *She's a cow!* or *What a slut!* or *Give me a chick with jumbo tits!* Each of his pronouncements a knocking on the door in the night.

I lean on the counter, and in these few moments of closer proximity, I spot the Mr. Burns of the moment, a man of about my age, starched and cuff-linked. He casually but purposefully drifts toward us. He—or his boss—has hired this troubled boy, this kid with bad luck. And the boy has worked out pretty well. But, of course, it's prudent to monitor him, and, in this instance, an eye must also be kept on me. After all, who might I be, this man chatting somewhat suspiciously with Tim, who seems to know him? A bad influence? Someone from whom Tim needs to be rescued? Tim *is* in that program, you know, with those other problem boys . . .

Were I in Mr. Burns' position, I would probably think likewise.

A friendly possessiveness now emanates from him. Tim is his charge. Tim is, I realize, perfect for the role, which may be why he is the only client from the TLP thus to be "adopted" by a mentor from the community. More than his race or his mild boy looks or his burred smarts—all crucial—his preeminent qualification is that he is orphaned and has been a ward of his hated HRS, and he has no criminal record (despite some routine teenage lawlessness). From the deck of possible sympathies—stacked with images of fearful youth—he drew a lucky stereotype. He has the right suffering. Mr. Burns can imagine himself as Tim, can see himself in Tim, and step onto common ground. Tim can be taken to dinner, to the symphony. He can forgo dudespeak for *May I help you?* He can be trusted enough to be an employee and enough to try to reward Mr. Burns' faith in doing good works.

I realize that I must let Tim go, so I select a bottle of perfume. He rings it up, double checking the change he makes, as Mr. Burns lingers nearby. He shrinks under our mutual gaze, bearing all those expectations from which someone like Matt flees.

He nests the bottle in a gift box and asks if I want a ribbon. Oh, yes. Christmas, after all. He struggles a little with the pre-tied elastic bow. It reminds me of the four women from the neighborhood association who, last year, bore fudge and gifts to the TLP for a tree decorating party. One of the residents foresaw the evening as a "stress test," and several of the guys tried repeatedly to slip off to their rooms, only to be shepherded back to the office by Frank and Paul. Perhaps because no men accompanied the visiting women—and the women themselves were mostly much older—the chitin of toughness gradually fell from some of the guys. A few eased into silliness. One wrapped a ribbon around himself like a sumo wrestler. Another made earrings of two six-inch snowflake decorations. Tim, who earlier had held his palm in front of his face and blew hard—to check his breath—fussed over the tree.

"I haven't had Christmas in two years," he said.

All the lights and bulbs on the branches came from a wicker bassinet of articles he had brought with him to the TLP—his salvaged remains of domestic memory.

"Some of this stuff is older than I am," he said, a moment later, overcome, slipping into the darkened back office to compose himself.

Now he hands me my gift.

"You should go into the museum," he suggests, somewhat stiffly, perhaps for Mr. Burns to hear. "It changes all the time."

"I've been through it," I reply, glancing toward Mr. Burns, then smiling at Tim. I hold up the perfume. "Besides, I've experienced enough art for today."

SEVENTEEN

PERCHED ABOVE THE LAWYERS and defendants, the judge—bearing his name into the third generation—stares over the top of his aviator glasses, a fleshly projection of the mauve marble slab that backs him with the ancient necessity of law, the great tomb door of austere edges and final punishments. The lawyers proffer their deals, and he sifts the lives into probations, programs, prisons, calling for the priors, demanding a "depo," postponing.

"The Young case," he intones and swivels toward one of the public defenders, ready at the somewhat distant lectern below. "Stan, that's yours. What's this all about?"

And the defender summarizes and asks for a continuance.

The judge looks down as he pronounces his decision, incessantly arranging the documents before him. He then rolls, in his grand leather chair, from one end of the bench to another. This morning's lengthy docket—displayed like airline flights on TV monitors in the courthouse lobby—spurs his pace. Even the bailiffs move with balletic lightness and economy, fingerprinting defendants, blocking the walkway out of the courtroom and the path between the lectern and the bench when a prisoner is escorted in from a side door.

Tim elbows me and points toward the front row, where Jason sits with his parents. I wonder where they were when he was first admitted to the TLP. He's spent most of the last eight months since the home invasion in their custody.

"Has he been brought?" the judge inquires of the bailiff.

Jason's attorney, a public defender—thirtyish and slightly overgroomed—approaches the lectern and explains the charges and argues that Jason be treated as a youthful offender.

"Where does he fall under those guidelines?" asks the judge.

"He was doing well in the program . . . ," the defender asserts and turns toward us in the back bench.

Frank rises and says, "It's a program for homeless youth . . ."

Jason and his mother peer back over their shoulders at Frank. Mother and son: no mistaking the resemblance, even the mouths slightly open, bottom jaws shifted sidewise.

"The victim has been subpoenaed," says the plaintiff's lawyer, "but he is not here, your honor. He has a tendency to be late."

He mentions also that another of the four who committed the crime was allowed to leave the state and that a fourth—a more violent offender—was not apprehended.

"We will deal with that defendant at the time he comes before the court," the judge replies crisply.

Tim and I nod at each other: Zachariah. Tim despised him but respected his toughness. I remember him slumped under the oak one evening, his knee rocking like a willow stem in a stream. His girlfriend,

Trisha, lay in a delivery room in Tampa and he was trying to arrange transportation across the water to her.

"I just want to show my manliness and my maturity as a father figure," he said, urban, bottom-end Kentucky slurring his speech, "Just put out the whole father role, ya know. I'm gonna have a beautiful son . . . or a daughter maybe. I'm gonna have a house and good job . . ."

He'd met Carlos at a shelter and followed him into the TLP. He'd met Trisha two months before that.

"I've seen more shit than anybody in this place put together," he bragged, eager for my eyes to widen. "Killing, robbing, splacking cars . . . If my momma woulda been harder on me then I probably wouldn't be here. She helped me out *too much* . . . But then I wouldn't have been in the shelter and met Trisha . . ."

Ultimately, Frank arranged for him to take the bus to Tampa the next morning. Shortly after we talked, however, Karen, one of the hood rats, appeared at the top of the sandy alley, and Zachariah sauntered off to meet her before curfew.

The judge calls Jason's attorney and the lawyer for the victim to the bench.

A few minutes later, the defender, Jason and his parents, and Frank adjourn to a side room.

"Gee, I didn't know that Frank was going to be so involved," Tim whispers to me. "I thought we were just here for moral support."

While we wait for their return, the judge assails his docket. The night of the stolen car. The day of the vandalized store.

"Are we talking bags of marijuana or a roach in an ashtray?" the judge asks about one case. He later assigns a forty-year-old, indigent heroin addict—a perpetrator of a botched B&E—to a methadone program.

At last, Jason and his parents stand before the judge. Jason's father, in a puckering, gray Sunday suit, folds his hands behind his back and bows his head as though in church. Is he ashamed? Bored? Furious? Is he hoping for leniency for his son? Or a harsh penalty? Does he feel himself on trial? Or has he given up such sympathetic allegiance, if it ever existed? When he glances toward Jason's mother, who stands on the other side of his progeny, does he see an ally? An enemy?

Jason pleads no contest. Because he has no juvenile record, he is given a year in a level eight residential facility, out of town, followed by eighteen months' probation. Almost wallowing in his large, gold suit—and with the sides of his head closely cropped and the one long flop slicked back—he resembles some character out of a '30s movie.

In a stuffy, muted voice, Jason says to the judge, "I know what I did was wrong."

"I hope that what you're saying is genuine," the judge replies. "I suppose you know your parents have undergone anguish standing there with you. You don't want to go to jail." His voice softens. "It's a nasty, rotten place. You don't ever want to go there."

"You'd think the judge could come up with something a little more original than that," Tim whispers.

While Carlos is being brought, the judge initiates another hearing. A twenty-eight-year-old black man—who has been sitting behind us in the chamber for more than a half hour, mumbling with one of his companions—is charged with having sex with a fourteen-year-old girl. His attorney tells the room that the defendant has an IQ of 89. Neither the girl nor her mother are in the courtroom; they never want to see the young man again.

"The sex," says the victim's lawyer, "was consensual, but only because the mother believed that the man was eighteen, not twenty-eight."

The judge wrinkles his forehead and casts an ironic but unsurprised gaze over his glasses. "It was all right with her for an eighteen-year-old man to have sex with a fourteen-year-old girl but not a twenty-eight-year-old?"

"That's right, your honor," replies the attorney.

Two black matrons sitting in front of me, one of them hooked up to an oxygen tank, turn toward each other in mutual amazement.

After finding out the defendant has no job and no home, the judge remands him to a residential facility for a year, with a year probation. The defendant, who faced seven years in prison, blows a sigh of relief as he retreats from the courtroom.

Through a side door, Carlos appears in prison blues, a broad, faded *Max* stenciled in white across his back. Last week, Frank took a pair of dress oxfords to him at the county jail, since Carlos had a suit for his court date but no shoes. Evidently, the judge has decided against such sartorial niceties. After waiting 231 days in jail for this hearing, he is thinner, his face angular, a handsome rack of shadows. Not the gauntness of a boy about to heft into his full manhood but a raptor-ish, maturing tightness. Not so much an arrogant aspect as a worn one and, as the old ladies used to say, "harder." Frank told us that when he delivered the shoes, Carlos held up his picture ID bracelet to show how much he now differed from that rounder, buzz-cut boy we knew. That boy whose nose ran as he nibbled wings drenched with his favorite pickled pepper sauce. Who prided himself on "standing up" when it was necessary. A leader.

"County jail is worse than the penitentiary," Frank said. "He's in a cell with fifteen other guys, some of them crazies. And lately, as he was getting close to his court date, some of them have been pushing him."

Unlike Jason, flanked by parents, Carlos stands alone in the dock. His only relative—an aunt—and his girlfriend sit in the front row, behind him.

Carlos is sworn in, and the judge asks him if he understands the plea he is making.

"No," he says.

The judge, slightly irritated, turns toward the public defender, who says, "I have explained it to him, Your Honor."

The judge repeats the scripted question, and Carlos says, "yes suh," his accent new and odd, maybe acquired in jail.

Like a priest eager to speed through yet another lightly attended dawn service, the judge hustles through the balance of the liturgy: questions to ensure that Carlos is aware of what is going on, that he is not high on drugs, etc. Yes suh. Yes suh. The judge concludes his call and response recitation by asking Carlos if he understand that the charges against him carry a maximum sentence of life in prison.

Yes suh.

The judge gives him five years' probation. In addition: no alcohol, no guns, no leaving the state, no consorting with the people involved in the crime.

Carlos offers no apology, but turns toward the bailiff, who leads him toward the end of the desk and the papers that will document his release.

While he is being fingerprinted, the public defender comes over and asks the aunt and the girlfriend, Crystal, if they can pick Carlos up in three hours to take him home to Tampa. Their eyes confer. They seem to be coaxing the other to volunteer. Then they decide. They write down a phone number, and the public defender presents it to Carlos.

As we file out of the courtroom, Crystal—hauling a teddy bear backpack by one of its arms—whispers to Frank and Tim, "Carlos didn't even look at me."

We walk out to the lobby. Frank reminds them that he still has a few of Carlos' things, and they can come and get them any time.

"She's got a rude awakening," Frank explains, as we head across the lot. "Carlos doesn't want to see her. She never visited him in jail. In fact, she even called him once and said she was coming over and never showed up. He's done with her . . . Well, maybe not until after tonight. He's been in 230 days . . ."

Tim snickers, "Yeah . . ."

As we follow Frank's truck to a restaurant for a late breakfast, Tim says, "Frank looked like he was not enjoying himself, whatsoever. He looks stressed."

True. But Tim, too, is askew. He can't banish the image of Carlos transformed under the faded white *Max*. He repeats over and over that Jason appears unchanged by the intervening months. He remembers, no doubt, that he sensed Carlos and Jason were heading off the property for trouble that evening, and that he didn't warn the TLP staff.

"You know how some people have a fire in their eyes," he says, as though poking a stick through bars caging some perplexing beast. "Carlos was always looking for an opportunity. Not always thinking about the right things but, you know, he was always out there. Now he looks dead."

The extra gleam in the blackened eye. That personal gem. Is it now a diamond crushed back into coal? Home to a more ancient, deeper heat? A sorrow?

Tell that to the victim . . . if he shows up.

"You okay, Frank?" Tim asks at the restaurant.

Frank appears surprised at this, though he restrains it.

"You just seemed a little stressed," Tim says.

"Not stressed," Frank says, refusing Tim entry here, "just concerned."

I ask about Carlos' future. He wasn't living with the aunt before he came to the TLP. She doesn't seem interested in keeping him long.

"He's got no GED," Frank says, "so it's probably manual labor, though that may not be too bad if he gets in the right line."

I wonder aloud how well he'll fare with people in the workplace. "You wouldn't want him banging someone in the head with a shovel."

"If he can survive nine months in jail without getting into a fight," Frank replies, "he can survive in the workplace."

"Every time I crack my neck I think of Carlos," Tim says.

The notion of Carlos flourishing from manual labor inspires Frank to conjure the example of his future father-in-law, whom he idolizes. Impoverished, from a large family in Columbia, the man went to sea at fifteen, traveled the world, and became a first-rate baker. He took up carpentry. He taught himself the real estate business. Wide-open eyes and an eager mind colluded with luck and wild toil to make him prosperous. He lives part of the year in Florida now. He's offered Frank a partnership in a house-refurbishing concern.

Talk of travels gets Tim thinking about the Germans and the French who come to his counter in the museum—one of his openings to the world. He asks Frank about Alaska and Australia, both of which Frank has mentioned as possible honeymoon destinations, though no date has been set for the wedding. Frank sings about the Great Barrier reef—the old surfer—and discourses on the temperature of the waters and the times of year when the sharks come close to shore.

Tim listens, suddenly hooked in the current of exoticism and danger. He's still intent as the conversation veers and Frank reminisces about a thug he knew in his old neighborhood, Al DeCarlo. Frank's sister had been beaten up by her boyfriend. Al asked her what she wanted done to the boyfriend. Broken leg? Broken arm? The son of a major racketeer, Al lived in a palace until the police nailed him. Though in his late seventies, Al's old man got life in prison, and Al and his brothers thirty years each.

"He was the nicest guy," Frank says, delighted with this former acquaintanceship.

"You should write a book, too," Tim says, impressed. "You've got the cool stories, Frank. Didn't you get trapped underwater in a cave?"

Frank shies slightly, since I'm present.

"No. I was just stuck in the back of a cave."

"And you've got the gangster background, and you're talking about going to Alaska . . . or Australia."

Frank coughs a little nervously.

"You've done it all, Frank!" Tim exclaims. "What a life you've had!" Odd that Frank's life would already be past tense, but then Frank is older than Tim can imagine.

Frank leans behind a smile which points as much inward as outward. A man nearing forty.

"I would have done things differently," he says.

Yes suh.

EIGHTEEN

IN AMERICA, SOMEONE in a chicken suit stands before a fast-food restaurant and waves at passing traffic. This person has been hired to delight and distract, and, of course, to persuade those seated at thirty miles per hour to slow and divert from their routes: stop in and chow down on the white and dark meat—with the entrepreneurial approval of the devoured. Chicken sells chicken. What else has chicken got to sell?

The person in the chicken suit flaps the allotted wings. Occasionally, a driver honks or waves back. Less frequently but with some regularity, a driver curses or flips the bird to the bird. More than once, a motorist hurls something handy, a cigarette butt, or maybe an unopened can of soda. These objects sometimes bounce off the beak, and the person inside glares with rage and humiliation through that aperture, partially consumed, in that moment, by the maw.

As Tim and I roll up US 19, toward the driver's license bureau, he remembers his first encounter with the chicken suit in America.

"I screamed something at this guy," he says, tossing his head back, laughing, "and my mom got so pissed at me that she turned the car around and took me back to apologize in front of the whole big street. I had to shake this guy's feathery hand, I swear to God."

We're heading to the license bureau because Tim phoned me this morning, very early, and asked if he could use my decaying VW Rabbit for his driving test. Though he didn't say it, I'm nearly his last choice. Still, I agreed, eager for the time alone with him. Tim has not exactly eased into anyone's company, but he has, in the weeks since I visited him at the museum, pestered me about selling my car to him. He's also nagged Frank and Jen to promote him to Phase Three, since he's been working steadily for over a year and has been admitted to the local community college for the spring semester. HRS will provide him with some of the financing for school, and he's saved up the rest (including his portion of the missing $300—which has been replaced quietly by the central office, apparently without further investigation). Now, having given up on the likelihood that I'll sell my car to him, Tim lusts for a gold 1970 Malibu offered by a neighborhood seller, a beautiful, impractical conveyance when new and now, well into its twenties, utterly so. Still, Tim is determined to get his license, get his insurance, get the Malibu or some other vehicle, and get going—out into life, to work, to school, all around, you know?

The feathery hand his mother made him shake belonged to a "middle-aged guy," Tim says. I imagine the man, most likely too old to have anything but bitterness or self-mocking laughter about finding himself sweating in that woolly gullet. He slips off the chicken head—like an astronaut removing his helmet—and takes this boy's hand with appropriate gravity. He listens intently to the boy's enforced apology, maybe withholding the urge to smile at the quaintness of the mother's intention. Maybe a sudden surge of lightness and hope surprises him, the dreaminess of the actual. The boy, though he can't know it, requires the man's sobriety—because the dark, corrosive grin can always find them both, later. The man thanks the boy for the gesture of repentance and pronounces him absolved. In this moment, a world is affirmed where even a middle-aged man in a chicken suit garners respect, where maybe such a man—more than most others—reminds us how necessary such decorum is to help us live wisely among our implausible fates.

I follow Tim's directions northward. I defer to him because despite his usual brusqueness, he often shies from asserting himself directly and prods others to decide for him—as a way of procuring their approval and reassuring himself. I fancy that he should have the opportunity to exercise independence. I think, too, that I should take advantage of the chance to learn how to cede control of such a situation as this. Tim, however, confuses the streets, and we are lost. We stop at a garage, and he asks for directions, and I—against my habit yet trying to set an example and instill confidence—again follow his orders. We head south.

Since he mentioned his mother, I ask him again about their last years together. Perhaps his mistake and my subsequent show of composure temper his habitual peevishness. With uncharacteristic calm, he explains how he and his mother moved to Florida from New York, and how his grandmother—his only relative—still survives though Alzheimer's now spurs her ceaseless wanderings around a nursing home. I edge him toward the last year with his mother, and Tim repeats the story of hearing his father's voice, that once, on the phone, and the story of how he was told of her death by good Mr. Green, the school counselor, and the story of the violent foster parent who made him sleep under the bed thereafter. He fingers all his mythic treasures, an inventory of his defining events. As if he can't proceed without everything in its place, such as it is.

"I was pretty pissed at my mom," he says finally. "We were going around with hardly any clothes, everything dirty. She would cry. She cried a lot. I used to think that she needed to get out and get a job, or maybe a guy, or something. We used to fight about it."

"Did you ever wonder that she might have been lonely?" I ask, spurred by his candor. "Maybe she couldn't find anybody . . . an adult, I mean . . . who was interested in her . . . I mean, what did she think about after you went to sleep at night?"

"Yeah . . ." he says, letting these possibilities rise like some strange fragrance.

At the license bureau, we discover that I've left my insurance card at home. Embarrassing, as well as a problem. We might have to return on another day. I restrain my frustration, perhaps more than I might were I alone, certainly more than I did years ago in similar circumstances, loutishly demanding to see the manager, shouting, strutting. Tim fidgets, scowling, and I put my hand on his shoulder to urge patience—in him and myself. It's the first time I've dared touch him, and he doesn't buck against my attempt to impel him toward actions more mature than I once could muster.

Perhaps our tone gives grace because the officer says she knows my company well and thus verifies my policy with a quick phone call. During this interval, Tim again examines his learner's permit and birth certificate. On the permit, his first name is misspelled—"Tom" instead of "Tim."

"I got it just after she died," he says, cranky. "I wasn't in the mood to proofread."

His birth certificate looks wonderfully old, bearing an aerial photo of the hospital and vaguely medieval script. And this comforts me somehow, though I didn't fathom I might want such comfort. A brown stain mists the bottom third of the document.

"It's coffee that that redneck bastard I had to live with spilled on it," he growls. "He got it on my only picture of my mom, too. From her driver's license."

The only picture? I know it must live in his wallet, but I don't dare ask to view it. Besides, even if he complied with my request, I'm not sure I want see her now, sentimental, maybe, about preserving her incorporeal power.

When Tim and the testing officer drive off at last, I try not to watch, a bit paternal about him . . . and embarrassed—though I should know better—about owning such a ratty car at my age.

"What do I do?" Tim had asked me as we'd pulled in the bureau parking lot, somewhat flustered by the reality of his imminent exam.

"Just do everything slowly," I'd said. "With some poise." Worthy advice, now, for me.

From their wall mounts, the TVs testify, and we in the waiting room stare up as if in reverence or bow down as though ready for beheading by the imperial executioner of infojunk. The weather minute with Brunette proceeds. Tim told me, "I met her once. I got her autograph, too. I was just a kid then, so I cared about that kind of shit. You know, she adopted this kid like they did me at the museum, but he fucked up big time, and she dumped him. The dude was stupid."

Brunette among the highs and lows, the upper air disturbances and fronts. Her hand passing deifically over the land and the waters. Voluble Brunette in her perfection suit, rather than the chicken suit.

A short while later, Tim steps through the waiting room door, his mouth tucked up in one corner, a failed attempt to suppress his obvious bliss.

"You've got a turn signal out," he announces. "But the officer let that slide."

I congratulate him on his rite of passage, proud and gratified that he'll accept my pride in him, and that such a tame victory as passing a driver's test can stir us together, even briefly. While we wait for processing, he jams his hands in his pockets and occasionally glances at me in triumph. He dances around a little and comments, gleefully, inanely on the surrounding scene. He reminds himself to get his insurance this week. This week! And did I know that the Malibu has an original spare tire in the trunk?

A few minutes later, the woman at the license pick-up counter declaims through the PA, "Tim Winston. Mr. Tim Winston," as though introducing a new, just-arrived character to the public world.

"Mr.?" Tim asks the ceiling, as if addressing some confused voice from another plane of existence.

"Better go get it . . . *Mr. Winston,*" I say, and he jabs me playfully in the ribs.

Dipped in glory, Tim insists on buying me lunch. I let him drive, and in his excitement, he nearly snags a bridge railing.

"I almost killed us!" he shouts.

"That's okay," I say, breathless, recalling my father's floorboard-stomping fear when he first let me drive the family station wagon on the vacant pavements of the local fairgrounds, "just as long as it's *almost*."

At a chain restaurant near the TLP, Tim the First, King of All, rolls his eyes sarcastically at the exaggerated courtesy of our waiter and mocks the sentimental main street scene depicted on the cover of the menu.

"I wonder how long it'll be," he says, "before we all have to wear bulletproof vests, with all the gangbangers around."

Over burgers and fries, he recounts selling his mother's Valiant just after her death—and his regret now at not having that meek but dependable beater. I try to encourage him to consider other cars than the Malibu. Frank has refused to help Tim search for a vehicle, telling me that Paul poured too much quasi-parental energy into his relationship with Tim, and that Tim must learn to do important things on his own. Obliquely sermonizing, I tell Tim of a high school friend who totaled his car and about my experience years ago on the "seat belt convincer" at the state fair. Ultimately, the mention of high school leads us onto the subject of girlfriends.

"My problem was that I was almost always the friend," I say. "You know, the funny friend?"

He nods. "Did you ever have a girl that would be with you alone but didn't want to hang out with you in public?" he asks. "That's when you really hit the bottom of the barrel."

"Yeah, I know."

"Denise was her name," he says, with Bogart's world-weariness in *Casablanca*. " I was at the bottom, or next to the bottom."

"Really? I don't believe that. How do you know?"

"I was like . . . I was like Glen Grub," he says. "He was the bottom . . ."

"What a perfect name . . ."

"A tough little kid, man. And he was so stupid, he tried to follow all the trends, like sagging his shorts and stuff, which I'm not saying I'm any better than he was. God, you know how you do. I don't think he could afford it. It was bad, man."

The waiter arrives with more water, pours and goes, pursued by another of Tim's exasperated winces.

Suddenly, Tim says, "You'd make a pretty good dad to some kid. Most parents send their kids to Daytona Beach, but you'd send your kids to China or someplace like that."

Unprepared for this—and making too much of it—I splutter something about having plenty of kids already, in my classes at the university. I feel as though I'm giving myself away somehow, and yet it seems that whatever reply I might muster would give me away—though I can't fathom what I've exposed. Maybe I've revealed nothing particular but have discovered merely the possibility of my want on view without my permission—an unspecified, maybe purposefully unnameable want. I suspect that beneath it lies an old, intimate cowardice and an older fear. Still, I steer hard away from all inclination toward epiphany when with the guys—those "meaningful" moments that the volunteer to organizations like the TLP might quickly glean from contact with the deprived or troubled. That tinny jingle of stingy insight. Generalization, conclusion. The poets speak memorably of terror entwined with joy in beholding their children, and I am moved by this. But I don't really know the first iota about fatherhood, and the TLP is not a lab in which to presume to learn.

My fluster is superfluous, however. Tim has gone back to Tim. He pulls out his license and again studies it.

"I was so much younger when I got my permit," he observes. "I'll probably look a lot different in six years when I get a new license."

He pauses as if to honor this recognition of the future, of time outside of memory.

"You look good," I say about the picture. "A little like Emilio Estevez."

"Thanks," he replies with disdain. He brings the image closer. "Shit! See how it goes right?"

"What?"

"My nose. When I was two months old, my mom told me that some HRS woman came to help her take care of me. It sounds weird, but it must have been some experimental program or something like that. Anyway, this woman came and then . . . well, my mom said this woman was some kind of lesbo or something. I mean, my mom was kinda flaky. Anyway, this woman came on to her or something, but then the woman and HRS took me away from my mom for two weeks, and when she got me back I had a big bruise on my nose, like it was broken."

Another familiar treasure in his inventory.

"Broken?" I ask, this time offering some doubt about the detail.

"A big bruise, broken, maybe."

"How did you know this happened?"

"My mom told me. And my grandmother said that HRS tried to take my mom away from me."

"That's what you have to go on?" I reply, my tone pushing past bewilderment into mild scorn.

He rubs the crook in his nose, that trace of injury or heredity. I desist from pursuing the prospect of his mother as abuser or, at the very least, propagandist. I think of Jen's remark about her one day in the office: "From what we know, she was evidently some kind of burned-out hippie. But in the middle of all her substance abuse, she taught Tim some values. That's what makes him different from some of the other guys."

The feathery handshake?

Yes . . . in America, where you get your license and try to stay out of the chicken suit. And if you crave success and begin to acquire it, you sense the chicken suit always near at hand, being outfitted for you. And maybe, behind the wheel, you wave back at the chicken suit, to propitiate the spirits of absurd undoing which it fastidiously houses. Or maybe you curse, or flick a butt. Or maybe you drive on, believing the suit has nothing to do with who you are and where you live, where you started and where you end. Or maybe you're the one—a Glen Grub?—for whom that suit is, well, a paradise compared to your previous life in traffic.

Tim insists on buying me dessert, but as soon as we finish, he's eager to get back to the TLP. He knows that Salim wants badly to see him—or any of the guys—fail. A flop relieves him from trying. Salim, and maybe Andre and Matt, will be waiting, hoping to gloat, and Tim wants to drive up, fully bold and composed by achievement, even though the manual steering on the Rabbit causes him to grunt "Jesus!" as he labors to yank the wheel on tight corners.

"Give me the keys," Tim commands in the parking lot, then hears his gruffness. Embarrassed, he shakes his head and says, "Listen to me. What a jerk!"

Then I hand them over.

NINETEEN

THREE DAYS LATER, near dawn, Sam enters Quovonne's room and thinks he sees Quovonne in bed.

"I called to him," Sam tells me, "but he didn't budge."

Uneasy but drawn toward the mystery, he approaches and discovers Miss V attached to a body of fluffed, blanketed pillows. Within minutes, he finds Quovonne asleep with Andre in the latter's room.

For some weeks, David has lobbied to "terminate" them from the program, as has Betty, a senior administrator at the home office. Jen and Frank have argued for a reprieve, partly because they felt the TLP was spinning into chaos during the lengthy search for Paul's replacement, and, thus, it was no time for more failure. They've also resisted because they resent the apparent leisure—and incompetence—with which David and Betty are conducting the job search. They suspect the candidates championed by those making the final decision.

Increasingly, Jen and Frank and Sam understand that they and the guys have been included in the "interview process" only as a procedural gesture. The TLP staff is, bureaucratically speaking, reduced to being one more among the guys. They will have no real say in who the new manager will be. This circumstance irks them all the more since they have—as a matter of professional integrity—compelled Andre and Quovonne to sign new contracts stating that each would stay clear of the other and submit to extra watchdogging, such as bed checks. Professionalism is the staff's only bulwark against the guys' constant bids—individually and as a group—to transform them into the unreasonable, cruel parent tormenting the hapless, forgivable child.

"We haven't told Andre and Quovonne that they're gone," Frank says later in the day after the discovery. "Jen's trying to place them first. But then it's good-bye and good luck. Tomorrow, most likely."

Indeed, weighted by an exasperated gloom, Jen crushes the phone between her cheek and shoulder as she dials up the usual agencies. She feels guilty, she says, because the program she has helped construct "isn't serving" the guys. Andre had come to the TLP from Beach Place in Tampa, because he had nowhere else to go. Maybe he can return there. For Quovonne it is the runaway shelter, or the street . . . or maybe back to Miami.

Just outside the office, Andre and Salim prepare to catch the bus to a mall in Clearwater. Since Jen and Frank have decided on termination, they've said little to Andre and Quovonne about being caught by Sam. A pretense of routine has been more or less preserved. If Andre and Quovonne read in the special lunchtime office powwow their impending separation, they haven't exactly shown it. The familiar agitation ripples around them and then thickens. Andre tosses some fake tae kwon do kicks toward Quovonne, who sits on the steps. When Salim swaggers up, Andre sends him ahead to the bus stop. Andre and Quovonne each wear a smile, like a clamp, and stare at one another. Quovonne stands. There is a murmur or two, and then Andre, in his starched jeans, moves toward the street. Quovonne follows, like a child wanting to be allowed to go along. Andre whirls, his mouth still like the clamp. He leans forward and flips Quovonne the bird. Quovonne, now so much resembling Miss V, holds out the ring on his left hand, thin, cheap silver bearing a small heart. Andre turns away. At some remove, Quovonne follows him out to the sidewalk and then watches him stride off to meet Salim in the distance.

He then turns back toward the TLP, still smiling, though his mouth seems about to sink inward like a rotting jack-o-lantern.

"What?" he says to me in the doorway. "I know you're thinkin' something."

It takes another day to sort out the details of their departure because Matt complicates the situation. Nearly everyone knows that, on occasion, he's sneaked a girl into his room after curfew, but Frank and Sam have never caught him. The night after Sam finds Miss V dreaming for Quovonne, Frank discovers Matt in his room amid halos of candles, performing a ritual—perhaps an exorcism—on a neighborhood girl named Cat. Also present is Lex, whom I'd met at the Dairy Queen, and Randi, the exotic dancer and Matt's fuck buddy from the banyan tree. Mostly naked, the four are clearly sexing the midnight. The girls scatter, snatching up what they can, though Cat is somewhat delirious, zonked on chemicals or the worship of the goddess of mystery.

"I can't tell you what we were doing," Matt replies each time he is questioned the next day. "It's something . . . very complicated. You . . . wouldn't understand it. It involves . . . too many things. But it was something that was very serious. We *had* to do it." He winces, the frustration of yet again having to fend off the clueless.

I coax him to show me his book of Wicca magic. Stamped on the cover: *This is for fictional and entertainment use only.*

"I can't tell you about what happened," he repeats, alone with me under the oak.

"Try me," I plead, hoping our history might win me a confidence not earned by the staff.

"If I told you," he says, his eyes wet-rimmed plates. "I'd have to murder you."

While Frank cleans Quovonne's vacated room, I help a little, but mostly loiter and mull the fates: Andre installed temporarily at the north shelter; Quovonne put on a bus to a family member in Miami; Matt splitting from the TLP before he could be terminated, later apprehended by the police and transported to the south shelter, running away from there the first night. It's unseasonably cool for December in Florida, the pinkie of winter brushing over us as its whole, blizzarding hand clutches the Carolinas and places north. Here, whitecaps under the old Frankenstein. Gray, bedrizzled windows. Damp sweaters and jackets. An appropriate ambiance for our current business, which has the somber order of washing a corpse.

"I felt close to Andre, but we need to follow the rules," Frank sighs, dumping the contents of a wastebasket into a bag. "On the way to the north shelter, we talked. He said, 'I could have done this program, and I chose not to.' It was . . . tough. I told him how I felt and he told me—and then he stopped. He couldn't go farther. I didn't linger. I just dropped him off. Best not to draw it out."

I nod in agreement. Somewhat out of apprehension, I tell Frank about a professional friend of mine—a former alternative art gallery owner and well-known Bay area bohemian—who just a week ago was robbed in the neighborhood where Andre and his father had mugged the lady at the ATM. My friend had strolled to the grocery store for a few items, and on the way back to his apartment, a black kid not more than fifteen rode up to him on a bicycle, pulled a pistol and demanded his cash.

"I'm checkin' ya," the kid said, after my friend gave him all the change he had from the ten spot he'd taken to the store, "and if I find anything, I'm gonna kill ya."

My friend said he wondered, with odd calm, if he had forgotten a stray bill in his back pocket or some other change. To die of absent-mindedness and a feral kid's double standard about truth and false-hood, cooperation and contempt. The kid meant what he said. He mugged two more pedestrians within the hour, shooting the second one to death.

"Yeah," Frank says, shaking his head, as though given old bad news. "And it bums me out how we're just enabling them here." He switches on the vacuum.

To be honest, beneath a complacent sadness at the general folly, I'm relieved that Andre, Quovonne, and Matt are gone. Several of the dozen or so guys who've been sent packing over the past year and a half fought for one more chance to remain at the TLP. Somewhat like people who pass through the stages of the grieving process as described by the psychologist Elisabeth Kübler-Ross (denial, anger, bargaining, acceptance), those guys underwent a pitiful struggle which ultimately brought them to at least a temporary resignation. Unlike them, however—and somewhat uncharacteristically—Andre and Quovonne took the news of their banishment without comment. They'd foreseen. Maybe they wanted to be thrown out. To have it over with? After all, they couldn't bring themselves to run away—alone or together. Andre was given an hour to pack his few things, and he did. Quovonne left the next morning.

Most of the remaining guys were happy to see them go, though Salim and Galvin have discovered that it's difficult to talk to each other now without the third in their posse between them. My relief is partly vindictive. Increasingly, I see now, I'd longed for Matt, Andre, and Quovonne to vanish because the more they bumbled and suckered the staff and themselves, the more they tested my compassion, which I soon found unflatteringly callow. They stumped my understanding. They invited me to despise the obstinacy and fearful failings in them. They made it easy for me to forget that they have only this one life, and it's wasting—that we puzzled humans all have only this one life and we labor to realize that fact and act accordingly. They demonstrated, too, that I didn't even know how to be usefully hard. My unacknowledged wish to jettison them—through their banishment from the TLP—was the wish to jettison the intractable. It was their kind of kid's stuff and maybe their parents' kind.

Not that these things would matter to them, or anyone else. After all, I'm not a professional, not schooled in the cool management of situations, in wielding the therapeutic wrenches and batons. No social service tax dollars leap into my pocket. I'm just a citizen, an onlooker, a cautioner and questioner under the live oak tree, someone to catch the football, the book guy. Of course, more and more tax revenue has begun to flow toward citizens like myself—away from professionalized social work—as government decides that communities know best how to ameliorate their social problems, with more volunteerism and local cunning.

Maybe the money should flow that way. One of the staff at Beach Place noted with some surprise that Andre had admitted his fault. She claimed that this recognition on his part is something of a success, an indication that he won't easily forget the TLP. It seems to me, however, the same cloud-with-silver-lining-ism that has doctored my vision of the program. The Beach Place people and others like them seek hope, it seems, as often as results, believing the former might announce the imminent appearance of the latter. Of course, they need hope to keep filling out the forms, to keep up the house of positive reinforcement—

which is the substitute they can offer for family. They need it for the spiritual moil. I've distracted myself from the more miserable arrangements of the TLP, its clear failures, because I like and respect Jen, Frank, and Sam. They've trusted me, and they try. They're the pros, though bewilderment visits them as it does anyone. As for me and my neighbors, we're busy people; we give ourselves elsewhere. I'm not convinced that, with or without tax dollars, we know what else to do about an Andre or a Matt, or that kid with the pistol and the double standard—beyond demands for better education . . . or more policing, more prisons, more throwing away of the key at every level of infraction; beyond the childish cravings for poetic justice and the sentimental longings to simplify reality with a club. And what phase of the program would we then be in?

Frank and I pull off the bed sheet and find *NO!!!!!!* inscribed on Quovonne's mattress in twelve-inch penciled letters, underscored three times.

We share a quizzical look.

"Your guess is a good as mine," he shrugs.

I think of the pages of the fantasy novel Matt claimed to be writing. At first, I thought he'd merely copied them from one of his *Forgotten Realms* books. He admitted that he'd "borrowed" some of the character names. In re-reading the pages, however, I believe they're his invention. The self-appointed shrink in me also wonders if they offer an obscure commentary on him like that *NO!!!!!!* does on Quovonne. Just after Matt left, David mentioned coyly that some previously unknown portions of Matt's files finally came into the TLP's possession.

"There's a substantial psychiatric history there," David said, proudly sotto voce.

He claimed that Matt's most troublesome records—a history of violence and severe disturbance—had been withheld by another agency that wanted the TLP to take Matt off its hands. Matt wouldn't have been admitted to the TLP had the staff known of his "problems."

Possible. But it's also possible that the records had been forwarded to the TLP and then secreted, to ensure Matt's admission and raise the program census.

David pushing *Shoeless Joe* on Matt . . .

I didn't tell him of these pages:

Artemis Entreri stalked along the alleyways of Calimport, the southern equivalent of Waterdeep, with Cattie-brie in tow. He never made the slightest whisper as his slight, yet well toned body moved around corners and other obstacles in the pitch black maze-like network.

"The pasha will be disappointed if we're late," he said though he showed no indication of concern. Cattie-brie remained silent. She could care less about this disappointment.

They rouned a corner and came to a cul-de-sac at the head of which was an old, rundown looking house with two apparent beggars sitting on either side. As they walked up, though, one looked up at Entreri. The one on the left said, "Pasha Pook is in his quarters. He's expecting you."

Entreri only nodded and continued in. They headed to the right and up a short set of stairs. The few people they passed kept their eyes respectfully averted, or was it out of fear? She did not know. Always heading up, it seemed to sort of spiral. Then they came to one plain looking door which Entreri knocked twice then thrice on. A bolt was thrown, tumblers fell and the door opened. There were exquisite pieces of art covering the walls, floors and even the ceiling. One piece of furniture dominated the oval shaped room, and in it sat Pasha Pook.

"Ah, yes, Entreri. Good to see you." And he was visibly pleased. "I see you have the girl, Cattie-brie, is it?" She simply glared at him. "Ah, well, you will get used to being here. I am not surprised to see you back. Entreri, you know the usual payment for my prized assassin."

"I was thinking of a short term pay increase," he said.

"Oh, really? What did you have in mind?"

"For this one I want your head," Drizzt said with unnerving cool. Cattie-brie cut her bonds with a concealed knife she was carrying. She swung her bow, Tamaril the heartseeker, off her back and notched her arrow.

"And I'll second that," she said as she took aim at the pasha's wizard assistant.

Scimitars flashed out and Drizzt stepped toward Pook. "You sent Entreri to kill Regis and capture Cattie-brie, you've terrorized me and my friends for a ruby pendant? Do tell." By this time the tip of Twinkle was resting just above his Adam's apple.

"You've misunderstood me. I didn't send him after her," Pook said as best he could with the sword tip at his throat, drawing a drop of blood.

"And the pendant?"

"I . . . uh . . . ," he was shaking visibly now. "It was a very expensive ruby, and I didn't want to kill him. I just wanted to toy with him for stealing it from me!!" The words exploded from him so fast Drizzt's sword almost impaled him through the throat, but he eased back enough to avoid too much harm. "I only wanted Regis, not to bother you or your friends. I told him not to go after her, but he wouldn't listen. I told him I'd pay for her alive, and I would have treated you o.k. No torturing or berating or anything." He was babling by now, and sweat was pouring down his face.

"You planned to keep me here against my will. And, what, use my body for your pleasure?" Cattie-brie was now aiming at Pook's forehead and advancing. "What do you think, Drizzt? Quick or slow death?"

"I think you should drop that bow!" Rasister said from the doorway. "Or should I let them shoot your dark friend?"

Three of Rasister's cohorts were were-rats and all had crossbows trained on Drizzt.

"Impecable timing, Rasister, my friend," Pook look relieved.

"Anything for my Pasha Pook," Rasister returned.

Cattie-brie looked to Drizzt for conformation. He gave a slight shake of his head and looked at the hilt of twinkle where his hand was, three fingers extended. He slowly, one by one, started lowering them. Cattie-brie tenses and glanced at Pook's wizard, who was so excited to be alive he didn't even notice. When she looked back Drizzt was just lowering the third finger.

As soon as his finger touched the hilt of his scimitar, Drizzt exploded into action. Snapping his scimitar into its sheath, he tumbled into a wide roll, drawing a concealed bootknife and throwing it at the closest of the were-rats, embeding it to the hilt through the windpipe and fell down, clawing at his throat.

A few days later, Jen announces that, in three weeks, she's taking a job on the other side of the county, with an agency that works with small children.

"At least we've got a chance there," she says to me privately, her dimpled chin again set with the wish to have new resolution. "I feel bad all the time here. I can't deal with the guilt, I guess. And David is driving me crazy. I'm also thinking of having my own children. It's time to move on."

The sooner the better, no doubt. "Both of our moms are dead!" Tim screamed at her when he heard the news, "and you said you'd never leave!"

Now she stares into a tray of Christmas cookies. "I haven't suggested it yet to David," she says, turning to me, "but I wanted to ask if you if you might not be interested in running the group sessions—as a temporary thing . . . until the new program director comes on. You could do it . . ."

In the air between us, I see David diagnosing the program's problems as a failure to make public in the house meetings the conflict between Andre and Quovonne. I see me, Mr. Citizen, offered a chance to define Life Skills. There is also Matt's Cattie-brie and her possible connection with the real life Cat. There is the missing $300, and Sam's long-standing desire to get the next full-time opening, and Salim, Galvin, Bill, and Tim pestering Frank with the question: When you gonna leave us, too? Suddenly, there is the demand for the sound that each of us wants, the sound which will complete us, heal us, change us, show us, embody our truest and clearest and most crucial name; that resolving note which is our note, that saves us from ourselves and all the dopiness brimming in our cells never more than seven years old, in the genes reeling back into the plasma of the void to the Ur-kaboom . . .

There is, too, the honey-gold rubber pacifier I found while Frank cleaned Quovonne's room, and, most of all—and most conveniently—that penciled *No!!!!!!*

Four days before Christmas, Matt appears at the wide-open office door.

"I wanted to get my tomato plants," he announces, as though expected. He refers to two small plants in plastic cartons which Frank and I found in his closet.

Frank leans back in his chair. "All of the stuff left in your room was put into the trash."

"But my tomato plants—"

"Those weren't tomato plants," Frank says, "and you know it. What, do you think we were born yesterday? I've smoked more herb than you've ever dreamed of."

Matt stares hard at Frank and Sam. His upper teeth flash out as though, at any second, they might devour his lower jaw.

"Fuck," he mutters, finally, and shoves the door jamb and vanishes. A moment later, I step into the doorway. He's nowhere in sight.

"You wonder about someone like that," I say, relieved. "He scares me."

David's disclosure about Matt's past—combined with images from slasher films and tabloid tales of murderous satanic teens—has helped my imagination transform Matt's wormy smile into a more sinister sign. Matt's fascination with knives, his sophistry, his attempts to coax me across the deep drop in the banyan: all collude, now, in anxious retrospect, to have him shove me from that tree onto the rocks below, a crashing reward for all my snooping around pitiful fuck-ups who might need to teach this pitiful adult a lesson about presumption.

"You never know about someone like that," Sam agrees, his mystical, superstitious side drawing up to meet my creeping. I peer at the scar branching along his muscled forearm, another map from the Gulf War, and I welcome its familiarity, though I know almost nothing about it.

"I'll have to murder you," Frank snickers, a bit too intently. "What shit! They should Baker Act that guy."

Two crossbows fired, both bolts flying harmlessly over Drizzt's head. They dropped the crossbows and went for their swords.

Cattie-brie whipped around and fired at Rasister, taking him in the shoulder. The blast of the magical arrow lifted him off his feet and spun him around to slam into the wall next to the door. She drew Khazid'hea and advanced on LaValle.

The wizard's face suddenly drained of blood as he looked at Cattie-brie as if she wore the body of Bare, God of Strife.

The tip of her sword met resistance as it came into contact with LaValle's magical shield. A flicker of hope flashed through his eyes, though passed quickly as Cattie-brie brought Khazid'hea back for a mighty blow.

As she brought it down on the shield the sentient mental voice of Cattie-brie screemed out in agony and exultation. The spell shield shattered into brilliant, blue-white shards of harmless magical energy.

As the shards winked out of existence, Cattie-brie advanced like a panther closing for the kill.

From behind the rooms on the other side of the green, Matt appears with his stash: a cloth drawstring bag, which he tosses over his shoulder, and a pool cue. Like Drizzt and Twinkle, or Cattie-brie and Khazid'hea, Matt and the cue saunter away toward adventure—past the bus stop, the Dairy Queen, the interstate bridge.

TWENTY

WITH THE FROSTING of Jen's good-bye cake still glomming the taste buds, the TLP gets another chance. A new year, a new manager.

"This is where the place turns the corner or goes down," David tells me casually on his last day in the office. I ask if the parent organization is still backing the program.

"They're submitting a grant for re-funding," he assures me, "and it will be well written."

Later, I mention that I'm still dogged by a little grief over Andre, Quovonne, and Matt.

"I used to feel things like that," he observes, "but now I think about what's best for the program."

Of course, I say.

He then lifts his gaze toward the window and titters. With a mildly regretful tone, he announces that he'd wanted to make a suicide/homicide assessment on Matt but couldn't get Matt to react.

"He was playing it very cool," he concludes.

Of course.

"There were two candidates with successful records managing programs like this," Frank says bitterly the next morning. "Either would have been perfect, but they hired the guy who wore the tie."

The guy with the tie, Webb, arrives to find unlikely quiet, since all the remaining residents but Bill have found work or are at school. In the office, Frank introduces us, saying merely that I'm a long-time volunteer. Bearded, fiftyish, Webb gives me a black-Irish Santa Claus smile as he forages through file cabinets. He's large—maybe 350 pounds—soon earning him the sobriquet "the Big Guy" from Tim. Not many days elapse before he abandons the tie, and often during our various talks, he suddenly pushes up from the broad leather chair to shake his slacks around and try to make existence a bit more comfortable. He employs his bulk to his advantage—having dealt with it as he still deals with it—and no doubt it's a metaphysical as well as historical substance. Certainly, it's rhetorical. As he says about the residents who will resist the changes he is bringing to the program, "The guys can say what they like. Hey, I'm already discredited. I'm obese."

It's clear why Webb has been brought in. "Not everyone can make it here," he announces, "but that's too bad. I'm as much a businessman as a therapist. I'm a taxpayer, too. These guys think that we owe them a free ride. They're surprised when I tell them we don't. We supply the basic needs, food, shelter, safety. They have to start to work to change their social skills, to become more responsible. I see an incredible need for aftercare. Yeah, you get them employed, you get them a place to live, but they're going to need a lot of work. Seminars, groups, things like that. Dealing with crisis, asking the right questions. I'd like to see graduates from the program involved."

Later, when familiarity has nudged us away from such official visions, Webb offers me a cup of tea.

"In my former practice," he says, interested by my interest, "my clients were mostly alcoholics, children of alcoholic parents, or people in bad marriages. It's gut wrenching. You regress them back to two years of age, where it all started, and you see very capable people go to pieces. You know, you either got what you needed by about the age of two, or you didn't, and most of us didn't.

"People come into counseling and I ask, 'How many books have you read about childrearing before you decided to have a kid?' None. Or they're thinking about getting married. So I ask how many books they've read about that? They say, 'We love each other . . . that's enough.' And I ask, 'If you're going to buy a car, you read *Consumer Reports* or *Car and Driver,* don't you? Or, 'You're a CPA, right? How many courses did you take to become a CPA?'

"I'd give people assignments about being a better parent or a better mate. I'd say, 'Take ten or fifteen minutes a day to do them, something like that . . . or more, of course.' I'd tell them that being a good mate and a good parent were the two most important jobs they'd ever have.

"And they'd bring me a little scribble, something they did in the car on the way to the session."

He laughs, quaking, a grim, knowing Santa.

"What about the notion," I ask, "that you can do everything right as a parent and still have a messed-up kid?"

"I don't think you can measure parenting," he says. "Most parents want to feel like they've done a good job. Many are in denial. A guy smacks his kid, and he thinks he's a great parent. You get that kind of stuff all the time. They laugh at the idea of therapy."

"So people can't know if there's anything wrong?" I ask.

"I think people know what's wrong with them," Webb replies, tugging on the collar of his turtleneck, rubbing it across his lips. "But I don't think they're sophisticated enough to know their defenses."

Truly. I toss out a line or two to show Webb that I've had some experience with therapy. I'm buddying up, yes, slipping possible punches, launching my coy effacements—hoping to scope to the marrow of this new institutional stepfather. Each time I enter the office, however, I feel a little more the outsider. Suspect, despite the cordiality. I resist the burgeoning intuition that I belong under the live oak, that I have alliances there.

"You strip people down and take them back to where they really are, where the damage took place," Webb says one morning, after I've asked about his use of regression therapy, "A five-year-old needs something different than a twelve-year-old."

"What *does* a twelve-year-old need?"

"Attention, or maybe he needs to say, 'My father was a no-good sonofabitch.' I don't care how old a man is. He's a person first, and I'm gonna hug him, if that's what he needs, and offer him the security.

"I had a patient, once, who regressed to about two years of age, and he was underneath the dining room table, hiding from his mother and dad fighting. So I went over to the sofa, and I just put my arm around him. If I were a two-year-old kid and I saw him, I'd get under the table with him. So I sat there with him, and I tried to talk him out of his feelings. He just needed to be with his feelings . . .

"Of course, as a therapist, you can't bite the bait of letting your ego get involved with the patient."

He peers at me over those high, red cheeks.

"In therapy, I wouldn't make you go someplace I think you ought to go . . . or where *you* think you ought to go."

"I know," I reply, hoping to beguile, as the residents do. "I've come to sessions with an idea of what to talk about. Of course, I was trying to be the good student, too."

He dunks his tea bag. "So let the counselor earn his money. Make it hard on him."

Webb's vision of regression therapy seems a time machine fantasy: one reels back to the moment of his undoing, understands the situation as an adult, and takes the necessary action to rewrite the moment and thus the future to which he'll be returning. Magnanimous god-magic. One of my psychologist friends, however, claims that it only works—if it works at all—with the terribly disturbed. I also can't imagine, say, Tim allowing Webb to hug him back to the cradle of his mythic broken nose—though Tim needs hugging, and more, mightily.

"I think that most of the people who got into this field are like me," Webb says one afternoon, unprovoked. "They had problems. And unless they got into some general therapy, to deal with their anger, then they're like the person who says, 'Well, if I'm focused on somebody else, I'll never have to deal with myself.' All that person did was make altruism a defense. He can always look good because he can always look to the people he's working with and say, 'This guy is screwed up.' That's one of the reasons I don't bum around with a lot of clinicians. Because I've never yet gone to lunch with them where they stayed talking about themselves or something that interests them. They always end up giving me an analysis of their clients.

"Either you've gone through your shit in therapy and you really have something to offer your patients, or you haven't and you're practicing because it covers up your problems. I think most counselors are damaged goods. Everybody has some baggage because their parents weren't perfect, their grandparents weren't perfect, society wasn't perfect. Maybe we don't need an overhaul, but we definitely need some fine tuning. In my case, I needed an overhaul."

Alcoholic son of an alcoholic father, with a long hang in gangs, Webb recounts what he wishes of the story he can tell of himself, which he's labored, no doubt, to compose. The fretful, receding mother, the high-school jacket, the pecking order of street fighters and the gangs encircling a pair of their leaders in a Saturday night rumble: quaint stances out of *Blackboard Jungle* or *West Side Story*. Except this was the early '60s, with dope dealers fighting motorcycle gangs and, eventually, a couple of Webb's friends on the floor of a beer joint, drooling dead from .32 caliber slugs.

"How did you finally turn things around for yourself?" I ask.

"I guess I had a strong work ethic," he replies. "I was a musician, a drummer. I quit the gangs when I realized that there was another choice than just slugging a guy."

So Webb was a smart tough?

Or maybe a square, fictionizing coward who's appropriated his vicarious fascination with bad acquaintances in childhood?

Like Webb's unexamined clinician, I try to think of him rather than myself, since I feel I'm starting to appear to him as though I'm on a little neurotic mission at the TLP. Too often as he and I talk, it seems I draw the parallels between his story and mine: the Midwest, the drunken parent, the myriad inner violence, the siblings scattered like decimated tribes, the endless running away, the touch broken into jagged shards for each embrace—and the broad, commonplace need to sound it all out, reassemble, heal.

"When I was in advertising," Webb says, "I would go to my counselor when it got later in the year, since my insurance paid for a set number of sessions each year, and I'd lose them after January first anyway. I'd do it to get in touch with a new part of me. You may be going for a Band-Aid, but you might get more. It's good to go to an expert. They've done the research."

Of course.

Now Webb burrows into reviewing the program, poring over reports, attending meetings—as though preparing the TLP for some profound therapy. As the weeks pass, however, Frank wonders, with increasing dismay, why Webb can't find a replacement for Jen—someone with the requisite counseling. When Webb suddenly rises from the leather chair with its newly broken back now lashed to the seat with a rope, as he shakes himself and adjusts, I wonder how he'll try to get rid of me, the volunteer who's maybe had too much access for his taste, who's one more irritating variable in every new equation. Santa smiles, Santa confides and offers tea, but Santa, I think, would like me gone.

Tim sweeps off at the wheel of his Suzuki Samurai—115,000 miles on the odometer—to his first days of classes at St. Pete Junior College. (*Change Your Life* says the catalogue cover.) After the customary bureaucratic hassles—and Tim's customary goddamning—he's in midsoar. HRS provided tuition and book money, and he used his savings from the museum to purchase the car. Webb advised him in his search for insurance—since Tim is still six months short of eighteen and a ward of the state—and Tim found a willing underwriter. He's also been promoted to Phase Three, only the third resident out of the thirty who've been admitted to the TLP to reach that level, and the first in more than a year.

For weeks Tim had badgered Frank and Webb about the promotion, until one day in the house meeting Webb said, "I don't see why Tim shouldn't go to Phase Three. What do you think, Frank?'

With the room utterly quiet, the other guys waiting, Frank replied, "I'd like to talk with Tim in private."

"You have objections?" Tim said, edgy.

"No," Frank said, with quiet austerity, "just some things to go over." Since Webb's arrival, Frank had been forced to re-establish the stricter order which had prevailed before Paul and Jen left. A precarious agenda, since familiarity drew most of the remaining guys toward him in the face of the changes a new manager would bring. Frank had to commiserate with the guys over each new imposition without really doing so, since he was also enforcing the order. His disagreements with Webb—personal and philosophical—complicated his tone. More and more he believed that Webb's exclusive experience with adults gave the latter a set of assumptions that would prove useless in his relations with the residents. By offering Phase Three so casually, Webb might be pandering to Tim—to gain some rapport. For some time, Frank had wanted to promote Tim to Phase Three—to inspire the other guys—but he wasn't sure Tim was entirely ready, and he didn't want Phase Three to seem a gratuitous achievement. Now he had to bestow.

So Tim abounds in the emerging Tim, far from his angers about Jen's departure. He stands before the mirror, after showing his new school duds. Shirtless, with his jeans down to his thighs and his orange athletic shorts ablaze, he pinches his lower back. "Hey, man, I'm getting fat! Pouches!"

Not quite, though some muscle invests his arms at last.

"God, there are so many chicks at JC!" he sings. "Maybe I can meet an older woman . . . not one of those thirteen-year-old teenyboppers, but a broad with a brain in her head." His reflection turns to me. "I've got $133 dollars in my checking account," it says. "You think I ought to buy a watch, to get to classes on time and stuff?"

Developmental math, freshman composition, ethics—the books for his three courses lie on the floor of his room and then the floorboard of the Samurai.

"I can help with the comp," I say, "if you ever need it, that is."

One day after work, Galvin sits under the live oak, passing a cigarette back and forth with Bill.

"If people thought the way kids thought and knew what the old people knew," Galvin says, a far-off whine in his voice, "it would be a better world."

Since Andre was terminated, and Salim has grown remote from him, Galvin's dropped the thug nigga stance—even exchanging rap and hip-hop for R&B. Thug nigga doesn't play at the computer factory, either. He's lonelier than usual. Hence, the company of Bill.

"I just have the feeling of existing, of existing real slow," Galvin says. "Very impatient, for me."

"What do you want to happen?" I ask. "You're twenty. You've got a job. What next?"

"Live . . . with more bills. Right now I just got a foot in. When I get out of here, I'll be swimming in it."

From behind the new high fence around a house across the sandy alley comes a hammering: the rhythm of a refurbishing begun just this week. Interior gutted, new windows . . .

"I can either not control myself and do what I want, and screw everything," Galvin says, "or go day by day and practice control, knowing that I can have that ability to do it. It's kind of just . . . existing. If you didn't grow up with all that violence around, you wouldn't have the ability to just go bursting off and doing what you want. Your conscience would say no to it, I think. My conscience is like 'Forget it, you ain't gonna let it slide, right?' So many times I've let it . . . go by . . . a lot of stuff that my stepfather did. I had to let it go by. I wanted to change it, so bad. I wanted to do a lot of things that I couldn't do about him. He was Italian and very strict. But he was only as strict as his father was on him."

"How long did you live with him?" I ask.

"Fourteen years. We get along now, but there's no possible way you can ever say 'I'm sorry.' You can't change the past. It's like you never remember . . . the good shit . . . but you never forget the bad."

"You'd say you're sorry to him?" I ask. "Or do you want him to say he's sorry to you?"

Galvin's voice lifts in astonishment. "He already did say he was sorry . . ."

He takes the cigarette from Bill. "He calmed down," he says. "His body started aging. He couldn't do the stuff he used to do, or something."

A whiff of sarcastic pity.

"He learned a part of life from me, and I learned a part of life from him," Galvin continues. "The rough way. As many times as he's told me don't go the hard way in life, we made it hard, actually, for each other. He was like a big . . . brother that could do what a father could do."

"What a father could do?"

Galvin winces into the sunlight. The hammering.

"Fatherability," he says.

Fatherability.

Frank and the mowing business. Webb and hug therapy. Sam and God's good military.

What kids think and old people know . . .

"Life isn't gonna be here for me," Galvin says a little later. "It wasn't made for me. It was made for me to comprehend what it could be like, and go through it. Understand?"

"That's pretty mystical," I reply. "I don't know if I understand. Who's making the decisions in your life?"

"I do."

"Even though it's a mysterious life?"

"Yeah. To think of it another way, if there was no God, who would man fear?"

"Why do we need to have something to fear?"

"Because we're animals," he says, softly, as if offering condolences over the casket. "Don't you think?"

I look toward Bill, who faces the grass between his toes.

"Well," I offer, "we're certainly creatures . . . What's wrong with that?"

Galvin scoffs. "You live in a world with billions of people that say, 'What's wrong with being an animal?' and see how rough it'll be."

"So you think people are animals and they're trying to destroy each other?"

He leans back into an assured weariness. "There'll always be someone on top of things."

"Is that necessarily wrong?" I ask.

"Yeah," he chuffs, almost choking on a laugh that I would bother with such a question. "It depends on what type of leader it's going to be. First, if they have no God, some of the stuff that happened back in the 1400s with King Arthur and all that might happen. But their army was under God. That kept everything, that kept the peace, that kept evil intruders out."

"You mean the slaughter of a lot of people in the name of God?"

"Yeah," he says, "People back then were also not as intelligent as we are. Maybe in the ways of artistic abilities. But not logical, in the ways we do now."

"Who do you think invented a place like this?" I ask, sweeping my hand across the TLP grounds.

"Some people who cared," Galvin replies, with some solemnity.

"They needed to be leaders to do that."

"Yeah, they were leaders in a small way. But I'm talking great leaders."

"So you say we need things to fear—like great leaders—because we're animals?"

"Would you want to live under a leader who taxes you and all that stuff?" Galvin asks. "It wouldn't be God's world, I know that."

"What? You want total freedom—"

"I'm a rebel at heart—"

"While at the same time you want God."

"Yeah," Galvin says. He taps Bill on the shoulder, and Bill hands him the last of the cigarette.

"So, you're really not wanting to be free," I say, trying to pin him, urged maybe by that obscure dislike for him.

"I am free when I leave this world," he declares, "but until then I have to live in this world."

"Just like everyone else," I say roundly, as if able to conclude with this premise which always fails to impress.

Galvin squints again into the sunlight. "I've talked to older people . . . when I was shaken up about . . . Revelations. And they said it's happened before. People thought the world was going to end and it didn't. One guy told me this. He was pretty old and wise and he lived a good life. I listen to old people when they talk—"

"Yeah," Bill suddenly says, drowsily, "some of them know what's up, man."

"I watch kids and how they act," Galvin continues, "'cause that's supposed to be innocence. They're born into sin. The innocence is still there, but they do sin. You just have to know how to describe innocence and sin."

He pauses, reaching somewhere within.

"I think I'm a pretty good judge of that," he concludes. Mild confidence.

"A judge of innocence and sin?" I ask, pursuing him. "Or of other people's innocence and sin?"

"I mean just looking at it and describing it," he says. "I think I give a good opinion on it."

"Everybody gets judged, man," Bill says gravely.

"Yeah," Galvin replies, "but there's like one major fork there. 'Cause even though a leader or someone else thinks they're right, they could be insanely wrong."

We sit and listen to the hammering for a while. A power saw.

"You'll be twenty-one in a few months," I finally say, "and then you're gone. This really will be the last time you get to spend so much time on yourself. Once you're out of here, no one is going to care much about your psychology, your past. You'll have to pay a therapist for that."

"That's why I don't like therapists," Bill rumbles. "I'll deal with them and respect them, but I don't like them. They do it for money."

"They should do it for free?" I ask.

Bill shakes his head. "I'm just saying it's easier to talk to friends 'cause your friends aren't in it for anything."

"Quite the reverse," I say. "You're not going to really tell your friends the truth. Because when you talk to a therapist, you talk about things that are secret."

Bill hawks and spits. "I don't give a fuck. How many people do you think wanna hear my philosophy?"

"Not just your philosophy," I say, "but taking an honest look at where you're going, who you are."

I hear myself echoing the aspirations page in the TLP handbook—that first idealistic, callow handbook ditched long ago. I'm still trying to keep the guys on the straight, trying to help the program, maybe wanting to believe it since I feel so out of kilter and incongruent with their reality. Are these the alliances I sometimes feel are real and deep when listening to Webb? I remember Frank observing, after one such meeting with Webb, *Well, we wanted to make the therapeutic component larger, so here he is.*

"Everybody needs to look honestly at themselves," I declare. "Galvin, you have a job now. You don't seem as arrogant as when you first came in."

"When I first came in," he sneers, "I was the nicest person here. Did everything for everybody. And you know what happened? I got screwed. Like I always do. And you know what I did?" His voice thins, becomes chalk dust rubbed off the palm. "I went back to myself . . ."

"But you can't live alone in the world," I reply.

"This program is a buncha bullshit," he says, still dusty and soft. "You look a bit closer. People are leaving. They know this program ain't gonna be here when the grant runs out. So . . . I have to do what I have to do. Thank you for what you're trying to help me with, but it ain't gonna work here 'cause I ain't gonna let my problems out in this place. They aren't going nowhere but in the air and coming back down to me."

"Sooner or later," I say. "You'll have to deal with them. You've got six months before you're out. You might as well make some use of it."

"A therapist is trained to understand from all aspects," Bill says suddenly. "They can teach you about yourself."

"In Job Corps, I took a college course on psychology," Galvin replies, lighting another cigarette. "I learned a little about how the brain works. That's all I need to know. Therapists try to take away the way I look at this world, turn me into a little zombie. It works for some people. They want to live a little hunky-dory life."

"What's that?" I ask.

"I just want to live a humble life, not do it their way. I'm not gonna go out and rob and stuff like that. That's not my first goal, that's not what I'm looking at."

"You talk to a therapist about yourself," I assert. "No mind control there."

Galvin sits up in the chair as if given an electric shock. "You can call up these *psychics,*" he says, singing out the term, "and they can say stuff and it just *happens* to relate to your life. The only reason it sounds so cool and sounds like it's so true is because something in the back of your mind is pushing out this chemical juice that's making you think, 'there has to be something in there.' Your mind is trying to force it, saying, 'You know, it's not going to be real, it's not going to be real,' but something in the back of your mind is looking for it and makes you believe that a psychic really tells the truth. Sometimes psychics are kind of on track. But if you got about twenty people together who'd been to psychics, fifteen of them would say he was on track—except then they'd find out that he'd said the same sentences to everybody."

"I've been to therapists," I say casually, though the experience wasn't casual, and I was much older than Galvin. "They've helped me. Of course, I learned things I didn't like about myself. I learned things that scared the shit out of me."

"It didn't scare the shit out of me," Galvin spouts. "It made me mad. They were telling my mother that I was going to be a *psycho lunatic* and I was gonna lie straight to her face when I get older! The therapist said this like she was upset because I came in and bothered her with my . . . *problem*."

We sit for moment. More hammering from beyond the fence.

Galvin snorts. "My mom told me later in life, after she'd seen how I was not gonna be that way, that she didn't believe the therapist. She'd kept it as a secret 'cause she thought that it might be true. But I made her wrong.

"So I guess that's all I need . . . to stay away from therapists. The only kind of therapist I have is my counselor, a good friend of mine. He helped me when I ran away. He became a friend, not a counselor. He just had a lot of wisdom that he passed on."

"Wherever you can get advice is fine," I say, conciliatory. "But getting it from friends is sometimes a problem. Friends have got to live with you in the future, and, as you guys have pointed out, many of the people you call your friends aren't really your friends. Why not look for wisdom in other places. . . ."

"I find wisdom almost everywhere I go," Bill declares, seemingly roused.

"But sometimes you're misled," Galvin says. Again, the chalk dust voice. Sorrowful.

"How do you know you haven't already been misled in a hundred ways?" I ask.

Hammering. Sunlight.

"I know . . ." Galvin says. Dust.

TWENTY-ONE

BACK AND FORTH, up and down, the splaying brush in Frank's hand lays down a creamy coat of white on the laundry-room door. Part of Webb's new order, the meticulous strokes abut and blend, or cross and double-cross. The bristles daub, jab into the snagged and pitted places, or heap more paint to finally drown stubborn, resurfacing grains.

This must go, Webb had written on dozens of Post-it notes he then attached to chairs and tables—old before and more battered now—in the rooms vacated by Matt, Andre, and Quovonne.

"I don't know where the money's coming from to replace the stuff," Frank says. Back and forth. Up and down. Beneath the dragonfly wing of fragrant Florida spring.

Galvin has been terminated. He was caught with a girl in his room—a girl from the runaway shelter . . . underage, no less. The girl's mother swears she'll pursue an investigation. No one believes her.

"Galvin was almost twenty-one," Webb said the day after the booting out. "He had a job, and he'd accepted all he wanted of the help we offer. It would've been time for him to go soon, anyway, and make room for more willing clients."

And Sam is gone as well. Turned in his keys, surreptitiously. The girl in Galvin's room claimed that Sam had bedded her. Sam disappeared then, leaving a message that his father and brother had been killed in a car accident. Frank later received a phone call from Sam's mother asking about her son. Frank offered his condolences. The woman told him he was crazy—there had been no accident. The next day a man looking for Sam arrived at the TLP. Sam owed him money for a car.

"I don't think Sam was with the girl," Frank says now, brushing over the rusty droplet stains on the vents. "Galvin didn't say a word about it, and it wasn't like him to take the heat for something without blaming everyone involved."

Frank's withholding the rest of the story, and the blade in his manner waves me away from further questioning. Instead, I think of Sam's resentment about not being hired full time, of being passed over, he believed, because he was black, and of his resolution to quit if it happened again. Webb's arrival hadn't improved his prospects. Sam filed long hours, but he—like many applicants—didn't meet Webb's qualifications to replace Jen. He and Frank managed their association generally well, but in any discussion—about sports, local politics, the world at large—they often opposed each other, and Sam always, at some point, demurred, while Frank never retreated, certain of something in Sam, assured by it.

"He might have been in the Gulf War," Frank says. "But do you really think he's in the military now? I doubt it . . . but I can't say for sure. I didn't hire him."

I recall Sam's story about sharing rations with an Iraqi who'd lost his arms in a missile attack, the man eating out of Sam's hand. And then there was the scar along Sam's thick forearm. If not from the Gulf, as he said, then from where? The B&E days with his old gang buddy Horace? *Was* there a Horace?

Yes, I tell myself, absolutely. And this prayer for the existence of Horace—the dead surprising Horace and the boy Sam was while hiding, wounded, under that parked car—is a prayer for truth I can know, that won't abandon me. It is, I see now, the clients' prayer.

Frank's brush laps at the can of paint. Renewal. Maybe inspired by the house under refurbishment across the sandy alley.

Tim is still attending classes, though he says he hangs too much in the student union, shooting pool. Also, a new force has looped Frank and Salim, pairing them. Almost daily, Frank has recruited Salim for early morning landscaping jobs—as he did Andre—often overpaying him for his work. Thus, Salim frequently barks proudly at Frank from across the green, and he chants, "Frank is my big dog!" A line of their work stories has perked into casual gatherings under the tree or on the stoop, echoing the sweeter myths of co-worker comradeship and small father-and-son business love. In one tale, Salim stomps furiously around the parking lot of a plant nursery after he and Frank have come for an order which is supposed to be ready but is not.

"I'm paying him to stand there," Frank laughed when the anecdote arose, "and he's shouting, 'This sucks!'"

In another tale, Salim literally digs into his labor, shoveling three gallon holes for quart-size plantings before Frank notices and slows him down.

"It's that chromium picolinate," Salim explained, "that new thing for weight loss. I have a slow metabolism. But, man, if I forget and drink a Cherry Coke after I've taken it, that stuff jazzes you. You gotta be movin'."

For us, Frank and Salim have shared again the ruthless heat and thorns, the oleander sap like old scabs. They've busted ass and been blackened with dirt, and Frank has gotten all those caterpillars on his arms, and they've tried, unsuccessfully, to persuade a city worker to dose the lawn of one of Frank's clients with the pesticide he's laying down next door.

In each instance, Frank has pushed into these anecdotes with an enthusiasm I haven't seen for some time. He's big dog happy. Especially about the tale of Lunch in the Supermarket Parking Lot: Salim, in the back of Frank's pickup, reaches into the cab and snatches a French fry from Frank; before he can eat it, however, he's swarmed by gulls—"like in the movie, *The Birds,*" he says; he howls and cowers and swats, and Frank races the truck all around the lot, trying to escape the ravenous flock.

This narrative good will has extended into the house meetings, as well, sheathing the usual frictions. Beautiful mundanities. Frank recounts an incident during his days working construction: "At lunch hour, a guy bit into his sandwich and said, 'This tastes like shit. You want it?' Now why would I want it if it tastes like shit?" Tim says: "Yeah, but men are into nasty smells, you know, 'Get a load of this' and the like." And there is the ongoing oration from Frank about sign-out sheets and the need to keep the laundry room spruced . . . and Salim musing about how the guys could save their money and, maybe, go to Busch Gardens for a group activity. Before he was terminated, Galvin even proposed a weekly game of "Stump the Staff," in which the guys would offer a question and win a prize if the staff couldn't answer it.

"The question couldn't be on things like rap music," Frank responded, "because I've got no clue."

"No," Galvin assured him, "it would be stuff like, 'What color was Grandpa Smurf's suit?'"

"What would be the prize?" Frank asked, a little cautious.

"What will you give me?" Galvin replied. The sidelong look.

Tim cackled. "Soft toilet paper!"

"Yeah, I could use that," Salim agreed, shaking his head.

Tim's new Samurai also roused, temporarily, the brotherhood of the car.

"When I got my first one, I came home only to eat," Sam said, as the guys matched horsepowers one afternoon. "The rest of the time I was rollin'."

"I had a Honda, once," Salim chimed. "You could go to Egypt on half a tank of gas."

Even Webb, still mostly remote in the office, angled into this association, telling of a '41 Ford he'd purchased for $25. "I had it about three months before I wrecked it," he said. "Only one door opened. It went to five miles an hour in first, sixty in second gear, sixty-five in third. I just left it in second and called it automatic transmission."

Generally, Webb has urged the guys to higher responsibility, over and over labeling their unacceptable behaviors "pathological." Then one day he heard himself and reached for a joke. Salim had been praising mushrooms over all plants: "Those guys are troopers. They've been around since before grass. They're cooler than grass, especially when they stick up above it."

"Sounds pathological," Webb intoned, and rolled his Santa eyes, almost mocking himself.

"Pathological!" the guys moaned, swaying in their chairs. "Pathological!"

Thus, our grace. With two new residents due at the end of the week.

Now Frank turns from the paint can. A pickup truck, splotched with clay-colored primer, edges up the alley. A lanky weed steps out of the passenger-side door: Brad, terminated nearly a year ago.

His hair is short now, strandy black spinach tossed on his forehead, his face sprayed with pimples, some headless and red. He saunters to the edge of the property and asks if Tim is around. No, everyone but Bill is at work or school. He sways on the balls of his feet and asks about Paul and Jen. Frank tells him that they're gone, then resumes brushing the paint, listening. Brad thrusts a cigarette into his mouth. I ask him how he's been. He and I often talked when he was in the program. Like then, he clicks the barbell in his pierced tongue against his teeth, laughing out his code.

"I got arrested," he brags, the words popping out in clusters like notes in a drum solo, "for beating up a cop that I never beat up. I was walking down the street, and he pulled a gun on me. He jumped out of the car and yelled, *Hey get down on your hands and knees!* I was like, *Whoa! Hey!! What's up, man? Leave me alone!*" He sucks on the cigarette, guffaws. "And then he found out I was the wrong guy! He had some witnesses in the car. He picked my head up and said, *Is this him?* Then he's writing up his little report, and he writes in the report that I hit him, and stuff, so I served three or four days in jail. But I still ain't gone to court yet."

Speed metal music stomps from the cab of the pickup truck.

"That's my friend Robert," Brad explains. "He's uh—"

"Impatient?" I ask.

"Handicapped," Brad says. "He has this disorder or something. I don't know what it's called . . ."

"So where are you living these days?" I ask.

"Over on Tenth Street. Tenth Street and Ninth Avenue. That's me."

More music.

"Hold on!" Brad shouts at the truck. He sways back toward me. "He's kind of impatient, too, I guess."

"Yeah."

"That kinda sucks, sitting in your truck doing nothin'," Brad observes. He pops his fist into his opposite palm, then discovers something else to say. "We're redoing his truck. That's his work on the side there. And we redid his interior."

I look over. Blotchy primer and some dents, and dusty blue carpeting, hirsute across the dashboard. The driver's hands swing out toward the radio, into view: each bent severely backward at the middle, like those of a cartoon character whose paws have been slammed by a piano lid.

Brad steps over to the hands, mutters something and comes back.

"He's funny," Brad says, as if confiding. He leans against the wall near the laundry-room door. "I like him. He sees pretty girls and stuff, and he thinks he's gonna get 'em. So it's always humorous. He's got a lot of confidence."

"Watch out," Franks says. "That's wet paint."

Brad jumps back, checks his sleeve.

Since he'd been a resident at the time of the home invasion for which Carlos served nine months in the county jail, I ask him if he's seen Carlos lately, or if he's heard news of Zachariah. No contact with Carlos, Brad says, but plenty with Zack.

"I had just got a job and everything," Brad explains, jamming the smoke into his mouth. "I was kicking off real good and I was gonna have an apartment of my own. I was hanging out at my Aunt Sue's with some people, and then these two girls I knew from before started hanging out . . . See, there's a split-up family: stepmom, stepdad, another stepmom—you know what I'm saying, the whole nine yards . . ."

"Many steps . . ."

"Many, many . . ." Brad concurs. "They all got together and decided nobody wanted the kids."

"Uh-huh."

"And this one girl—Randi—I started going out with her, and

then she and her friends moved in with us like a week later, and she knew Zack, and then all of a sudden he was there and we couldn't get rid of him for nothing."

I wonder if this Randi had been Matt's witch woman, the accomplice in the mysterious ceremony with Lex, fuck buddy of the banyan tree, nude dancer, hood rat, girl . . .

With great strut, Brad announces that Zack was arrested at last for the home invasion.

"How did the cops find out?" Franks asks flatly, playing along. He speaks to his moving brush.

"I'm not saying!" Brad snorts and bounces. He pulls himself up. "Let's just say he shouldn't have ran up and hit my girl Randi. She didn't like it . . . so . . . payback was hell. They got him. They got him good. He didn't even expect it. We were sitting in the house playing Nintendo, and this guy came up to the porch, dressed just like you." Brad snaps his fingers and claps, one thick pop. "He started talking to Randi, and she was telling him information. Five minutes later he came walking in, three cops behind him, two at the back door. Ugh! 'Zachariah Klager, you're under arrest' for la-la-la-la-la. And then they found out Zack had other criminal charges, and they shipped him back home to Kentucky.

"So Florida got him for theft, and assault and battery, and breaking and entering, and whatever else he got charged with. And then he went to Kentucky, and from what I understand he got charged with something else. Not manslaughter, but something where you beat somebody up real bad and they're near death."

He clicks the barbell against his teeth. "He'll probably be in the cooler big time, like Carlos." He laughs. Those picked-at and squeezed cheeks.

The truck starts, but Brad seems not to notice. The driver slips it into gear and rolls idly away from us, down the sandy alley.

"Hey, but here's the thing," Brad says, as if coming to the point. "Tell me, if you were a little kid, and you were out robbin' people, and you took somebody's ATM card and found you didn't have the right PIN numbers, would go back to ask for them again?"

At the end of the alley, the pickup turns and disappears.

"I have the items that they stole," he boasts. "Zachariah told me where they hid the stuff. There was two bottles of wine, tons and tons of CDs, Super Nintendo, and some other little knickknacks . . . gold watches, necklaces, bracelets, rings. I told Randi about it, but I'm not gonna risk myself to go get it. I didn't think she would go get it, but about five days later we're walkin' downtown, and she goes to where it was at, by a garbage can covered with this mat thing. She and her sister brought it back. Wine from like '07 and stuff. I stuck them in the cupboards. Zachariah didn't know we had the bag. He told us later that there was another bag that the cops found. Partial evidence. Regardless to say, Zachariah eventually found out we had all this stuff. If the cops asked me now, I'd say I don't know anything. He assaulted me, that's what I'd tell 'em. He was really a dickhead, and he deserved what he got. He liked to mess around a little too much."

Brad sways and claps. Pow! Day done. Case closed. I'm beginning to remember why so few of the residents liked him.

"So, tell me," I say, trying not to sound too . . . acerbic, "why does someone like your Aunt Sue let someone like Zack stay at her place?"

Frank glances from his brush, then returns to evening the strokes. Back and forth, up and down.

"My Aunt Sue has this theory," Brad says, eager, "that all my friends are good guys 'cause she's met like billions of my friends, and half of them are good people and she never knew different. She figured that since Zack was my friend, I wouldn't *mind*." He yanks the word wide, like some sarcastic goo. "Nobody would *mind*. Zack's a good *guy* . . . Turned out to be *wrong*. He destroyed her *house*. He did a lot of *things*. She got *mad* . . .

"Actually, when he got arrested, she bought a whole bunch of that alcoholic stuff, and we literally had a party. We didn't get up and say, 'Let's have a party now that Zack's gone!' It was like you just put two and two together, and it comes to a party . . .

"It was nice, though. It was fun. And ever since then, my life has straightened up a little bit. Had a good job for a long time."

"Yeah?" I ask. "Where?"

"I was assistant manager, making twelve bucks an hour at a telesales room down in Clearwater. Then I get arrested for beating up a cop I never hit. I never hit that cop once. Never. Served three days in jail. Had to be three working days, didn't it? Couldn't been on like a Friday, where Friday night would have been my first night and then Saturday and then Sunday, and then I was out Monday morning to go to work."

He jams a new cigarette into his mouth. He strikes and strikes his lighter. "Damn!" he snorts, and shakes the lighter. Three more strikes. Flame.

"I'm getting off the hook, though," he declares. He seems to suck in his bony gut to make room as he slides the lighter into the front pocket of his shiny jeans one size too small. "I have two other witnesses, so I'm relatively in there, and I got a good lawyer kicking up. I'll be out in no time. I gotta wait another month for my court date, something like that. My lawyer's cool, I like him. I can get money from this, he told me, 'cause I missed work and I got fired from my job, and I can make the cop pay a form of restitution. Isn't that nice?"

At the other end of the sandy alley, the pickup truck appears. Back from around the block. The driver, curly haired, maybe thirty, doesn't look at us as he approaches. He stops just after passing us, so that his back is to us.

"You still teachin' college?" Brad asks.

"Still at it," I reply. "Frank and I were just talking about that since Frank is getting ready to change his relationship to this place."

"Why is he changing his relationship to this place?"

"He's getting married in about six weeks."

"Frank, you getting hitched?"

"Yep."

"Congratulations! That is a very good thing to hear. What's her name? Cindy?"

"Margo."

"How long you been engaged?"

"A couple years." Frank doesn't look away from the brush. The friend in the pickup shoves open the passenger-side door.

"Yep, a new life for Frank," I say, awkwardly chipper.

"Then he'll leave this place and get a real life!" Brad crows. He leans toward Frank, almost taunting. "Then you're gonna leave this place and get a real life, huh?" He laughs, clicks the barbell in his tongue at me. "I think he's about ready."

He asks us to tell Tim that he'll come by again, some time. Then he climbs into the truck and rides away, the damaged hands at the wheel.

"If he didn't have such a big mouth," Frank says, "Carlos and the others would have let him in on whatever was going down. And he'd have been right along with them, in the front seat, too."

As Frank washes out his brush, we talk about the duplex that he and Margo have bought in the north end of the county, near the beach. It needs paint all around. They want to start a family right away. That's why he's quitting the TLP. Time for Phase Four. I think of the outward changes he's undergone in the more than two years I've known him—from aging surfer dude in bleached, crew cut Mohawk to this older, bearded, burnished desert dweller, with the look of a handsome prophet or certain simple, decent men.

"I'll come around to the TLP," he says. "I told them I'd do a little contract work, maybe."

"You really ready to get a life?" I ask, happy for him.

He grins. "Sounds pathological . . ."

TWENTY-TWO

"HONEY, YOU CAN'T make chicken salad out of chicken shit," Carmelita says about Galvin and the other guys terminated from the program. She frowns knowingly into the distance as she sings this assertion and concludes with the slow head shake which punctuates each comment she deems true and deserving of a responsive laugh. She slips a long cigarette into the middle of her mouth and, like an egret sipping lake shallows, leans over her lighter. Carmelita is here, beside the oak tree on a Monday morning, because the girls' group home operated by the parent organization—and of which she has been the night manager for the last six years—has been closed. Part of the restructuring at the home office. A change of strategy.

"They're going after more prevention issues, focusing on littler kids," she says, "and the budgets just aren't there for those adolescents anymore. Most of those kids just have to go back to their families now. There's no place for them."

Neither Jen's replacement exactly, nor a candidate for Frank's role, she's been brought in to support Webb's new order. Greater control, more structure: sign-out sheets, a demerit system for chores, room inspections—all enforced by a mildly martial female presence, a little iron mothering. With her buzz-cut Afro, and her personal uniform of khakis and light blue button-down-collar shirt, she seems to harmonize with the program's emerging tone. She has the saunter.

"It's basically the same situation here as at the group home," she says when I ask about her new role at the TLP. "I'll be doing the same things I'd be doing if I'd gotten that job teaching health at the high school. Life skills and stuff like that."

She smiles, takes a puff, the same pause as when I met her three years ago while conducting poetry workshops with the group home kids.

"All of it falls into place," she croons, "oh yeah. Not a job I'm

gonna get rich at, I'll tell you. But the self-satisfaction is more to it. I had a cleaning business on the side that I did during the day, to make the ends meet. Hell, anybody can make money. Are you happy with what you're doing? That's the key."

From across the sandy alley, the first blows of a hammer echo in the house being refurbished these past months.

"You gotta get into your work, really," she declares. "Do I have any regrets over working with those kids for six years? Not a one. I've had some nasty ones, don't get me wrong. But the good ones outweigh the nasty ones. I had a girl, she was terminated from the program in '90. She came by Saturday night before last, knocked on the door at the group home, and I wondered who is it this time of night 'cause usually my friends call before they come over. Here she is with her husband walking in the door. I said, 'Hold up, sister. You were the one that told me you weren't never stepping foot in this damned place again. Do I see you at my front door?'"

Her laugh scoops up some deep pleasure.

"Yes, lord, she really looked good. Got a job, gotta little girl just as cute as a button. She stopped by to show me the child. So now I'm a grandmother. She says, 'What days can you baby-sit?' and I said, 'Uh-uh nooooo, dear. Give me the ones that are walkin', smokin', cussin'. Don't give me the little ones.'"

She shoves her hand into her pocket and smiles at the grass.

"Is it easier," I ask, "to bond with girls than the guys, since the guys are into this teenage macho stuff?"

"I don't see any difference," she says. "They gotta trust you first. These boys haven't been helped by a lotta mothers, from what I've seen, so it's gonna be kinda hard, at first, but I think that eventually they'll come around."

She mulls the question further, then observes.

"Boys will throw their clothes on the floor. Girls will place them in the basket nice and neatly, even though they're clean and dirty clothes *together* . . . A lotta changes, dear, a lotta difference . . . You say what you want to boys, and they just blow it off. Girls have a tendency to sit and whine and pout about it for . . . about twenty years . . . and then they get over it. Uh huh."

The brown chow from the apartments across the sandy alley—the one that Tim wanted to beat—draws near us. Carmelita calls to him sweetly. He keeps his distance.

"There are ones who bond, and there are those ones that don't bond with anyone, and you can't make group home kids out of them. Can't do it . . .

"Lord, if they'd had places like this when we were kids, I think I'd have just checked in."

Head shake.

"Forty bucks a week for food. Privacy. Honey, all you got to do is keep your room clean, get a job, and complete your high school education . . ."

She sings out this last line, almost testifying to its healing power, and also somehow frustrated by it.

"I had one girl when I first started working at the group home. I'll never forget her. A little black girl. Her name was Senika. The kids were sitting in the hallway one night. They weren't doing anything wrong, but the rules said lights out at nine o'clock and everybody in their bedroom. And so I just came and set there, and the kids were telling about life experiences, and Senika was telling about how her momma used to try to drown her in the bathtub when she was little, and used to take extension cords and beat her on her back. And she even showed the kids her scars and everything like that. I just set there for about fifteen or twenty minutes, and then everybody jumped in and shared it. And then all of a sudden I walked up, and I touched Senika. All the girls took off, hauled ass . . ."

Head shake. Smoke. Puff.

"When I put the light on, they said, 'We were in our rooms! We were in our rooms!' and I said, 'If you were in your room, honey, why are you in somebody else's room?' That was genuine. None of it was on the record. Senika used to tell me, 'My family will never change because my momma will never change.' She stayed about six months, and then we wound up having to terminate her because her mom wouldn't work with the program. The woman wanted help, but she didn't want to do anything to help herself. It's like that sometime with kids. You have to let go. I learned a long time ago, dear, that some are salvageable, some are not. And we can't save all these kids. No chicken salad out of chicken shit."

Or chicken suit?

The brown chow stares at us from across the alley.

It isn't long before the guys' complaints about Carmelita spring into the house meetings.

"She's got to lighten up," Salim moans. "This isn't the group home. She's always calling me down, saying, 'C'mere, Slick!'" He scheemers the words, with some comic zest. "Frank, you gotta talk to her."

"What?" Frank replies, smiling. "You're afraid to ask her to chill?"

"When she hit you on the back of the head, did that hurt?" Webb asks, with some irony.

"It stung," Salim says. "But I don't care about that. It's her acting like she's gonna die or melt if I don't clean my room in a second."

"If you come to her with something better than a complaint," Frank suggests, "maybe she'll compromise."

"How about 'Carmelita, kiss my ass!'" Tim announces, and the guys laugh.

Salim winces. "If she puts one more of those lists in my room . . ."

"Just look for the truth," Webb says, "We all know when we're messing up. Admit it, and just do what you need to do."

"Carmelita has some adjusting to do," Frank adds, trying to soften the changes. "Work with her."

Salim leans forward, his palms pressed together as though in prayer. "Since I'm eighteen and it's legal for me to drink nonalcoholic beer, can I drink it here?"

Always this wearisome testing of the edge, this echolocation.

"No," Frank replies, "it's got alcohol. I can't control what you do off the property. I wish I could. But if I smell beer on your breath, we'll give you the pee test. If it comes up alcohol, you could be terminated."

"The 'non' in 'nonalcohol' is just a marketing approach," Webb says.

Salim leans back. "I was just giving you a hard time. It's a waste of time to drink that stuff."

"Sound pathological," Webb concludes.

Salim moans, but without his earlier camaraderie. Between him and Webb, a pressure is advancing, a crack in the bearing.

Later in the week, I encounter Salim on the green, swinging through existence, jazzed by his control of the universe and, perhaps, more inscrutable powers. "I heard we got a new resident comin'," he crows. "I gotta show him the ropes, show him how it is."

"You sound like a con," I say. Actually, like a B-movie con.

"I gotta tell the man upstairs how it is," he declares, nodding toward Webb's office. But he doesn't want to meet the man upstairs, this boy popping his daily diet pill.

Over the next couple of weeks, the crack between Webb and Salim deepens, widens. Salim and I linger under the balcony during an afternoon shower. He tells me that he wants to buy a motorcycle and keep it, secretly, off the property. He relates how his mother nearly bankrupted herself with credit card debt, how that debt consumed all his earnings from his work at a kennel one summer, how he didn't really need all those toys she bought him and his older brother for Christmas—bribes, they were—and how maybe he blames her for his father leaving so long ago, his father whom he's seen two or three times, who sent him the pager from Ohio.

"This shit thing," he snorts, shaking it when it goes off again arbitrarily. "I put a new case on it. I must have fucked it up." It finally goes silent. "I should just throw it out."

The rain thickens, a monologue of sorts, and he emulates its mood.

"I left home at about sixteen," he says, "and my friend's dad kind of adopted me. You could say that's my father now. He works hard as hell every day, bustin' his ass. But he does the same thing I do to relax. He comes home, has a couple of beers, and smokes up a joint. And I see nothing wrong with it. 'Cause as long as you're working hard and pay your taxes . . . this guy was even in the military, and he still works. I see his son working hard as hell. He gets straight A's. I call him my brother. He lives in that environment, and he gets by. I just don't see nothing wrong with it . . . as long as it doesn't keep you down. People who do that stuff, who work really hard but they're doing it because they hate the work they're doing or they . . . No, this guy loves the work he does, landscaping, and he owns a nursery now, so his life is his plants. He loves his plants. And I can talk to him about it 'cause I do landscaping. I was talking about plants and what to do and all this stuff, and he really is a cool guy."

A lie, of course—no . . . a fantasy, a dream, a myth . . . at least, a hope . . . of allying some of his conflicting aspirations: school success, drug pleasure, father love, worthy work, respectability. And Frank's shadow haunts the edge of this fabrication, though Frank is moving on from the TLP in just over a week.

"My mom always insisted that I never realize what I do," Salim continues, "but she didn't see when I take responsibility for what I do 'cause I don't think she wanted to hear me say it. I remember one time, Webb . . . oh man, I could have hit him . . . he came in my room. I hadn't called him to tell him I was coming back late. So we're sitting in my room, and he's jumping all down my back about it, and I was saying, 'You're right, man. I should have called. I fucked up. It's my fault.' I told him that straight out, and then he kept going on and kept pushing at me. I stopped him and I said, 'Webb, did you just not hear me say I fucked up.' He said, 'No. No, I didn't hear you.' I'm like, you can't be that dumb. I didn't say that but I wanted to . . .

"I know I messed up, and I apologized for what I did, for being so irresponsible, but he just didn't want to hear it. Sometimes people just don't want to hear you take responsibility. They just want to keep having a problem with you."

"Maybe because of your inconsistencies," I say, "it's hard for them to believe you."

"That really aggravates me a lot," Salim replies, "What do they think I am, a clown, and that I'm just bullshittin' in everything I say? I know I have to prove myself, that I am a credible person . . . See, they don't know me around here. I mean, they read my file and decided to see how I am from that. Whatever I've ever done, they've put it in that black book, and that black book follows me wherever I go. And that book was started when I was a little kid. But I just feel lucky that some of the stuff I've done wouldn't even be in there. If it was, I'd be behind bars. I mean, someone was looking out for me. Whoever it is, I thank them for letting me get to my point now where I know sooner or later, if I fuck up, I'm gonna have to stand in front of somebody that's gonna make a decision on me. That's why I feel that I'm lucky. I cannot have someone else in control, me standing in front of this person and them telling me what I'm going to do with the rest of my life."

I think of Frank a few days ago, packing boxes in his apartment. "Webb is trying to play tough guy," he said. "He wants everyone to see him as the boss. He wants the guys to look at him and tow the line because he can terminate them. Of course, you have to make them accountable, but that tough stuff . . . he's going back to square one. We learned that from the beginning. It doesn't work. You pound these guys all the time, and pretty soon they're just going to say, 'Fuck it.' Webb thinks these guys should be angels. He's setting them up to fail. He's setting up Salim. He says he's got some kind of struggle going on with Salim, that Salim is going to affect the new guys coming in, some weird struggle. Webb doesn't know anything about working with kids. He's never worked with kids. He just can't sit there in the office. I told him that if he wants Salim to fail, he doesn't need to push him. Just give him a chance and he'll fail under this system, if that's what he wants."

I think, too, about Webb clamping me on the shoulder at the end of a recent house meeting.

"Some of the guys," he announced, "asked me to ask you what you're doing at the TLP and what kind of book you're writing."

The adult lie. This request had nothing to do with the residents, but with Santa's turf anxiety.

I gave a little speech, more or less outlining what I'd told the guys anytime they've inquired. Their interest was piqued as usual.

"Is it going to be like *Boys Town*?" Salim asked. "Or maybe it'll be more like *Kids*. That movie had no point, but people liked to watch it. I watched it just to see someone more fucked up than me."

"I'm not so sure about that," Tim said, laughing.

Webb waved me into the office the next day and thanked me for my explanation. He said he understood the concept and he believes that we think alike. Later, he tossed several "fucks" around the room—perhaps to flatter me with some revelation of his ease—and he asserted repeatedly that he must continue to work on his weight, take charge of it. He also fumed about his "countertransference" with Bill.

"I'd love to bop him on the head," he said. "I'd like to lock him and his mother in a room downstairs, and give them no food or water, until they sorted things out."

This must go, he'd written on the Post-it notes he'd attached to furniture he'd consigned to the junk pile—part of the Santa Claus Clean Slate Program, of which Salim and I, and maybe Tim and Bill, are future participants. Webb's weight problem: the new beginning, no old influences, no historical precedents, no attitudes from "before"; the quest for a purified form, with Salim driven off like the son of those parents making a new start. And, in this drama, Salim's worst intimations are confirmed. One possibility for a different life is given up, and Salim settles back into a familiar set of rules as onto a saddle broken in by his characteristic shape and usual motion.

And must Salim go, as Webb suggests, in order to bring in those more likely to succeed, and to make the program more successful?

The waiting list teems with clients, though no one vouches for their quality.

A few days later, at the house meeting, Salim appears with his hair razored on the sides and buzzed on top: a dwarf mohawk. On his belt, a cellular phone.

"What do you have it for?" Frank asks, motioning toward the phone.

"Long distance. My friend's father pays for it. He says I'm like his son."

Frank remains silent, editorially, then turns to the subject of minimum levels of cleanliness in the rooms.

After the meeting, I approach Salim. "You know, Webb's trying to piss you off so that you'll do something that will allow him to terminate you."

"Yeah, I know. He says stuff."

"Why not frustrate him by keeping control of your anger? Don't let him control you. *You* control yourself." Easy for me to say, part-time hypocrite. I flinch within. "Think about the way you discredited that guy in the gang. Think about those guys in the corporations, the guys in the blue suits, who get even like that. Think about that kind of control."

Blue suit control. Chicken suit control, as well? But then, these days the world brokers in the blue suits don't have to wear blue suits; they've become wise in the ways of marketing rebellion—hipper, in their fashions and poses, than their daddies were, and yet no different. How to explain *that* to the guys?

Salim chews his sunglasses. Grunts. The ancient, obtuse bitterness. That weight. Beside the cellular on his belt, his defective pager beeps.

Tim is faltering slightly in his classes at the JC, and he readily provides his analysis of the causes. Stupid teachers, of course, and stupid administrators, stupid assignments, stupid books . . . and, oh yes, too much pool playing in the student union. I concede to him, after reviewing some of his class handouts, that a few of the assignments seem puerile and dreary, and I suggest that, for his English class, he write about something that matters to him, like the TLP. He declines, claiming that the subject doesn't fit the course requirements. More insidious than unimaginative professors or syllabi, however, is Tim's reliance on fallacious comparisons to the other guys at the TLP. He offers Galvin and Matt's failures and Bill's grouchy, intermittent catatonia as benchmarks by which to measure his accomplishments. He invokes the image of Salim, still not in school, racing a little, radio-controlled model car over the micro-dunes of the sandy alley to advance the premise that *Tim is the smartest of the residents, the most mature, the most likely to succeed. On his way, in fact.*

He spits and hisses for greater independence, though his callowness beyond the museum shop and the JC classroom abounds. His inflated self-image urges him to redefine his role in Phase Three by trying to reduce his involvement with incoming residents and the remaining guys.

"Staff wants to incorporate that TLP do-boy crap in me," he grumbles. "No way. I'll talk to each new kid *once!*"

Like Salim, he, too, has slid into conflict with Webb, though under different terms, since Webb clearly believes Tim is more valuable to the program than Salim. One day, Tim announces that he won't go along with the others on the weekly group outing.

"I want to do my own thing," he says.

"But participating is part of the program," Webb contends.

"Are you trying to put a guilt trip on me?" Tim howls.

"Okay," Webb replies, suddenly annoyed, "this program has not followed through on a lot of agreements in the past. Granted. But we hope that in the future, the so-called graduation into a particular phase does not allow a person to do whatever they want to. If they want to do that, then we can eliminate all the phases, and each person should be individualized as to how far they go. We could eliminate group nights, too, because the reality is that most of you guys don't have the skills to interact with other people. The attitudes are such that I don't see any realistic growth."

Tim delivers his next words deliberately, laying them out like wares in a shop window. "I don't see how you can put a fox in with the chickens and expect them to get along together by the next morning."

Salim and Bill laugh but quickly swallow their glee when they sense the room squeezing inward. I find myself wanting Webb to shake Tim with some riposte, for the good of the larger order, though I'm not sure just now what that order might be . . . or maybe I'd just like to give Tim a salutary bop on the head.

"I think a better analogy," Webb says, "would be putting all the foxes together . . . But we don't want Phase Three used as a mechanism to get your way as opposed to understanding responsibility to the personal community and to the general society."

Tim slumps morosely in his seat. "A lot of the time you guys don't see my point of view. I don't believe I'm better than anyone else because I'm in Phase Three."

"Yeah," Webb says, thumbing his beard. "But what about the attitude right now?"

"What do you mean?"

"You have the attitude that's often condescending," Webb says. He peers at me then Frank, and then at the other guys in the room, seeking a coalition in our irritations with Tim. "The attitude that you're somehow in a superior position."

"It's just my personality," Tim responds. "It's been like that for a long time."

"But my question is: Does it work?"

"Not always."

"So if you do something and it doesn't work and you repeat it, what would you call that?"

"Agh, I don't know . . ." Tim growls.

"Insanity." Webb announces, his torso bouncing slightly on this burst of breath.

Tim sneers and twists himself around. "If you're gonna pick my brain like this, Webb, do it in a private session, will ya?"

"Why should you dictate that rule?" Webb says, pursuing. "You're telling me that I can't interact with you the way I want to interact with you?"

"You're telling me how to act!" Tim shouts. He races into a rhetorical cul-de-sac. "You're telling me that I shouldn't be so condescending! I don't care! I'm not really in the mood to sit around here and chitchat about personality! I can't even get my thoughts out straight right now, I'm so pissed off."

"So leave Tim alone . . ." Webb says, in a mocking whine.

Tim laces his arms together. "Please," he hisses.

Webb stares reproachfully at him, his tear-them-down-to-build-them-up stare.

"Done," he declares, letting the word spread into silence. Then he slaps his thighs with the palms of his hands. "You've got your isolation."

That night, I dream my family must flee town. An army, or something similarly ominous, approaches. We must pack the little we can carry, the things we will need. I see a red pinstripe dress shirt from my college days. It must remain behind, though it seems in perfect condition. An aching sadness and an excitement pervade the scene. I must choose fast. Only one shirt, one pair of pants. Tim is somehow part of my family. I want him to meet this old man who is also with us and also an orphan. I want Tim to hear the man's story because I'm sure it will help him. The dream streams along in its aching—a blurry current of images, unconsummated longing, and the titillation of abandoning possessions. Then my father, almost three years dead, stands, facing a public bathroom urinal—except that he is black and his bare back, broad as a stingray, is damp with sweat and flecked with dirt and grit. He's a heavyweight boxer, narrow waisted. Standing at the urinal beside him, I feel my spray wetting my pant legs, clear droplets, almost like water my mother sprinkled on clothes stretched across her ironing board when I was a child. Then before the wide mirror, my father—now looking like himself in middle-age—sits behind a small, thick-set black boy and seems to fuss over the boy's hair, doting on him. And all is peaceful. Yet I awaken wrapped in the aching.

 "Kevin. He's a fast tracker," Webb observes about one of the new residents he's admitted to the program. 'Fast talker,' however, seems a more apt description. Febrile, proud marcher for his gayness, simulator of agreement with whomever is in charge, Kevin seeks his shining nest in the given. He also calls his chatter down to extricate him—deus ex machina—from infractions wrought by dreams of a sun-rocked convertible and swamp-love highs in a jammed, anonymous Jacuzzi.

And then there is Leon, testing a gospel of positive thinking derived from the football coach who's convinced him that, small as he is, he can be a halfback for the high school team. Daily, Leon grinds through spring drills.

"Footwork, it helps" he says, peddling, dodging imaginary tacklers, his speech sloshing around in his mouth so much as to be nearly unintelligible. "Every game is really about mind control. You give 'em the eye like, 'hey, I'm gonna take you'." He lunges and spins and tears toward an imaginary goal line.

"If you run the forty-yard dash in 4.2 seconds, you might make the pros," Webb says, trying to encourage. "But if you run it in 4.4, you aren't gonna be a multimillionaire."

"You can work at it, and you can get some speed," Leon maintains. "It's a difference between quick and fast. Fast is just straight." He zigzags out the office door. I imagine him crushed by larger, swifter linemen, a towering wave of self-discovery.

"He'll make a great bartender," Webb says, positing this fate for Leon. "Yeah, teach him to be a bartender. He's got a living for life. I don't think he's gonna do much more."

In the white chairs under the oak, Kevin holds forth.

"We're a socialist democracy, like this program. Welfare," he proclaims.

"What about the tax breaks we give to companies?" I ask, wanting to spar a little. "Isn't that welfare? What about the tax break people get on their mortgages?"

"But that's not socialist," Kevin contends. I veer from this old argument.

"Webb tells me that you go to college," I say.

"Yeah, at JC," he replies. "All we do is talk about the police and how crappy they are. And the New World Order, and how it's coming to power soon. They said that they banned it in the '70s, but they had votes on it again two years ago in Congress."

"What the hell's the New World Order?" Salim asks.

"It's one power," Kevin responds, suddenly resembling Matt in this eagerness to command through explanation. "It's like the United Nations . . . like the Monarchist's Party. It'd be the parliament, basically, and we would all be bound by that organization. There would be no different countries. There would be no money. They'd put a bar code on us, and we can only spend what we earn. It eliminates drugs. You can't buy drugs because you have no money. New World Order. It tells about it in Revelations . . ."

The hoot and coo of the season's first mourning dove turns me from the group. It cheers me, a Proustian envoy from my childhood. But it also reminds me of the day I met Andre and Matt and Galvin nearly a year ago, here beneath the oak. The guys' debate then and now sounds as familiar as the bird's call, but unlike that tune, its essential sameness pains. More and more, I realize that I'm generalizing Kevin and Leon and the other newly admitted residents, abstracting and grouping them into a single set, hearing in their tales and the terms of their fury, in their self-deceptions and shortcomings a simple repetition, an ultimate redundancy, the expression of type. It reminds me how, after some months of conducting poetry workshops at the runaway shelters, I began to ask the counselors there how they kept themselves from losing the sense of each client as an individual, as the protagonist of his or her unique, exacting epic—and not just another instance which confirmed the existence of a certain demographic. I'd seen various perspectives in the poems produced by the kids there, but the kids themselves began to seem more and more alike. No counselor had an answer to my question, except that one must remind himself not to forget the person, the face. To my prideful dismay, there are at least eight Donald D. Morrills listed in the Internet phone directories. With how many others—not carrying my name—do I share the same taste in color, the same pheromonal proclivities or intimate imaginings? Yet what more common belief does each of us Americans hold than: *I am unlike anyone else—my two hands have mingled with the earth differently than all others.* For no good reason I can name, in the presence of the new guys, something of the distinguishing heart in me resembles that fat fish which the cartoon cat dips down his throat like a sword swallower and pulls back into the light as a stripped bone. Is this what Jen felt, or Paul, when they were deciding to leave the TLP?

At Frank's good-bye cookout party a week later, I still dwell on the image of the stripped bone, wondering how it's linked, if at all, to my refugee dream of Tim, my father, the black man, and boy. Burgers swell and glisten on the grill. Frank jokes with Tim about the recent breakdown of the Samurai. Salim hustles around the scene, occasionally howling, "Frank's my main dog!" The lack of solemn ceremony seems Frank's choice. He and I will see each other again, so this is no good-bye for us.

Later, as a last call on Frank's status, Salim asks Frank for permission to go somewhere in the north part of the county that night.

Frank turns to Carmelita, to reaffirm the transfer of power, "What do you think?" he asks.

Stern, she looks straight ahead, though Salim stands at her side. "Didn't you miss your curfew last night?"

Salim shakes his head yes.

"You gotta do some things, first," she says, with the scripted concision of a drill instructor. "You work with me, and I'll work with you. You screw me over, and I'll nail you to the cross." She shakes open her lighter, cups her hand around it like a harmonica player working into a blues riff, and then snaps it shut.

Frank opens the card from the guys and staff. It contains a gift certificate from Home Depot, to help refurbish the duplex. Teasing, Salim asserts that from his days working for Frank—before he took his current job at the car wash—he learned that everybody at the Depot knows Frank; it's been his *real* home away from the TLP.

Frank thanks everyone, giving an extra nod to Salim—a gestural respite for them both, a parting from a kind of care. He's convinced that Salim is selling drugs via the new cellular provided by his "friend's father," but Salim hasn't been willing to admit this to him, even in confidence.

As if to enter a closing wish into the cosmic record, Frank mutters, "If I wasn't getting married, I probably wouldn't leave."

The guys gather at the picnic table and eat. Tim makes sure that he sits beside Frank, even though they haven't gotten along well lately. Earlier this morning, Tim told me, "Frank's been here a long time and done his thing and helped. I don't blame him for going. Now, Jen and Paul, they just walked. They didn't have any reason to go, especially Paul. They just left. They can have that shit."

I think now that my refugee dream is partly a wish for a similar sanction from Tim, though why should I need permission from him, or Salim—or anyone—to leave this place behind?

A week after Frank's last day, Webb announces that Bill has been transferred to another program. This news raises brief cheers from Tim and Salim and a few of the new residents—all of whom view Bill as a slowly wandering, occasionally belligerent statue. I agree with their relief, since Bill could do no more at the TLP, it seemed, than pace the perimeter of his emotional cage and sit.

Also, Webb finally hires Jen's replacement, Benny, a transplanted New Yorker and reformed gang member in his mid-twenties who's most recently worked with kids in lockdown. I meet him, awkwardly, on a weekday morning, stepping into the office to find him alone at the desk, uninformed as to who I am. He peers at me suspiciously, the lids yanked low over his eyes, his skull denuded save for a wee wreath of hair which circles and squares the crown, giving his head the appearance of having been lopped off at the top. As if he'd stepped from some antique gang fashion magazine, he wears double-laced shoes and tight synthetic slacks, the cuffs of which flare like fins from his muscular calves. I feel like it's my first day at the TLP, though I'm not even expected. I race through names of clients, allude to the most recent events, trying to sound at ease though I hear in my voice an intruder, or a jettisoned party from Santa's Clean Slate Program.

But Benny—though he continues to look explosive—quickly eases and is pleasant. Soon, we're talking about the weather and his suffering.

"Too hot for me!" he says. "Five minutes is all I can take out there." He tosses a glance toward the window.

"It's cooler today than yesterday," I brag. "Don't you think?"

We chat about the program, and I stay close to what I believe Webb wants for the place—towing the party line—but I try to let Benny know I'm no neo-volunteer bearing a guilt-gush of sympathy for the guys. Within a few minutes, I see how bored he is by the general quiet of the place this morning and how grateful he is for any company. We relax. I ask him about his experience in lockdown—a highly structured program for criminal offenders—and, eventually, I ask how the TLP residents differ from the guys there. He pauses, then observes, "The guys in lockdown got caught."

Later in the week, I arrive to find Salim packing his clothes. He's been playing quite by the book, deflecting himself from any proddings toward a confrontation with staff, but he also hasn't gone back to school or managed to find full-time work. Webb seems sometimes to have been split in his concern about Salim—now apparently wanting him out, now wanting to give him another chance. Evidently, that division has been resolved.

"What do they want you to do?" I ask.

"Forty-hour-a-week job, get my GED within thirty days. Which is what I want to do. But I can't get it. I have a job, and it's not forty hours, and I'm chasing other jobs. It ain't gonna work out. That's, basically, why I'm getting ready to leave."

His voice flickers. Between his eyes, above their blind spot, his brow puckers vertically—a cleft in the rock. He's scared. It's the first time I've seen it, and he doesn't care that I see. Why isn't he singing of his older brother and the glory of the Burgus, the big shit in Orlando? He claims he can't go there, though he's leaving in the morning.

"Well, I gotta get ready," he announces, wearily, trying to end this encounter . . . or perhaps to coax my sympathetic intercession? As if I could intercede. Like Frank, Webb believes that Salim is selling drugs, or transporting them.

"Take care of yourself," I say. We part without a handshake.

"Salim's smart enough," Benny says later, almost as if reminiscing about himself. "At least he's smart enough to have some cash stuffed away." He casts a questioning, cowled eye at me, as if for verification of this hypothesis . . . or for some special knowledge I might be harboring. "Of course, he's not that all that smart. He used this place as a pit stop rather than a stepping stone."

"Still," I assert, "it's a pity, at least partly."

"So you can take him home," Benny says. "How's that?"

TWENTY-THREE

AT THE JC, Tim's dropped his composition class. He's failing ethics, and the B he's managing in math won't keep him off academic warning. He hasn't taken me up on my offers to help him with his studies, either. But to encourage him to see a larger world, and to disabuse him of his foolhardy comparisons with the failing guys at the TLP, I invite him to cross the former Frankenstein and attend one of my evening classes at the university. Incredibly, Tim's never been on the other side—my side—of Tampa Bay, only fifteen minutes by Samurai. As I write out directions, he hedges, already anticipating his errors, rigid with reflexive fear.

"Here's my number," I say, giving him my business card. I decide to push him around playfully—to level this mountain of potential debacle he's raised in order to consign himself evasively to its foot. "Call me if you have a real problem. But *don't* call just to tell me you're wimping out."

"So this is required?" he laughs.

"Hey, it's Hitler night." I say. A little curricular pandering here, of course, but what can an old prof do?

At the appointed hour, I stroll to the front of Plant Hall, the main building on the university campus, where Tim is supposed to meet me curbside in the Samurai. But I find him already seated on the steps and eager to boast that he's been waiting ten minutes. We're both nervous. He relates the miraculous adventures of his making the correct turn off the interstate, into downtown and then to the campus. He shakes his leg and diagnoses "clutch knee" from driving so much. I see that he's assiduously combed and decked in the appropriate swaddling attire of pierced and tattooed youth—a figure lifted from the pages of a fashion catalog or our university's view book. He fits here, except that he's not in his home place but in mine—at least part of mine—and judging it.

I give him a halting tour of the building, dumbly half wanting him to fall in love with it. Originally a 500-room hotel built by Henry

Plant, a Gilded Age railroad baron, it sprawls and swirls majestically—as though its architectural alloy of Gay Nineties fancy and an orientalism inspired by English Romantic literature might have welcomed the variety of human difference in America and this grubby, shacky port town in 1892. Here are tall verandahs fringed by gingerbreading and shadowed by stainless steel Moorish minarets. Here Teddy Roosevelt and his minions rocked in wicker before invading Puerto Rico in 1898. Here Babe Ruth signed one of his fat contracts in the '20s. Here, also, the discreetly wealthy imbibed afternoon string quartets, and, in the thickly timbered *Reading and Writing* room, one solitary quest or another dozed in cool winter sunlight. Here is the bright, tinkling ballroom where the long-dead promenaded, and here stretched the medicinal gardens, and here stood the casino which burned to the ground. Here and here and here, variably glorious and deplorable, privilege shook its due from existence until the Crash of '29 sent Mrs. Plant, then two years a widow, permanently back to New York, her personal possessions packed in more than seventy rail cars.

"She gave the building to the city," I explain, "and the city adopted the minaret as its symbol and started the university here."

"You've done this a thousand times, I bet," Tim says. "The tour, I mean."

"No," I reply, surprised. "Never." Never like this, at least.

We swing across the campus, among the more conventional buildings. We stop at the library, where I pick up some Internet information on the Royal Shakespeare Company from one of the reference staff. I linger, hoping that some nourishing curiosity will hook Tim and draw him toward learning. I show him the university film studio and TV station. I point out the new residence hall under construction.

Jittery, he tries to joke. Later, he remarks about my being an Assistant—not Associate—Professor, as I had told him when he'd asked. He then pulls out the business card I'd given him. From an old batch in my desk, it does say *Assistant*. Suddenly I realize more deeply how he probes for the flaw in things, including himself—for the pathetic shortcoming, the hem unraveled. Now here's the prof ashamed enough about being an *assistant* that he had to lie about it. Maybe Tim believes he's getting a brief tour of my humiliation now, and this bolsters him. Maybe he feels closer to me because of it. Maybe he's discovered his usual illusory truth: *No one who is a success could be interested in me.* Yet Tim wants to succeed and, ultimately, knows what to do. For instance, when Salim aimed his elaborate fury at Carmelita, Tim counseled him to consider his options, finish his Life Skills for Carmelita and move on. All very rational.

Painstakingly casual now, I explain that I thought I'd thrown out those business cards after my promotion a few years ago. But it sounds like a lie, so I say no more.

Tim claims to be hungry, and we drift over to a campus pizza joint. When our order arrives, however, he only nibbles.

"Carmelita's always emphasizing how negative I am," he declares. "I know I can be negative . . . but she really goes on and on, telling me how hard everything is." He pauses, sips from his soda. "Maybe she's just trying to get me ready for more shit."

"I think a short black woman might know something about the knocks of the world."

"An ugly woman," Tim swears.

"Ugly or pretty, it's not easy."

I ask him what he wants to do with his life—the inveigling question—and what he will do once he leaves the TLP.

"I used to want to be a marine biologist."

"Yeah, I saw it in your file," I say excitedly, hoping this slightly exaggerated revelation might conjure the intimacy and fellowship which has flickered at times between us.

His mouth gapes sickly: kid punched in the gut. "How did you get into my file?"

The tone and face of the first days after we met, the days of his fresh, twisting grief. I scramble. Idiot. Fool.

"Actually," I say, directly, with all the pleading pressure of the truth, "I haven't seen your file, but Jen gave me a copy of your career essay. Ninety-five percent of what I know about you derives from what you've told me. You're Mr. Privacy."

"That's what you're calling me in the book?" he asks, his voice suddenly springing forth unburdened.

"Not exactly. But that's your story, and you're entitled to it."

His angry features withdraw, leaving a dignified boy face. I want to say something about that essay and his file which will rectify the situation, but I can only tear at torn tissue. Though he's confided other, more personal history to me, I feel unscrupulous about the essay. Yet he now appears satisfied that I haven't invaded his privacy. It seems he doesn't really want to hate me, not for this blunder, at least. And this restraint is unprecedented. He sips his soda and advises me to buy a Jeep.

"It'll look good with your mustache."

Within, I throw myself toward the image of his enraged, betrayed countenance, trying, without luck, to earn its absolution.

The class, First-Year Writing, convenes in a room in Plant Hall. Students form the usual large semi-circle, and Tim slides into a desk on my right, near the front blackboard. Two or three times a semester, a student brings along a sibling or a friend from the hometown, and I welcome these visitors—after discovering their identity and introducing them to the group. Usually, I tease these potential students gently, sometimes turning to them during class discussion to pose a preposterous question, or some such frivolity. This evening, however, I cast no spotlight on Tim. (I've forgotten to ask him if he would like to be introduced and decide not to be unilateral about it.) He remains the nameless stranger, and the students note this with occasional, curious glances.

I march through the usual business at the start of each session and then lecture briefly on the most recent stage of their semester research projects. The objective of the course is threefold: to introduce them to research methods, to improve their ability to think critically, to improve their prose. In other words, to resocialize them a little: lure them somewhat from the larger culture (from the savvy, reduced, market-driven mind devoted to the image and the sound bite, the irrational appeal and deified quantification) and ally them with the university's questionably defined ideals of print-based humanism and rational discourse, historical inquiry, aesthetic judgment. I hope to help them better spot the smiling whim-wham, the worming come-on of contemporary America; to navigate past the indefatigable Cyclops of publicity posing as knowledge, the lotus blossom of information as power—all that busyness which keeps them abreast of the latest stats on third-tier NFL quarterbacks and the gross of the most recent hit feel-good movie, that prides itself on its lifestyle choices and wanders the malls and the bandwidth far, far from the internal music of the soul's solitary questions. *Been there, done that* goes the recent sass intended to demonstrate that the individual uttering it is not merely existing but richly alive. Even to such blather I'd like the students to be able to add, truthfully, *thought about that*.

So I'm still hoping to gain a little liberty for the individual consciousness, still sentimental about the prospects of self-making, even in the fluid medium of postmodern identity, despite the devouring, wholly adaptive sophistry of consumerism.

The class is *my* come-on, of course. The agape offered by a crank. A believer in democracy. An antique, nagged by a soul-whispering sense of mediocrity. How can one not feel mediocre when so much of

the larger surroundings are mediocre? Of course, this is a thought error not much different from Tim's belief in his superiority defined by the bumbling of his peers. Maybe it's also merely a condition of adulthood, or of mid-life, that logy confusion laced with time's retribution on one's earlier dreams and ambitions, an occurrence which doesn't always filter down to our children as the kindness and wisdom of their elders.

I stalk the class—performing, I realize now, for Tim. I want him to affirm the world I want to believe in, the world I represent here. His presence tinges my exhortations, jokes, analyses, explanations, inspirations. It compels me to understand that as I speak to the class, I also speak to myself, to that fellow whose name and title (*Associate* Professor) gleams on the door to the office with the shabby carpet which I'd proudly shown Tim; to that fellow who Tim then said some of the guys at the TLP believed must have been a drug-blasted hippie back in the '60s, "since you're always talking about ideas and shit like that." That fellow who—like all the Franks and Jens and Sams—attempts to provide a worthy model. And, in this case, here in a converted hotel room once much more upscale than those which now compose the TLP but otherwise not so much different.

I turn the class toward a discussion of the evening's reading, an excerpt from *Mein Kampf* which I presented, without identifying the author, at the end of the previous session. The piece blares and bleats and swaggers, arguing with all the flawed logic of talk radio: crosses between genetically higher and lower mates produce an offspring that is genetically in the middle; different races of people are, in fact, different species, and since species don't mix with species, people should be segregated; evolution is an ascent to increased human vigor and power, and mixing the blood of the weak with the blood of the strong can knock it down for millennia. Thus and so, on and on. Pernicious whim-wham.

I'd asked the students to make margin notes and then summarize the argument. Now line by line, puzzling and lingering, we comb and snag each knot of idiocy, each faulty assumption about the way of things. Mostly, I want to slow the group down enough for it to become more acquainted with nuance, with complexity even in this ugly thatch. Implicit in Hitler's view, for instance, was a harsh genetic determinism offered as a basis for social understanding: people are as they are by virtue of their inheritance and cannot become otherwise. The liberalism which gained prominence in the West after the fall of the Nazis—which spurred some of the social reforms of the '60s in the US and elsewhere—was a reaction against this grim premise. But in the past two decades in America, a subtler form of the same idea has returned on the tide of new studies, mostly about twins, which suggest that genetics commands much of what we call character. Such an assertion now invites some to relieve themselves of their social compassion, to propose that public coffers withdraw assistance to the poor or the homeless or the jobless, since, in effect, destiny has assigned these parties to those stations and nothing more can be done.

"We are what we behold . . ." wrote that '60s icon, Marshall McLuhan, "We make our tools, and thereafter our tools shape us." Our instruments of perception, I assert, are still far too blunt to yield many assured conclusions about the nature of a person. I think of the great novelist Nabokov's remark that in the shaping of individual character there are the genes and experience, but most of all there is the "X factor" which is wholly unknown.

As we continue to untangle the excerpt, I survey the room and give myself a brief tour of the X factor, glossed by the little I know of these students from their writing and talk: here a young woman whose metaphysic derives from beach cabanas and pink drinks; here a single mother always slightly late to class from her day job at an office downtown; here a young man who insists that the "illuminati" control the world (probably since such paranoia comforts him more than the recognition of a world with no masters); here another young man, well-to-do, irreverently tailored and wholly conventional; here a young woman, to whom Tim whispers now and then, who earns her tuition by dancing nude in a club out near the beach. The results of our class sessions are incalculable, as is the future of this group. I can only try to answer the exasperated question of the slouching guy in the corner, "Don't words just mean anything you want them to mean?" (Echoes of Matt!) I try to coax their own smarter answers to such questions. And I strive for pedagogical patience and gentleness, since I'm also fortunate to be among them.

After we finish our discussion, the class pesters me to reveal the identity of the author. Those who had been in some agreement with him are abashed and quiet. After we adjourn, Tim presents his notes. They're good as far as they go, certainly acceptable.

"I'm surprised how dumb some of your students are!" he beams. "There were a couple of times I wanted to raise my hand."

"You should've," I reply matter of factly.

We walk down to the Rat, the campus bar and eatery, where I drink a beer and he sips coffee while we play pool. For all the time he claims to have wasted at the JC tables, he's still a poor shot. As the game unfolds, he meanders around a recap of the class.

"Damn, you're one kick-ass teacher," he declares. "Are you always so hard on them like that?"

A small shame turns over in me, that I've somehow betrayed the group by demanding more of it than usual because of Tim's presence.

Later, he grins and confesses that he was surprised I uttered a curse word in class. He's impressed. A curse word: my modeling.

Suddenly, a 40 Days 'Til Graduation party spills into the room. Somewhat undone, Tim leans on his cue and assesses the tanned young women in sun dresses, wielding long cigarettes, their gestures already geared for country club cocktails at forty-five . . . and the senior guys, thick and assured among friends and the sweet male networks that lead to opportunity. The room roars with confident glory, with the X factor, scented by platters of finger food. It's a special event, but I decide not to explain that to Tim. Let him imagine it commonplace here. Let him remember that this, too, is on the other side of the water he'd been reluctant to cross.

A few of the revelers stop to chat on their way to board chartered buses bound for various affairs around town. To each I introduce Tim only by name. Among those who linger a little is Lyle, one of my former creative-writing students. Lyle, fully happy to be Lyle. Impenetrable yet in his Lyle-universe. Whether strumming his guitar, or turning out a verse or two in no need of revision, blonde Lyle just chillin', always, and invariably mediocre. He announces that he has nine parties to attend. He and Tim stand side by side, Tim watching him as he banters. Not quite perfect opposites but close enough . . . and both fragile in their own ways. At last, Lyle's latest girlfriend arrives, beautiful and golden and quick to the nuzzling. His hand snakes around her waist, and he bids us good-bye.

"I wish I knew some people here," Tim mutters after they depart. "I'd try to go to the parties."

He leans into the table and fires one at the corner pocket.

TWENTY-FOUR

THE BEST MAN offers a toast to Frank and Margo, who smile, elegant amid white lace and veiling and roses swirling over wedding cake. At the ample, round tables snug in this oaky banquet room overlooking the Bay, we, the assembled party of family and friends, respond in kind and raise our glasses. Frank lifts the champagne to his lips. Here it is: a draught of the past, the boy he was on the cusp of that sinkhole long ago, hiding from his life, high and yet already falling. Does he taste that old descent now? Does he fear it? He sips.

After cutting the cake and dancing with Margo for photographs, he box-steps with his mother, staring off over her shoulder with great dignity as they turn slowly through lambent sparkles on the portable parquet.

"We get along fine," he'd told me, tightly, many months ago.

Later, she and his father—who have not seen each other in decades—come together to dance. His father, thin and somewhat hunched, eyes widened into alarm by thick lenses; his mother, in the draping, muted-print dress, solemn and furrowed, with that man's hand clamped to the middle of her back. Reunited. The tune from the eager DJ: *Color My World.*

Phase Four. Frank and Margo have stepped from the church along a suburban waterfront and collided with bubbles hurled by their loved ones. Now they part and, moving from table to table around the banquet room, shake hands and kiss and hug their way through those gathered lives.

A few days later, Tim complains, "I know Frank comes by to do the lawns. But I never see him. He could at least leave a note or something."

I say nothing about the wedding since none of the guys or staff had been invited. Instead, I nudge Tim toward talk of his new, second job: he's the voice on the other end when you call to activate your credit card.

"It pays $7.50 an hour," he announces proudly.

Since Frank's departure and his visit to my class, Tim has drawn somewhat closer, though we meet only on those occasions when our schedules brush against each other. He's finished the spring semester at JC with that B in math and D in the ethics course. I'd offered over and over to help him with his work. No go. He's registered for classes in the fall—including a second try at the composition course—and if he succeeds, he'll retain HRS support for his tuition. Often, when he complains about the TLP, I encourage him to write about it—to give him some necessary practice at expressing himself on paper. I suspect that he's locked up by masterpiece-itis: the notion that perfect, "smart" sentences should flow whole from his pen. I urge him to just relax and let his own available voice sound its truths, as he did in his letter to Frank about becoming a marine biologist. He agrees to try, but thus far, no words have been forthcoming.

So we talk, and summer cumulus gleams and puffs in sunlight, and then rain busts over the roofs in silvery chains, later steaming up from wet streets as languid ghosts.

"Are you coming for group shit?" he asks me one bright afternoon, toeing the grass.

"I don't think I'm being allowed there anymore," I reply.

"Why not? Doesn't Webb like you?"

"I don't think I'm part of the new order," I say and then add with cowardly emphasis, "I wouldn't say anything about it."

"Oh, I see, typical bullshit . . . I like Benny on a personal level and I like Carmelita on a personal level, but I don't like some of their ethics for this place."

"Why?"

"They seem to treat it too much like it's just their job. They don't understand. I think you should come around here because there are some kids who might want to talk to you like I have. Maybe they would put out more than I do, you know? Like Kevin could really stand to talk to somebody like you, 'cause he's going through a lot of anger shit right now."

"I was going to talk to Kevin today," I say, chopped by a small guilt at my recent indifference toward him, "but then he took off."

I pause, then redirect the conversation. "About me being excluded from group—don't make a big deal out of it. Nothing overt has been said. I just think that Webb and Benny are trying to build the program along different lines. I'm an outsider and—"

"An outsider! You were here before they were. Before I was."

"But I'm an outsider to them."

"They're the outsiders!" Tim moans, seized by the old urge to vent. "And Webb, I hate Webb, period! The only reason I ever talk to him is if I need something."

"Yeah, but it *is* their program."

"This is just a job to Webb," Tim rants. "He might care more than I think he does, but I just don't like him. He doesn't trust us enough. A lot of things go on here that shouldn't. It's too, too distressful. Webb just wants to sit his fat ass up in his office all day and make some rules. He doesn't want to come down to our level, you know?"

"He wants you to come up to his level."

"If he's the most qualified for this job, I'd hate to see the other people. He comes in here just laying down the law—"

Tim peers into the grass. He shakes his head. A moment later, exasperated, he pitches his face toward the sky, and I notice the first scattered blues of beard on his chin.

"If you would have come to see me yesterday," he says quietly, "it would have been totally different. I was in such a good mood yesterday. You would have been wondering, 'whoa, what's wrong with you, you're so cool about everything. This isn't normal for you.'"

I insist that to have paused as he did just then and recompose himself is a triumph of sorts, a show of progress. I encourage him to focus his anger on asking questions about himself and his relationship with others and his direction in life. I tell him again about my father's rage and my own quick temper, how that fury injures the one furious as well as those who most care about him. Recalling "The Wisdom Program" on the ancient computer he'd resurrected, I quote Seneca, "Anger is like ruin that breaks itself upon that which it falls." To encourage him to lean a little toward the idea of accepting therapy, I recount how it helped me to better understand my rage, feeling oddly exposed to him by this mundane admission.

Tim listens, but soon he's dwelling again on problems with the program. I ask him then if he thinks the TLP is a failure. For a long time, I've been wondering about this myself, uncomfortably suspicious that I've become one of the sentimentalists, distracted by hope from the most obvious shortcomings.

"They say you're supposed to be a good kid to come here," Tim declares. "Boy, are they stupid! The largest failure is when the people leave that started it, you know? What good has this place really done? The idea was logical enough. They did tons and tons of work, but the plan was wrong."

"That's a pretty heavy assessment," I reply. "Does that mean it's failed you?"

"No. I'm talking about quantity," he says, somehow calmed. "A lot of guys leave here just with the past they came with."

"What could the staff have done to make it better?" I ask, shrugging my shoulders.

"I don't know," he says. "That's the thing. I don't know any more than they did. I just don't think it worked as well as they needed it to. Some kids get some good ideas here, but look at all the ones who've left. On probation. Back to the same shelters where they came from four months before. They come here and meet the neighborhood kids and that's it . . ."

"So has it helped anyone besides you?"

At first, he says no. But then he mentions the two other residents who made it through Phase Three in the days before Andre and Quovonne and the others were admitted. He then remembers another resident from the early days.

"Phil left on pretty stupid terms, but he even changed from when he first came here. I talked with him a lot. I spent a lot of time with him outside his room. Yeah, he didn't leave here good, but he left here with a lot more than he came with."

Four residents out of approximately thirty-five. Given the TLP's $300,000 grant for three years of operation, it seems that this "success rate," such as it is, might still be more cost effective than prison—if the program diverts even one of the guys headed for that kind of trouble into ordinary, legal, red-tape life. I think of Frank telling me that not long ago he encountered Phil at the grocery store. Phil appeared a little heavier—possibly clean of drugs—and he was, at least, cashing a payroll check.

"So, would you close this place?" I ask Tim. "Would you say it's not worth the tax money?"

Tim leans down and snatches up a twig, snaps it in two, and tosses the smaller portion away. "I didn't want to come here, but I'm happy I came here now."

"That's the first time I've heard you say that."

"I'm happy I came here and I'm not in a foster home or whatever kind of place. I have no idea what they do with a seventeen-year-old orphan."

A few weeks later, Tim announces that he's leaving the TLP in midsummer, after his eighteenth birthday. He's also quitting his job at the museum to work full time at the credit card company. This latter news is especially surprising since not long ago he thought he might be fired. A fray with his boss, a woman.

"She's a fat bitch," he steamed, then turned to Carmelita. "No offense. She's a fat, *white* bitch."

"Tim won't change," Webb said about these struggles. "He'll strut around with that attitude, and one day he'll probably marry someone he can bully."

Tim, however, was transferred to a full-time position in a different activating unit at the credit card company, and I find myself encouraging him to pursue his plan to leave. I realize now that in his forthcoming departure I hope to witness at least one instance of unambiguous redemption, a case of which I can be sure, where I can believe I understand that tear of human longing which brought him (and maybe me) to the TLP and which will now lead him toward a life story he needn't try to escape—all beyond my puny capacities to care or teach or model or merely support him. In this desire, I also realize my craving for The Comeback, the great scheme of American Individualism, the epilogue we seek to attach to all our American tragedies, inspired as it is by our most sentimental (and thus most potent because least examined) emotions. I realize, also—slowly—that in Tim's going, I'm seeking a way to leave the TLP as well.

Not long after this, I walk along the beach with Frank in Clearwater. Joyous, he tells me that Margo, strolling ahead of us in shallow surf, is pregnant. They've already begun shopping for baby items, picking out the color schemes. Yet his pride somehow remains aware of how easily what he has won from the fate of his lesser self can be lost. He's holding his happiness quietly, so it won't be taken. This restraint speaks of how long the way can be for Tim, for Andre, Matt, and the others. Here is The Comeback, if any—this beach, their modest, meticulous duplex, the house-rebuilding business just begun with his father-in-law.

"Tim is scared to leave the TLP," Frank observes. "He knows what's out there. Most guys don't. He knows he's stepping into manhood.

"Salim was just as scared to leave the program as Tim is, but he wouldn't give himself any other options. I thought about asking him to stay a couple of days here. But then I thought, 'What's the point? What will he learn?' So I just told him to call me sometime . . .

"These weren't the kinds of guys we had originally designed the program for. We expected guys who were more motivated. But these were the guys we got, the ones who were out there . . . They heard things from us they hadn't heard before. They met a different kind of adult."

I mention that Tim is angry that he doesn't see Frank.

"Tim avoids me when I'm at the TLP," Frank responds, slightly incredulous, "and he won't come out here, though I've invited him."

Margo turns and approaches us. If Tim would only witness this life, I think, if he only would see Frank and Margo's bright rooms beside the glittering waves, it might inspire him.

"I thought I'd miss the place," Frank says, as we head back down the beach. "But I don't. I sleep at night now."

Tim reveals that he won't be leaving until late summer, approximately a month after his birthday, since it will take him that long to amass enough cash to go. Still, he's frustrated because he's already found the perfect apartment, large and quiet, and he doesn't know how to keep someone else from renting it.

"Forget it," Webb advises. "There'll be other places."

But Tim broods, a neophyte, still, in Life Skills. I wonder if, when he finally rents an apartment, he'll just hide himself away there. Everything about him is so deeply planned and fragile—though he swaggers a bit and speculates that his experience with his mom and the flophouses is proving valuable, something useful now.

I brood as well. On the unaccountable gleam in the bruised, darkened eye. On the wet-rimmed eyes of Matt, almost like those of my troubled little brother. Matt, whom we've learned has gotten the goddess of mystery pregnant—she, in this incarnation, yet another neighborhood girl, only fourteen. Both of them are now, for the moment, back at his parents' place in the Panhandle.

I think, also, of Bill's slack stare as he strummed his guitar to a CD: Kurt Cobain backing the carcinogenic mutter of William S. Burroughs with a few chords of the damned. And I think of Andre's hidden eye and his saucy glance at me when he rapped out *I'm a muthafuckin' Ph.D.*—his tenure at the facility in Tampa now recently concluded when he turned eighteen and was released, adjudicated. I recall elegant Miss V glaring up from Quovonne's belongings as he zipped her into his bag and went to the bus.

I think, too, of the bulk mail solicitations from law offices which come to the TLP now—fourteen in one day—all addressed to Salim, a sign he's probably been arrested. (He'd left two hundred hits of morphine in the bottom of his closet when he cleared out.) I wonder about Galvin, maybe somewhere on my side of the water. And Sam, vanished. And Jen, who now makes notes on kids all day but is not compelled to intervene, since that's not her job. Who said, at last, about the TLP: *I wouldn't live near this place, and I created it.*

At mid-summer, I inform Tim and Webb and Benny that I'm leaving town for a month but that I'll return in time to celebrate Tim's independence day and help him move.

"You gotta end this book with me," Tim says, leaning on the cable stretched down from the light pole, rocking on it like a boxer on the ropes.

"And how would that be?" I ask.

"You know, going off into the sunset."

"Shit," I scoff and then laugh, "you mean going off into your life. *Your life,* man."

A month later, I pull up the to the TLP in the noon glare. The place resembles the usual empty stage set, but as I walk across the green toward the office, a certain vacancy approaches me like a creeping odor. No muffled bass lines thump from the rooms, not even the roaring wheeze of the A/C units, except in Frank's old apartment on the far end, now Benny's. I race up the stairs. The blinds in Tim's window laze open, revealing a stripped space. I hustle toward Webb's office and peer in. Nothing there but the impressions in the carpet—from the sofa, desk, and photocopy machine—and the strew of a few paper wads.

I knock on Benny's door. A dragonfly twirls in the clear heat. Beyond it, I see that the house across the sandy alley, the one under refurbishment, now stands chipper and spruced behind a *For Sale* sign. I also notice that the only other car on the TLP property is unfamiliar. I knock again, and then again. I'm nearly ready to leave when Clark, from the runaway shelter, opens the door. Sleep-rumpled and groggy from having worked the night shift, he's nonetheless cordial. He informs me that Webb was fired and the program closed less than a week ago.

"Our funding was not renewed," he says. "Thirty-two programs applied nationally. Only sixteen got it."

Kevin and Leon and the rest of the new residents were "placed" in various shelters around the area. Tim, so close to his eighteenth birthday and apparently close to moving out anyway, was ferried into a garage apartment not far from here, his landlords a middle-aged couple whom Clark thought might provide some familial aura.

"The parent organization is moving toward out-client community-based services," Clark explains.

He gives me Tim's phone number, which is all the information he claims to possess just now. The apartment is nearly empty, since he's only staying here until the parent organization can sell the property.

I pass the big banyan on my way to the former Frankenstein. Unaccountably, I notice, maybe for the first time, that the small ridge on my lip from Andre's blow has fully receded. Gone.

Phase Four.

A new, huge federal housing project is begun in Tampa, to replace the depleted projects in Andre's old neighborhood. The newspapers report that the Tampa Bay area now has the largest gang task force in the nation. President Clinton announces an $8 billion surplus in the federal budget, the first in thirty years. I can only speculate about the sixteen unfunded TLPs and how that federal surplus might be creatively spent to better the chances of young people in crisis—especially as the stock market climbs above 9,000 and the national wealth is sucked faster and faster into the richest quartile of the population.

I call Tim three times over the next two weeks and ask him to call me back. Maybe have lunch.

"I'm not at home," his recorded voice asserts coolly. "Leave a message with my secretary."

Beep.

"He's not talking to me either," Frank says when I inquire.

I wonder what Tim will do, ultimately. Learn to mother life? Or maybe search for a mother in every face he encounters, comparing it to his dead ideal? Or maybe try, blindly, to orphan each day, every minute?

I call him again and tell his answering machine that I hope he'll call back sometime. Then, trying not make it seem like good-bye, I wish him good luck, sounding for words more right, more magical than any I know. Impossible words.

I put down the receiver and think of those faces—the guys—and
I hear Tim one day beneath the live oak in late spring.

"I don't need the whole world watching me," he says. "But I hate to give up. That's my thing now, you know?"